Merryl Wyn Davies (1949–2021)

Born on 23 June 1949, in Merthyr Tydfil, Merryl Wyn Davies was a writer and broadcaster with some 40 years of involvement with Muslim intellectual life. Born into a city of coal miners, she wrote movingly in *Critical Muslim* of the Aberfan colliery disaster of 1966. After graduating from University College, London, where she studied anthropology, she embarked upon an illustrious career in journalism, during which she struck up a prolific intellectual rapport with the writer Ziauddin Sardar that would span decades. At the BBC she worked for 'Everyman', 'Heart of the Matter' and 'Global Report' and was a columnist and regular contributor to the Muslim magazine *Afkar/Inquiry*. Her books include *Knowing One Another: Shaping an Islamic Anthropology, Beyond Frontiers: Islam and Contemporary Needs*, and *Darwin and Fundamentalism*. With Ziauddin Sardar she wrote a series of books covering seminal events in recent history. These include *Distorted Imagination: Lessons from the Rushdie Affair, Barbaric Others: A Manifesto on Western Racism* and a trilogy on America: *Why do People Hate America? American Dream, Global Nightmare*, and *Will America Change?*

Appointed in May 2010 as the founding director of the re-launched Muslim Institute, Merryl continued her involvement with the activities of the Institute right up to her passing in 2021. Proud of her Welsh heritage, she was an unapologetically working-class woman down to her bones, yet with a taste for the finer things in life. Her larger-than-life Welsh humour, razor-sharp intellect, and wealth of knowledge contributed to the air of conviviality Muslim Institute events became renowned for. Whatever the occasion, her warmth and generosity of spirit did nothing to temper a unique ability to analyse pressing issues concerning Muslim communities in contemporary times. She firmly believed in the need for Muslims to be critical and introspective, so that they may be the architects of the solutions to the issues they face.

Merryl spent much of the 1980s and 1990s in Malaysia working as a speechwriter for the then Opposition Leader and former Deputy Prime Minister, Anwar Ibrahim. There she revelled in the Malay culture and cuisine and adored the living multiculturalism upon which the great cities of Malaysia are founded and ordered. Kuala Lumpur, the city of contrast and diversity, was always a dear place to her where many memories were formed. There she waved the flag for the Indian Ocean World and Indus Valley Civilisation, ready to deliver hours of impromptu lecture for inquiring minds. She was an East-West woman and cared deeply for people, particularly those who had been bullied by one civilisation or another (and she was not above making sure the bullies of this world got their comeuppance!). She passed away in February 2021 in Petaling Jaya, Malaysia, in a world she adored, surrounded by friends who loved her dearly. Her absence will undoubtedly be felt in Muslim thought, scholarship and research. May her soul rest in eternal peace.

KNOWING ONE ANOTHER

In the name of Allah, the Beneficent, the Merciful

We have created you all out of a male and a female, and
have made you into nations and tribes, so that you might
know one another... the noblest of you in the sight of
God is the one who is most deeply conscious of Him.
Qur'an, Surah Al Hujurat, 49:13

For the one who asked the pertinent question

Alhamdulillah

KNOWING
ONE
ANOTHER

SHAPING AN ISLAMIC
ANTHROPOLOGY

MERRYL WYN DAVIES

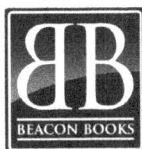

BB

BEACON BOOKS

Published in the UK by Beacon Books and Media Ltd
Earl Business Centre, Dowry Street, Oldham, OL8 2PF, UK.

First published in 1988 by Mansell Publishing Limited

www.beaconbooks.net

ISBN 978-1-915025-83-8 Paperback
ISBN 978-1-915025-84-5 Hardback
ISBN 978-1-915025-85-2 Ebook

Cataloging-in-Publication record for this book is available from the British
Library.

Cover design by Raees Mahmood Khan

Contents

Foreword..ix

Preface xix

Introduction...1

1. Idealism, Ideals and Ideal Types......................13
2. Enchained in Being..33
3. Revolution, Revival and Return 61
4. Islamic Anthropology in Words and Meanings..................95
5. Consonance, Concepts and Context 133
6. Discourse and Dialogue................................167

Bibliography 207

Index..223

\

Foreword

I met Merryl Wynn Davies through Ziauddin Sardar in Manchester. It was the early noughties and the peak of President George Bush's 'War on Terror'. Zia had edited a special issue of the *New Internationalist*, the left-wing magazine based in Oxford, UK; and Merryl had written a couple of articles for the issue. As a follow-up, the *New Internationalist* was looking for volunteers to organise a talk on 'Resistance or Reform' in Manchester. I was working as a volunteer youth worker in Oldham at the time, so I was able to organise the event, in addition to arranging several cars full of young men to travel to Manchester to listen to Merryl and Zia. The ensuing discussion was very heated yet productive as this was the first time many young people were able to discuss aspects of politics, religion and culture through a critical lens. Following my first meeting with Merryl, we developed a bond and friendship over the years through the Muslim Institute monthly round-table discussions in London and their annual winter gatherings at Sarum College, Salisbury. I have benefitted from Merryl's extensive reading, depth of political insights, and razor-sharp wit and analysis. My last meeting with Merryl was in Malaysia in 2019, two years before her death. As a tribute to Merryl's life, the Muslim Institute used its annual winter gathering to celebrate her life and legacy. I was asked to review and discuss the importance of Merryl's seminal book, *Knowing One Another: Shaping an Islamic Anthropology*.

As I read Merryl's book in preparation for the winter gathering, I was faced with the task of navigating the timeless with the specific. There were elements of the book which no longer reflected the author's changing world view due to the shifting nature of time or her own intellectual journey and development. This led me to ask much broader questions: are all written texts shaped by historical factors? Do texts relate to particular social, political, and cultural phenomena? Can texts be seen as having a political moment which are shaped by discursive contexts? More crucially, what is the relationship between the text and the author? What happens if the context leads the author to change their opinion of the text?

Reflecting on the *context* of Merryl's seminal text, it is clear that it is a product of the Islamicate world of the late eighties, which was largely shaped by epistemological ideas of the late Ismail Raj al-Faruqi (d.1986), termed 'Islamization of knowledge'. The Islamization of knowledge project was an outcome of the first international seminar at Lugano, Switzerland in 1977, attended by Muslim scholars with a view to addressing the pressing issue of the crisis of thought within the Muslim *ummah*. The outcome of the conference established a commitment to 'redefine the intellectual and academic basis for the Islamization of knowledge' (IIIT, 1988:vii). It wasn't until the Second International Conference on the Islamization of Knowledge held in Islamabad, Pakistan, in 1981 that a detailed perspective and a *Work Plan* was published, which included seventeen academic papers presented at the conference (IIIT, 1988). According to Ismail Raj al-Faruqi (1988:30) the first prerequisite towards the Islamization of knowledge required Muslim academicians 'to master all the modern sciences, understand them completely and achieve an absolute command of all that they have to offer'. Second, this knowledge should be integrated into the corpus of Islamic legacy, which is achieved through a systematic re-interpretation and adaptation of its components as the worldview of Islam and its values dictate. Finally, this should give Muslim academics the ability to act as pioneers, who then teach new generations of students, who in turn push the boundaries of human knowledge even further by discovering new patterns within

'Allah's creation and establish new paths for making His will and commandments realised in history'. By drawing upon a medical metaphor of diagnosis of a 'problem' and prescribing an antidote, al-Faruqi's 'Islamization' attempted to provide a crucial diagnosis to 'modernisation' and 'westernisation.' To meet the challenges of Islamization of knowledge for social sciences, several scholars attempted to 'Islamize' a range of disciplines, including economics (Siddiqi, 1988), sociology (Yunis, 1988), science and technology (Kazi, 1988), political and constitutional thought (Ghazi, 1988), epistemology (Abu Sulayman, 1988) and anthropology (Ahmad, 1986).

Merryl was a critic of Islamization of knowledge—one of the few who stood up to the project to point out its basic flaws. Her book was written as a critique of the notion of Islamization of knowledge. But it was also meant as a contribution to the intellectual revival that the project was aiming at and examined western social sciences within an Islamic paradigm. In contrast to many works on Islamization of knowledge, which tended to be rather shallow, *Knowing One Another* is based on a truly admirable depth and breadth of scholarship in both western social sciences and Islamic studies. It is also a sustained attempt at developing a Khaldunian theoretical framework.

Islamization of knowledge is no longer a viable enterprise. For many, its thesis has not lived up to its expectations and promises. For others the project was a reactionary response to the socio-political challenges of Muslims living under western hegemonic rule; and it failed to offer an in-depth critique of epistemology of knowledge (Sardar, 2004). Almost thirty years later, following a range of scholarly criticism, an important epistemological shift occurred from the ideas of 'Islamization of knowledge' to 'integration of knowledge' within the IIIT (Sardar, 2017), where 'knowledge, creation, life and humanity are perceived as integrated within a universal framework' (Sardar (2017:126). Sardar suggested a new paradigm, which is not inherently dichotomous and adversarial, by proposing a new model which speaks to the rapidly changing and complex societies, which demand plurality and inclusivity, and embracing of the Other. This requires us to 'revisit the philosophical heritage of Islam and develop a contemporary philosophical tradition of Islam, by engaging with contemporary philosophical trends of other traditions which are also struggling with complex issues of ethics and attempting to grapple with the moral ethical issues we face today' (Sardar, 2017:131).

All texts are produced in time, but *some* ideas contained within the text can transcend time. It is no doubt the duty of the critic to know the difference between the two. Indeed, it is a sign of mature scholars that they evolve and respond differently to changing times and circumstances. Sadly, there are many scholars recycling the same ideas throughout their academic careers, effectively presenting the *same* arguments by using a different scholarly vernacular.

There are many arguments in this book that should be understood within the context of time and the Islamization of knowledge discourse of the period. But equally there are many ideas and propositions included that are universal and withstand the test of time. Those who knew Merryl, or those familiar with her ideas, will no doubt know that she changed her views on some issues included within this text. In fact, I fondly recall our conversation on anthropology in which she discouraged me to read her book, stating that she had changed her mind on quite a few key arguments. This won't come as a great surprise, especially given that Merryl was true to the craft of a Muslim public intellectual.

The overall context of the book can be read as a detailed commentary on Surah Hujurat (49:13) in the Qur'an: 'We have created you all out of a male and a female, and have made you into nations and tribes, so that you might know one another… the noblest of you in the sight of God is the one who is deeply conscious of Him.' The nature of our interconnected world, due to the speed of globalisation, communication technologies and social media, means that there is a pressing need to make contemporary sense of the above Qur'anic verse. The increasing dislocation and re-connections between people and places made possible through free movement of capital, trade and cultural exchanges, assisted by technology and trade, means that the world no longer exists between *Dar al-Islam* and *Dar al-Harb*. The central trait of the modern world is interdependence. The 'knowing one another' referred to in Surah Hujurat is referring to a dialogue; the verse encourages us to look beyond our own emotional, intellectual, and spiritual comfort zones. As Merryl (1988:82) argues, Islamic anthropology should really be the 'study of mankind in society' and ought to be seen as an important mechanism through which Qur'anic mandate of 'knowing one another' can be actualised. Unlike western or secular forms of anthropology, which puts emphasis on knowing the 'Other', 'Islamic anthropology' provides opportunity for social scientists to know their *own* society and culture. More crucially, Merryl (1988:50) argues that the 'science of anthropology of western civilisation is the universal language of western civilisation only.' Part of the challenge for Islamic anthropology is that they must 'elaborate their own ways of knowing and use that as a vantage point to observe, evaluate and enter a dialogue with the dominant western civilisation.' Indeed, Islamic anthropology means that Muslims cannot take a passive role by simply knowing about other people, rather they have a duty to be actively involved in dialogue and discussion.

Her critique of western anthropology was more systematic and rigorous in her later works as in the case of *Barbaric Others: A Manifesto of Western Racism* (Sardar et al. 1993) and *Why Do People Hate America* (Sardar and Davies, 2003). Moreover, Merryl's reading and critique of western epistemology also shifted to recognise how disciplines are essentially a product of *episteme;* they are embedded in the epistemological framework of a civilization, and are a product of its social and cultural milieu. The challenge for Muslims is not to *Islamize* anthropology, which was developed in the West to facilitate colonialism and imperialism. Rather, the task is to develop their own culturally appropriate disciplines. Instead of anthropology, she argued, after Ibn Khaldun, for *Ilm ul-Umran*: studies of cultures and civilizations with emphasis on inclusivity, diversity and pluralism.

Indeed, a major strength of *Knowing One Another* is the insights it offers on culture and society. According to Merryl, culture is an integral part of human nature. This means that no nation can *think* of itself in isolation but only through dialogue with other cultures. Moreover, if culture, society, and diversity is inherent then 'cultural and social rights must inevitably stem from this: rights to autonomy, integrity and self-determination'. The duty of humankind is not simply to recognise, appreciate and celebrate diversity as an ontological reality. Rather, we are encouraged to see commonality and to recognise the arch of unity within diversity. There needs to be a recognition or a moral imperative which sees 'diversity as distinguishing our unity, not as complicating our commonality'. There is an emancipatory power baked into the fabric of knowing one another; that is, by engaging with dialogue and conversation one comes to know him/herself. It is only through the process of knowing the 'other' that we truly know ourselves.

The true understanding of verse 49:13, according to Merryl, can only be derived from a holistic approach to our duties and obligations, for both men and women. She insists that the essence of understanding culture and society is taken from Islamic ontology located within the Qur'anic worldview. In doing so, Merryl touches upon a range of issues which are not restricted by time and space. By dislocating or bracketing out 'Islamic anthropology' from its epistemological footing, this book offers a string of helpful reminders and indicators.

First, the concept of *fitrah*, the inherent nature or natural disposition of humankind, as articulated within the book continues to have meaningful currency. According to Merryl, through the concept of *fitrah* 'we see the dimension of capacities and endowments; the knowledge possessed by the *fitrah* is a capacity not merely for sensate existence, sight, hearing, touch and taste, but also a capacity for cultural existence with the power of articulate speech, language, conceptual thought and reasoning, intuition and imagination.' The concept of *fitrah* requires that we have an awareness of our own existence as a process capable of completion, that completion being the fulfilling of its debt to its Lord and Creator, and its ultimate return to God. In short, *fitrah*, through the potentialities of sense, reason, intuition and spiritual awareness, is an instrument of discernment between right and wrong, between true and false. Its highest dimension is the discernment of the existence and Unity of God. In summary, the power of understanding the concept of *fitrah* allows believers the capacity to rise to a higher state of consciousness.

Second, the capacities of *fitrah* allows the concept of *khilafah,* the vice-regent of God upon earth, to be fully enjoyed. Merryl sees the concept of *khilafah* as gender inclusive, applying to both men and women, but most importantly as an ideal ascribed by God to humanity. The ideas of rights or responsibilities from a Qur'anic point of view should be understood through human trusteeship of God's vice-regent on earth. Merryl shows how various Qur'anic commentators have demonstrated the dual implication of the status of *khilafah*: that of humankind in general succeeding as inheritors of the earth; as well as the implication that each generation succeeds the other in assuming the obligations of the status of *khilafah*. The concept of *khilafah* for Merryl exists as a relational term, especially given that the substance of humankind's trusteeship over the earth is a trust or *ammanah*. The concept of trust or *ammanah* logically entails responsibility and the notion of rights and duties implicit in the terms of the trust. Finally, the status of mankind as *khilafah* ultimately includes the return to God, which offers 'terms of mankind's covenant, the use of their faculties, *fitrah*, the exercise of the trusted status, *khilafah*, the living out of the operational process' through Islam.

Lessons from the recent Covid pandemic shows the interconnected nature of *fitrah* and *khilafah*. Covid has brought the interdependent and interconnected nature of this world sharply into focus, as we are forced to question geographical boundaries and to think of humanity as one, single *ummah*. Despite this realization of our interdependency, sadly this has not been matched with mutual understanding. In fact, 'the state of international relations, the subtle forms of xenophobia, and the festering sores of antagonism and animosity between nations would suggest not.' This observation made by Merryl over thirty years ago is as relevant now as it was then. The question of how individuals, and more crucially how nation states, deal with cultural difference is one of the key challenges of modernity and globalisation, and a major issue facing international relations at a macro level and community tensions facing local authorities. So, each generation have their own unique challenges of knowing one another, which continues to be a work in progress. The discussions on *fitrah* and *khilafah* is an imperative to contemporary debates and discourses. In fact, Timothy Morton has extended this idea of humanity. In his book *Humankind: Solidarity with Non-human People,* Morton (2017) shows us the importance of transcending the binary worldview between humankind and mother nature, as recent cases of global warming have reminded us that our relationship with the environment and other non-human beings determine the fate of our humanity. In doing so he questions the premise that the environment simply exists for the service of humankind. Instead, he argues that being human means creating and sustaining a network of solidarity and extending the concept of humanity to non-human beings.

The re-publication of *Knowing One Another* is most welcome. This seminal work needs to be read and re-read. It demands a re-reading through a critical lens which puts the 'Islamic anthropology' and 'Islamization of Knowledge' discourse within its socio-political and historical context. It also needs to be re-read for its highly original universal insights on culture, cultural relations, and the Other. As an academic exercise this book pushes readers to re-evaluate the relationship between changing global landscapes and its relationship with text and its author. In doing so, it reminds the readers of their ethical duty not to force works of literature and social sciences to meet the requirements of a theory by ignoring the complex relationship between the world, the text, and the author. More significantly, this book offers a Qur'anic framework that helps us to navigate a range of topics from environment and globalisation, to diversity and conflict.

Dr. Shamim Miah
2023

References

1. Abu Sulayman, A.H.A. (1988) *The Islamisation of Knowledge: A New Approach Toward Reform of Contemporary Knowledge*. In Islam: Source and Purpose of Knowledge. Islamisation of Knowledge Series Number 5 (Virginia: IIIT).

2. Ahmad, A. (1988) *Toward Islamic Anthropology: Definitions, Dogma and Directions* (Virginia: IIIT).

3. Al-Faruqi, I.R. (1988) *Islamisation of Knowledge: Problems, Principles and Prospective*. In Islam: Source and Purpose of Knowledge. Islamisation of Knowledge Series Number 5 (Virginia: IIIT).

4. Davies, M.W. (1988) *Knowing One Another: Shaping an Islamic Anthropology* (Mansell: London).

5. Gazi, M.A. (1988) *Political and Constitutional Thought: Some Guidelines for Islamisation of Knowledge*. In Islam: Source and Purpose of Knowledge. Islamisation of Knowledge Series Number 5 (Virginia: IIIT).

6. Kazi, M.A. (1988) *Islamisation of Modern Science and Technology*. In Islam: Source and Purpose of Knowledge. Islamisation of Knowledge Series Number 5 (Virginia: IIIT).

7. Morton, T. (2017) *Humankind: Solidarity with Nonhuman People* (London: Verso).

8. Sardar, Z. (2017) *From Islamisation to Integration of Knowledge*. In Sardar, Z. Thomas. J.T. (2017) Rethinking Reform in Higher Education (London: IIIT).

9. Sardar, Z. (2004) *Desperately Seeking Paradise: Journeys of a Sceptical Muslim* (London: Granta).

10. Sardar, Z., Davies, M.W. (2003) *Why Do People Hate America?* (London: Icon Books).

11. Sardar, Z., Nandy, A., Davies, M.W (1993) *Barbaric Others: A Manifesto on Western Racism* (London: Pluto).

12. Siddiqui, M.N. (1998) *An Islamic Approach to Economics*. In Islam: Source and Purpose of Knowledge. Islamisation of Knowledge Series Number 5 (Virginia: IIIT).

13. Yunis. I.B. (1998) *Contemporary Sociology: An Islamic Critique*. In Islam: Source and Purpose of Knowledge. Islamisation of Knowledge Series Number 5 (Virginia: IIIT).

14. Yunis. I.B. (1985) *Islamic Sociology: An Introduction* (Cambridge: Hodder and Stoughton.

Preface

The predominant characteristic of the modern world is inter-dependence. No nation can think of itself in isolation. What happens in one corner of the world affects the entire world. The apocalyptic warning of a Chernobyl is just one example that what happens in another country can become our problem, a problem requiring international action. The speed of communication, the interconnection of the world's economies, the increasing ease of travel and the numbers of people moving from one part of the world to another are all trends for the future.

The question: is this increasing realization of interdependence matched by an increase in mutual understanding? The state of international relations, the subtle forms of xenophobia, and the festering sores of antagonism and animosity between nations would suggest not. Although we may not be able to exist in isolation, we still think of ourselves in terms of our exclusive groups. The problem is not with having special identities, but in how we understand and operate them. Knowing ourselves is only the initial step that will help determine how we know other people. The more we can come to understand and respect other people in their own terms, to accept that our special identity can be secured only when we secure the special identity of others, the more likely we are to create a safe world for all of us.

In recent decades Muslims have realized that they need to find solutions to the onslaught of modernity and to shape the future according to the dictates of Islam. An essential part of this quest is the 'islamization of knowledge', a movement that seeks to ground the quest for knowledge in the eternal principles of Islam. This book is an attempt to contribute to that movement by offering a definition of Islamic anthropology.

Islamic anthropology has a special role to play in the islamization of knowledge. As the essence of Islam is universal, anthropology should be a way for Muslims to understand themselves and to treat non-Muslims with tolerance and understanding. Islamization should not mean retreating behind purist walls of isolation but should open out the Muslim consciousness so that Muslims can play a constructive part in the modern world's collective future. I hope that in some way this book conveys that objective.

I am eternally grateful to Gough Tonge, the teacher who provided the time, space and stimulus that led me to invent a rudimentary kind of anthropology for myself when I was nine years old. I owe a great debt of gratitude to my teachers and in particular, my supervisor, Peter Ucko, at University College, London, where I discovered that anthropology already existed. It would be impossible not to record how much I owe to a group of friends who have welcomed me as a Muslim, listened to my musings and rantings, and let me learn from their discussions. Finally, I owe an overwhelming and special debt of gratitude to my friend and mentor, Ziauddin Sardar, without whom nothing would be as it is. Certainly without his unfailing attention and supportive badgering this book would have never got started nor have been finished.

The ideas contained in this book have had a long gestation, and a difficult delivery. In all the crises attendant upon the writing, my mother has been a tower of strength, a great encouragement, despite the fact that I cannot expect her to be pleased with the line I must follow. I hope she will recognize I have been trying to live up to the standards I learned from a very special and remarkable lady, in my own way. If there is any merit in what I have done it has been nurtured in her care and love and in the efforts she expended in securing me my opportunities in life.

Introduction

*'To Boldly Go Where No Man
Has Gone Before'*

The Anthropological Enterprise

Why anthropology? The question usually arises from popular curiosity. The pursuits of academics are also the concerns of the public: they effect each other, and it would be a rash person who failed to notice they also foster and nurture each other. There would be no point in this book were there no link between the ideas presented here and popular general concerns.

Anthropology is a familiar and frequently used word, although its meaning and what anthropologists do remains vague to most people. The overwhelming response from a western audience is that anthropology must be fascinating, which it is, and that it has something to do with monkeys, men, and exotic rituals, which in some ways it does. People are talking about what has percolated out of western universities, where anthropology was formed, and pretty well the only place where it lives today.

There is another view of anthropology which has nothing to do with western society. In the developing world anthropology is a term of abuse, because it is seen to have abused those who were subjects of anthropological enquiry. It has made many countries inhospitable environments for further anthropological work. But there is a curious phenomenon now in evidence: in order to claim the basic right of self-determination, communities in the developing world must describe themselves in the conventional terminology of anthropology.[1]

One of today's best known anthropologists is Desmond Morris, a noted expert on monkeys and apes. Morris came to anthropology via zoology, and is best described by the even more obscure term, ethologist. His popular bestseller, *The Naked Ape,* is taken by the vast majority of people to be an informative insight into anthropological knowledge, though I have little doubt this view would make many social anthropologists wince. The problem arises from some complex confusions, the first that between physical anthropology and social or cultural anthropology.

Historically, physical anthropology is part of an integral anthropology where race and physical racial characteristics are viewed as traits linked to social and cultural capacity and behaviour; together they explained the peoples of the world. The labours of anthropology have made it clear that mankind is biologically homogeneous, more like itself than it is like anything else. The obverse has been the clear demonstration that biological racial traits have no direct bearing on culture, cultural potential or performance.

The second confusion is far more intractable, arising from the great debate over biological and cultural determinism as mechanisms ordering and explaining human life. Anthropology, the science of mankind, made it its task to prove the universal scientific laws governing the nature of mankind: to explain the diversity of mankind and the relationship between the diversities, and to distinguish the boundaries between mankind and other species.

Many social anthropologists are dubious about animal behavioural studies, which make too free a use of human cultural concepts when interpreting animal behaviour. Desmond Morris, whose popular success rests entirely on using this procedure, takes information from the study of primate behaviour, interpreted with human cultural concepts, as the evolutionary basis upon which human behaviour in a cultural context must be understood. Most social anthropologists would assert his analysis is simplistic and goes nowhere beyond the commonplace that all aspects of our physical being are involved in communication, that culture is a means of communication based upon signs.

In explaining culture in terms of acquired human behaviour, social anthropology draws on the mechanisms of physical and biological science. The result is an authoritative argument that all mankind is biologically unitary, with a unitary potential for throwing up cretins and geniuses. The significant point is that in order to abolish racialism, to stop some people being unjustly and unjustifiably seen as monkeys, anthropology, along with many other western disciplines, has had to make monkeys of us all.

For social anthropologists what differentiates mankind is culture, the distinctive human capacity that explains how mankind responds to its environment and history. The definition of this cultural capacity causes a predicament for anthropology when Jane Goodall films chimpanzees making tools and when Konrad Lorenz is deemed to have established species culture among animals. If mankind is an animal, mankind is not distinguished by being *the* tool-making animal, nor *the* cultural animal. There was an era when anthropology as a social science felt it had squared this circle by securing the triumph of cultural determinism over biological determinism. Derek Freeman's recent demolition of Margaret Mead shows how clearly this great debate underpinned social anthropology in the 1920s and 1930s.[2] Margaret Mead is undoubtedly this century's best known social anthropologist, and her books, *Growing Up in Samoa* and *Coming of Age in New Guinea*, are the most widely read anthropological texts, especially by non-anthropologists.[3]

Freeman makes it abundantly clear that the anthropological theory Mead set out to prove was that culture is a different order of magnitude, a different reality, one that transcends the biological nature of mankind. When it comes to people it is nurture and not nature that counts. Freeman demonstrates that Mead was an atrocious field worker, that biological determinism is alive and well and must be reintroduced into the annals of social anthropology where nurture must be rebalanced with the erroneously expunged nature. Quite why or how this is necessary from his alternative portrait of Samoan society, except that it is different from Mead's conclusions, he never makes clear.

Freeman's case is debatable, but the dilemma it poses for social anthropology is real. Confident of the victory of cultural determinism, most often assumed rather than argued, where does anthropology stand today in relation to the increasing strength of reductive biological thought? While the professional social anthropologist can afford to ignore Desmond Morris as mere commercial vulgarization, it cannot be said the questions posed by socio-biological anthropology are not serious.[4]

The student of popular culture will have to admit that the great upsurge of liberal consciousness in the 1960s markedly changed the presentation of 'other' peoples in books, films, television series and even in comic books, that is, the representations and stereotypes associated with the so-called 'native' peoples social anthropology has specialized in studying.

The classic instance of this change is in the cinematic Western. As the 1960s proceeded, presentations of the culture of the Indians became increasingly detailed and informed. Instead of just a war-whooping cast of extras, Indians began to become characters, and some were even allowed sympathetic speaking parts. This kind of presentation opened the way for European American guilt, a kind of sad inexorability about the nobility of the vanishing race. Such evocative names as the *Trail of Tears* and *Wounded Knee* came to evoke a reappraisal of European America's manifest destiny.[5] The result was a cinematic restriction of the gay abandon with which heroes could go about shooting Indians. Since then, more complex issues have emerged and led to the withering of the Western as a genre. The more the central heroes became torn and tormented by the clash between dominant European culture and recognition of the dignity, nobility and rights of the Indians, the more the Western became true drama, that is tragedy, rather than entertainment. When the message became 'white man bad, red man good', the stirring of the blood for European Americans was missing from the Western.

To look more widely at popular culture is to notice a similar movement in the representation of other cultural groups. The simple racism of 'foreign means evil' has become much more complicated. The presentation of black Africa has always been racist and prejudiced;[6] yet a television series like *Tarzan* of the late 1960s and early 1970s was relatively informed anthropologically. The actual diversity of African social and cultural forms was recognized, even if ludicrously incorporated. There were Africans who were 'good guys', without being music hall buffoons, there were aspects of African culture that were used in conjunction with Tarzan to achieve good.

The great growth genre of popular culture in modern times has been science fiction and here too anthropology has made an impact. Indeed, one of the leading science fiction writers, Ursula Le Guin, is the daughter of a well-known anthropologist, A. L. Kroeber.[7] A feature found in Le Guin's writing is also noticeable in *Star Trek*: a consciousness of the diversity of culture and society combined with an attention to detail in presentation which is central to the understanding of the motivation and action of the characters.[8] *Star Trek* actually provides an overt kind of anthropology course, wrestling with themes such as cultural evolution, parallel evolution, diffusion, the dynamics of cultural and social change.

American popular culture is a dominant force in the modern world. The central concerns of American society eventually get made into soap operas: everything from the Holocaust and AIDS to Alex Haley's *Roots*, and an American Indian version of *Roots* without the literary or dramatic distinction, *The Mystic Warrior*. These movements in popular culture owe much to the stirring of the liberal conscience. It should be noted that this coincided with the great upsurge in the teaching of anthropology, hence a greater familiarity with and wider circulation of its content.

By an examination of popular culture, I think we can assess the lessons of western academic anthropology: that cultural diversity is a reality based on reason and rationale and therefore must command respect. Comprehensibility is another matter. The overriding impression imparted by and expressed in popular culture is that cultural diversity remains bewildering, creating a barrier of 'otherness', which will always be an impediment to compatibility. This is not merely an aspect of popular culture, however; in Britain today it is a serious political issue. Many well-intentioned British people are fascinated about the differences of their Hindu, Sikh and Muslim neighbours, but they are loath to be neighbourly lest their ignorance of culturally sensitive etiquette causes offence. The world of their neighbours is bound up with an 'otherness' not so much alien as incomprehensible. Ultimately there will always be a choice to be made between 'their' ways and 'our' ways; you can accept the people but their 'otherness' is problematic.

A classic example of this lesson can be gleaned from *Star Trek*. For all its anthropologically-informed philosophy, and philosophically-informed anthropology, Captain Kirk is actually the embodiment of the 'American way', the ultimate product of White Anglo-Saxon Protestant evolution on a galactic scale. The principal message he purveys is 'niceness' in response to 'other' people. But the purpose of his niceness is clearly to demonstrate that other people should become like him, that his is the best way, the American way.

This sums up neatly the limits of the triumph of western academic anthropology. But I would go further; it is a triumph stemming directly from the epistemological base of western anthropology, and there is no doubt that it is a triumph. If America now accepts the nobility of American Indian culture through the dissemination of anthropological generalizations then modern professional anthropologists have worked hard and won. For western anthropology began precisely with the great debate over whether American Indians had any culture of their own.

Modern western academic anthropology is directed at interpreting 'other' cultures, making them explicable in terms of its own scientific categories and terms of reference. One of the most eminent contemporary British anthropologists, Sir Edmund Leach, whose *Social Anthropology* is probably the best popular introduction to be found on the subject, is rather at a loss to find any function or purpose for anthropology beyond studying the 'otherness' of 'other' people. This he declares is good in itself and provides eclectic joy to the anthropologist. The professional anthropologist may have passionate and committed views on matters arising from his or her study, but these are a private not a professional responsibility. It is the task of the politician, or policy-maker, or the voting public to convert meaningful anthropological knowledge into necessary action. The anthropologists are bound by permutations of their own non-interference directive.

Today anthropology is very conscious of being a discipline if not in crisis and terminal decline, then definitely in a *cul de sac*. Yet the subject matter of anthropology is of vital importance: how one defines the essential nature of mankind and the questions that arise from the diversity of human society and culture. The problems concern questions that should be asked and the capacity of the theoretical base of the discipline to generate relevant questions. The renewed theoretical debate, the tussle between the relativists and rationalists, certainly brings these issues into focus, without as yet offering any clear cut answers.[9] The wide academic interest in this debate offers the prospect of anthropology becoming a more lively, and potentially influential, discipline in the future.

For me, the 'knowing one another' on which I base my anthropology, is taken from a source outside western anthropology. Its meaning and interpretation give rise to a very different kind of anthropology. The phrase is taken from the Qur'an, Surah Al Hujjarat 49:13:

> O mankind! Lo! We have created you male and female and have made you nations and tribes that ye may know one another. Lo! the noblest of you, in the sight of Allah, is the best in conduct. Lo! Allah is Knower, Aware.[10]

The knowing one another referred to in the Qur'an is clearly a mutual process, a dialogue. This may seem a rather commonplace point—yet it is one of the greatest stumbling blocks in modern western anthropology. Indeed Ian Jarvie's most telling arguments about relativism revolve around this issue, for he sees the hidden agenda of anthropological teaching as the assertion that whatever is, is right in cultural terms.[11] With this criterion there can be no dialogue. He is obviously right, however, to assert that honest, informed disagreement denotes a greater respect than unthinking avoidance and silence on matters of disagreement.

The implications of mutuality are much broader than merely accepting the responsibility of the ethnographer to engage in debate with 'their' people. Ethnography, the *rite de passage* of professional anthropology, is a disorienting and frequently distressing experience. For despite the claims to scientific objectivity it is an entirely subjective operation as instances recorded by Pelto and Pelto make clear.[12] Beyond that it brings into question many of the cherished first principles of the entire discipline, a matter honestly and entertainingly dealt with by Nigel Barley in *The Innocent Anthropologist*. What he makes clear is that while anthropologists are seeking to know another people they are also forced to know more about themselves. While they stub their toes on other peoples' inability to describe and explain the self-evident, they also encounter the unconsciously self-evident about themselves. This element of the anthropologists' enforced cultural self-awareness is then expunged from the discourse of anthropology which is diminished by this avoidance. What the encounter with other people tells us about ourselves is often a significant learning technique, if used consciously. Our own intellectual, emotional, spiritual bases are the stumbling blocks to understanding others.

Anthropology provides the opportunity for anthropologists to reflect upon their own society and culture. This is an opportunity conventional anthropology seldom takes, regarding itself still as a discipline looking exclusively at 'other' people from a scientific base. While anthropology is best fitted to discourse upon the cultural basis and bias of the western intellectual tradition, it operates merely as a part of it. Anthropology could play a leading role in commenting upon western society in its relations with the rest of the world, but remains silent. This point has been forcefully made by Stanley Diamond in relation to western anthropology in the colonial era.[13] The task is no less important in the neo-imperialist era.

The culture shock on the return to one's own environment is experienced by all anthropologists. This should constitute the basis for the mutual learning necessary to set new parameters for the scope of Islamic anthropology, parameters that would engage a lively dialogue with western anthropology. The mutuality also means engaging in a dialogue with the people studied. The anthropologized are no longer silent objects of attention, their critique of the subject should become an increasing focus of attention.

When the knowing of ourselves becomes part of the objective and dynamic of anthropology then the import of what one learns about other people is likely to change. Rather than being a silent witness to the 'otherness' of 'other' people, the mutuality of culture that observer and observed possess in different ways brings into relief both consonance and diversity, things in common we share in different ways. If we return to the interpretation of the Qur'anic verse we see that knowing one another involves a number of essential propositions, and leads to a definite purpose. The unity of mankind is an established proposition, just as it is in western anthropology where the debate has been about the nature of this unity. God knows that He is the sole creator of all mankind, and this is His teaching to mankind. Then the phenomena of culture and society, our tribes and nations, are also shown to arise from the same source and are the original innate condition of mankind. Western anthropology, much of whose debate has been about the origin and growth of culture and society, has differed in this respect though it is now approaching such a concept of unity as an accepted proposition.[14]

If culture and society are inherent in human nature then they provide a necessary identity and means of action to the individual. Cultural and social rights must inevitably stem from this: rights to autonomy, integrity and self-determination, for example. But the dynamic of the verse is that culture and society are not ends in themselves, but rather the mechanisms for establishing right conduct related to the eternal values of cultural and social performance. The process of knowing one another and the acceptance of the mutuality of this process, enables us to distinguish and discern the relationship of social and cultural practice to values.

Islamic anthropology accepts that culture and society are inherent. It must also then accept that culture and society are fallible mechanisms, capable of failing to achieve collective wellbeing, and it should study how and why these failures arise and their consequences.

Relativism exists in Islamic anthropology because culture and society are diverse; but what they are relative to is open to debate by all: the conceptual base of Islamic values. This relativism can never flirt with the notion that whatever is, is right simply because it is cultural and social. It is, however, a study whose analytical tools are applied without discrimination to Muslim and non-Muslim cultures and societies. The essential openness of its conceptual base also makes it a dialogue where Muslim and non-Muslim can participate.

Mankind is richly diverse, but appreciating diversity for itself, just because it exists, cannot assist the human condition. Unless we can see consonance and commonality in our diversity then the tribulations comprising our history so far will continue to rumble on. Ultimately our need is for a moral imperative that orders knowledge to regard diversity as what distinguishes our unity, not as complicating or fracturing our commonality. Our need is for a system of knowledge actively engaged in clothing that moral force with practical, empirical meaning so that instead of being a pious hope it also becomes a mode of action, an active policy in contemporary reality.

Notes

1. In a recent television series on the history of anthropology, *Strangers Abroad*, shown on British television, the subjects of Malinowski's and Mead's ethnography spoke of their 'culture' as though it were an alien object they perforce had to carry around with them by way of self justification. The same syndrome can be seen in the essential advocacy and militancy of the indigenous peoples' movements of the world, such as the Australian Aborigines, Inuit and the American Indians' campaigns for land rights and social justice, where they have to perform their cultural authenticity, which many are ready to doubt, in order to get a semblance of a hearing and a redress that falls far short of genuine recognition of their rights. See also the review of *Strangers Abroad* by Burton Benedict in *Anthropology Today*, Vol. 3 (2) April 1987.

2. Freeman, *Margaret Mead and Samoa.*

3. Apart from these classics, Mead was an ardent popularizer and guru of 1960s liberal consciousness. She was, after all, purported to be the person who taught Benjamin Spock all he wanted to know about child rearing.

4. Morris's popular success is one thing, the upsurge of and interest in socio-biology quite another. Freeman espouses socio-biology in his work. For the opposing poles of that debate, see Wilson, *Sociobiology*, and Sahlins, *The Use and Abuse of Biology.*

5. Of course guilt and sentimental attachment to the American Indian legacy goes only so far. It has done little to provide political, economic and social redress for the remaining Indians who still experience oppression, discrimination and marginalization that undermine whatever has been repaid of the wealth expropriated, that is, of course, stolen from them. For an American Indian perspective of the West, see Brown, *Bury My Heart At Wounded Knee.*

6. The best example that comes to mind is *Sanders of the River* where black Africa is the home of evil, superstitious, natives. One also cringes at the squandering of the talents of Paul Robeson who sings the title song 'Sanders the Brave, Sanders the Bold'—you can be sure Sanders is the white hero shouldering his burden neath solar topee with fortitude, rectitude and a stiff upper lip.

7. Most notably see Ursula Le Guin's *The Word For World Is Forest*, a science fiction tale about cultural depredation. Her other novels such as *Rocannon's World, Planet of Exile, City of Illusions, The Dispossessed* and *Orsinian Tales,* all embody fascinating anthropological insight and detail.

8. *Star Trek* is not so much a television programme as a cultural phenomenon which has been orbiting the television screens of the world ever since actual production of the series was suspended in the 1960s. In recent years it has become a major box-office success as a motion picture series. The series also has its own hardcore organization of devotees known as 'Trekkies'.

9. For the best introduction to the various strands of the rationalist-relativist debate see Wilson, ed. *Rationality*; Hollis and Lukes, eds. *Rationality and Relativism;* and Overing, ed. *Reason and Morality.*

10. Pickthall, *The Meaning of the Glorious Quran.*

11. Jarvie, *Rationality and Relativism.*

12. Pelto and Pelto, *Anthropological Research.* See especially their chapter 'Science and Anthropology' for the famous Redfield/Oscar Lewis dispute over Tepoztecan when the two eminent researchers presented almost diametrically opposing views of the same community. They quote Redfield's revealing comment: 'The greater pan of the explanation for the difference between the tworeports on this matter of Tepoztecan life and character is to be found in the differences between the two investigators.'

13. Diamond, *In Search of the Primitive.*

14. This is best seen in Geertz's argument for a new conception of man in western anthropology in *The Interpretation of Cultures.*

1

Idealism, Ideals and Ideal Types

Anthropology is an accumulation of information, theories and techniques of study relating to the diverse practices and ideas of mankind in society. It is a mental construct dependent upon the system of knowledge of the anthropologists who have pursued their studies in this particular field. There is no inherent need in the nature of anthropology determining the questions, problems and debates existing within the subject or within the accumulated body of information upon which they draw.

The only thing that is neutral about anthropology is the word itself. It is there as a bland general description ready to be appended to specific definitions and content arising from the world view of the anthropologist and embodied in the theories utilized. The proliferation of double-barrelled anthropologies is a consequence: functionalist anthropology, structuralist anthropology, Marxist anthropology, and now Islamic anthropology. It is the meaning and implication of these double-barrelled relationships we need to clarify.

Economic anthropology, political anthropology, the anthropology of art, the anthropology of religion, the anthropology of Islam are a set of double-barrelled descriptions within the generality of anthropology. As such the terms are doubly neutral; neither word gives us a definition of the kind of anthropology being done. The crucial debate within economic anthropology, for example, is the substantivist/ formalist controversy. This derives nothing from the term economic anthropology precisely because it is a dispute over how the study should be pursued and what it should contain.[1] It concerns the question of whether classical economics, that is western economics, is, can or must be the basis of theory and interpretation. Some argue that western economics should be a starting point; but others argue that it has no utility. If western economics cannot be applied, then economic anthropology would undermine western economics which rests upon claims of the universality of 'economic man'. Economic anthropology would then demonstrate a fundamental rupture in humankind, with some segments of the human population possibly having a different kind of rationality, but being outside that rationality on which is based the economic practice of western peoples,

The anthropology of Islam is no more unified in approach as Abdul Hamid el-Zein demonstrates.[2] His analysis of some of the leading studies argues that it is the world view of the anthropologist that determines how he or she orders this field. The differences stemming from ideology affect how ethnography is undertaken, what the 'facts' are, what information is gathered, how it is interpreted, what conclusions are reached and what generalizations are made. Zein makes important points on the way religion is perceived and studied in anthropology; he questions whether, in fact, Islam can be comprehended in these terms. Implicit but unmentioned in the thrust of his argument is a matter given little attention in the anthropology of Islam, or anthropology in general: the status and meaning of the term civilization. The term is well developed in Islamic studies, most notably in the elegant and rigorous definitions of Marshall Hodgson.[3] Zein's conclusions seem to suggest anthropologists should give more attention to such concepts to enable them to deal with the complex phenomenon of Islam in the societies they study.

Functionalist, structural-functionalist, structuralist and Marxist anthropologies, to which we are now adding Islamic anthropology, are double-barrelled terms of a very different order. In these constructions anthropology is the dependent variable. It is functionalism, structuralism, Marxism or Islam which provide the world view described in theory and deployed as methodology, thus generating the anthropology done. The determining factor, whether functionalism or structuralism, but especially Marxism or Islam, is not neutral, however much anthropologists equivocate on the subject of commitment. Murray Leaf's history of anthropology, *Man, Mind and Science*, has focused on this issue very clearly. Whatever the anthropologists' claims, they are all working with conceptions of man, mind and science related to established epistemologies, philosophic systems, ideologies. Leaf is one of those who have pointed out that the lack of theoretical clarity and the wish to avoid theoretical rigour have been endemic in anthropology, consequently problems of theory have come to be regarded as problems in the general arena of knowledge. One would go even further and say it has led to that *fin de discipline ennui* that has for so long gripped anthropology.

Man, mind, and science are inescapable factors in the study of anthropology, and it is the conceptual fabrics of these factors which underlie and give meaning to the double-barrelled anthropological labels. It is hardly contentious to say the concepts of man and mind relate to epistemology, philosophy, and of course, religion. The history of the conceptions of man and mind in western anthropology will be looked at later. The really contentious issue is how anthropology relates to science, as a concept.

There has recently been a radical revision in the understanding of the concept of science. The two most important names in this field are T.S. Kuhn and Michel Foucault, both of whom lead us to the conclusion that science is a social construct, a conventional activity, a reflection and reflexion of particular themes of epistemology, philosophy, ideology and religion within a particular social setting.[4] Kuhn and Foucault have called into question the dominant, orthodox and still potent image of science and scientific activity as an objective, neutral, value-free enquiry in search of absolute truth. This is the kind of science in which complex processes are reduced to their constituent building blocks, whose properties are studied to uncover the mechanical relations governing their operation. This science is seen as the major achievement of western civilization, it is the idealized pattern for the acquisition of knowledge. To be 'scientific' involves a mode of operation which supposedly enhances the search for knowledge, making the output of any discipline 'superior'. From this perspective anthropology's predominant focus on 'small-scale' societies or the 'primitive' would be the logical place to seek the fundamental rules governing the social behaviour of mankind using the methodological rigour of science.

Real science consists of the pure branches of knowledge, mathematics, physics, chemistry, biology and their sub-disciplinary offspring. It is here that the objective facts about the world are established, creating the context of knowledge for all other information and with which all other information must be made compatible. 'Real' science, 'hard' science, 'pure' science is about demonstrable verities in the world 'out there'. Mankind is rather more of an enigma. Those disciplines which involve the study of mankind are tainted by the enigma, either irredeemably, in which case they are called humanities; or in such a way that they have to wrestle determinedly with subjectivity but can nevertheless be termed social sciences. C. P. Snow made popular the notion of the two cultures, science and the humanities, as mutually sundering and increasingly incomprehensible world views, but he seems to have underestimated the potency of science for western civilization.[5] For it is not just social sciences which strive to make themselves respectable by becoming more and more 'scientific'. Peter L. Berger's essay on recent trends in Christian theology is a case in point.[6] By the definition of science, and the foundation act from which it is said to originate, theology ought to be its antithesis, yet Berger shows that theology is now pursued 'scientifically'. The apotheosis of the development charted by Berger is represented by Don Cuppitt.[7] Cuppitt's stance is that religious faith, the concept of God, can be understood only through the world view created by the inexorable advance of science, the nature of faith is remade throughout history—taking its cue from science.[8]

The essence of science is reason and logic operated through empirical investigation, the testing of theoretical formulas and hypotheses in replicable and verifiable ways capable of proof or refutation. It is the methodological relationship of reason and logic with empirical enquiry that links them to the natural world in such a way as to establish the objective 'facts' about the natural world, The demonstrable verity of the 'facts' of science establishes reason and logic as the authoritative arbiters, the independent, objective, neutral and value-free means of knowing—which must be the basis of knowledge. In this scientific way of knowing, reason and logic transcend culture, history, ideology and religion.

Science is a universal system not dependent upon manipulation by the self-serving, or even the idealistic ends, of society, culture, ideology or religion. Science serves only science, science elicits knowledge about the knowable and defines their limits. The use of science is another matter; for then this objective, neutral knowledge regrettably falls into the hands of society, culture, ideology and religion, those lesser categories tainted by the fettering of reason and logic to limited ends.

The idealization of science has been based on an actual history of the growth of science. The point of departure for both Kuhn and Foucault were studies of what had happened in the history of science. They have shown the nature of science itself to be quite contrary to the widely held ideal-type definition. Foucault has dealt more generally with the nature of knowledge and the movement of ideas, Kuhn has dealt specifically with the culture of science as demonstrated through the history and practice of scientists. Foucault and Kuhn stand as just two leading names in a growing body of scholars who proffer a very different definition of the nature of science.

The critique of science is that it is a conventional activity contingent upon society and culture. Nature does not describe itself; no terminology, ideas, or concepts from the natural world impose themselves onto the mind of the scientist. It is the scientist as a member of a society, with a culture, and hence a conceptual fabric expressed in language, who imposes concepts and description upon the natural world. Science is the ordering of knowledge and information with the conceptual tools of language and techniques made available by a society and its history. Concepts and the resultant ordering of the natural world are subject to change, related not to any inherent necessity in the natural world but to the activity of scientists, as a community of specialists, a sub-culture, within the wider context of their society and culture.

The training of scientists occurs through the acquisition of paradigms, in Kuhn's sense of the term. A paradigm is more than a specific problem solution. It involves a connected body of information, a set of assumptions and definitions ordering reality, making the world familiar through categories which are amenable to study. A paradigm is a means of articulating a world view, a grooming of the mind in the use of information and knowledge that is authenticated not by the independent agencies of reason and logic but by a body of people constituting the scientific community. Training is acquiring an accepted body of assumptions, definitions, rules, conventions as the entry certificate into a field of discourse, the academic discipline, so that that discourse may be mutually intelligible. But it also means that problems, questions, answers, information about the real world are structured by discourse, paradigms and world views. Indeed Barry Barnes has argued that it is only because knowledge is conventional through and through that it can be manipulated for the accumulation of knowledge.[9]

Both Kuhn and Foucault have demonstrated how movements in the realm of ideas, concept definition and paradigms can be related to wider movements in society. Kuhn has pointed to the example of science in Weimar Germany, Foucault to the creation of the category of madness from which the study of psychiatry originates. The implications of such an understanding of scientific knowledge have been laid out by Barry Barnes and David Bloor.[10] Accepting this critique, we understand science as answerable not only to its own definition of itself but as the particular and specific product of a society. Scientific understanding can be seen as the accepted consensus of a body of people operating within the context of a particular society at a particular time in history. There are not even obvious scientific 'facts', for what stands as a fact, a question, a proof and how these are articulated scientifically are all subject to change and diverse interpretation contingent upon paradigms. In science one chooses one's paradigm, complete with its assumptions, and this becomes the framework within which one assimilates all new experience and phenomena and by which anomalies are identified or other people's anomalies are shown to be part of a coherent system.

Work in the sociology of knowledge has toppled the supremacy of pure science. The techniques of sociology, informed by the fruits of anthropological enquiry, which study the relation of science to wider societal influences such as values and goals, have been shown to be essential to make sense of science. It should be noted that Evans-Pritchard's study of the Azande is quoted as a seminal text by the bulk of writers interested in the sociology of knowledge.[11] One even gets the subliminal impression this is the final vindication of social science as legitimate knowledge. After all the soul-searching and inferiority complexes endured by the social sciences concerning whether they were real sciences or not, they have at last taken over the high ground. But if 'pure science' must be regarded as conventional, culture bound, subjective, then so too must the social sciences whose founding concepts and scientific methodology has been abstracted from 'pure science'. Kuhn and Foucault do not hold lessons for the understanding of 'pure science' only, but call for a revision of our assessment of the social sciences also, as well as our understanding of the concept of knowledge and knowledge generation.

What is needed is a vantage point upon this debate about the nature of science to help us to clarify the status of the various double-barrelled anthropologies we are trying to understand. So far we have seen that science, in the broadest usage of the term, cannot be explained by the abstract essences of reason and logic as an idealized autonomous realm. It must be understood as a way of thinking and action whose rules are devised by scientists. Sciences need to be understood via a body of knowledge about the action of people in society, sociology. Yet equally sociology is a discourse structured by paradigms. Knowledge is rooted in society, where society is taken to mean not just an assembly of people but the system of social organization, culture, values, goals and objectives, and a collective historical experience.

Just what does it mean to say that science and knowledge are conventional? Most certainly it means that the discourses of knowledge structure themselves within wide parameters. Yet equally it means that there are parameters acting to define the nature and quality of the ideas available, a repository of ways of thinking and knowing determining what ideas are manipulated and how they are manipulated. To say that knowledge is conventional means that what determine the answers to these points is not derived solely from 'the rules of science' or the dictates of reason and logic. Rather it is the way the 'rules of science', reason and logic, have come to be understood in a particular society, acting in conjunction with constraints generated by the economic and political formation of society, its cultural traditions, and the specific elements which have gone into the making of that cultural tradition.

The point is neatly made by Foucault in the Preface to his study of classification, *The Order of Things*.[12] The inspiration for the work, he writes, was a passage in Borges quoting the classificatory categories from 'a certain Chinese encyclopaedia'. What struck Foucault was the impossibility that he could ever think in that way, which led him to question what it was possible to think. The answer to that is contingent upon the interaction of a range of factors operating within the parameters of a society and its history. It is only through the assumptions of this lens that observation can take place. It is according to the rules and regulations of this system, which creates a hierarchy of valuational significance based on actual experience in history that discourses of knowledge are structured. Knowledge is accumulated and change occurs according to what the system deems possible and acceptable, useful and necessary within its own parameters.

Part of the problem with the debate about the sociology of knowledge is that couching the discussion in terms of 'society' as a general process obscures the crucial specificity of the nature of science and knowledge. If science and knowledge are conventional to a society, then it is not to a generalized abstract 'society' but an historically specific and particular one.

The sociology of knowledge has been a fundamental way of examining the process of change. But rather than uncovering general processes applicable on a universal scale, it deals with processes tying the nature of change in knowledge and science more firmly to a particular society. If knowledge is rooted in society then the society, as a conceptual fabric, must have a formative influence on the direction and nature of change. If one sets out from Rome to reach Washington D.C. the potential routes are numerous, but the experience of the journey is conditioned by the fact that one set out from Rome with the travel goods acquired there to sustain the journey. One's objectives influence the way one travels; the choices and decisions made are not merely contingent upon immediate factors, a boulder in the path or a stream in flood, but also contingent upon having set out from Rome with a particular idea in mind. If one had started from Ulan Bator one's travel goods would have been different; the experience of the journey would have been different because one would have traversed different terrain. Even if the paths of these two journeys cross, or come to cover the same terrain they do so with a different ancestry, a distinct character tempered by previous experience. What travellers from Rome and Ulan Bator make of Washington D.C. when they arrive is likely to be very different, both because their experience of travel and their starting points were different.

What is missing from the debate about the nature of the dominant orthodox science of today is not the fact that it is rooted in society but that it is rooted in the society of western Europe. To make science comprehensible we need not an abstract notion of knowledge in society but a term which expresses the actual historical interrelationship of science and scientific thought with the knowledge base that gave it birth, has shaped its growth and specifically locates and attributes its characteristics. Western Christendom was conceived as a unitary society, based upon Rome. Historically it shared a unitary knowledge base, indeed a single, if diverse, institution for learning and mediating knowledge, the Holy Roman Church. This was the civilization of the mediaeval West and from the fragmentation of this unitary framework emerged the processes and characteristics of modern western civilization.

Modern western civilization has a wider geographical extent than Western Europe having been shaped by the colonial and imperial experience. It has wide parameters which were established in the historical era of reformulation that pre-dates the emergence of the modern West and the rise of science and which destroyed the last vestiges of the unitary Catholic civilization. This should not obscure the fact the reformulation had a unitary knowledge base. If the formation of the modern West is seen as a fundamental rupture then it is a rupture defined and made specific by its interaction with the particular attributes of mediaeval Christendom. The action and reaction of the era of reformulation, the period of Renaissance and Reformation in Western Europe, are as crucial to understanding the growth of knowledge and science in western civilization as they are to understanding the growth of the nation state and capitalism. The process of reformulation produced diversity and fragmentation but they are comprehensible only within the unitary base of western civilization. The discourses of knowledge, in all their specialization, interact and influence each other today because they share a knowledge base, a common fund of assumptions, a conceptual fabric which transcends a single society and is not the product of an abstract or abstracted society but operates at the level of modern western civilization.[13]

There is another way of looking at this. Barnes has elaborated upon Kuhn's use of similarity and difference relations as the mechanism by which concepts are learnt. Implicit in this mechanism which he uses to explain the working of paradigms and paradigm shifts is the continuity of similarity definitions as the basis for the recognition of difference and the definition of different paradigms. Old and new paradigms are indeed different; they have major consequences for how an understanding of the world is ordered, they provide ways of contrasting different meanings of concepts. But in seeing how the shift was effected, how discontinuity was created, one is not looking at a scientific revolution as a single instantaneous event, one is looking at a process in which aspects of old concepts are given a different interpretation: a shift of emphasis is given to themes within the potential meanings of an old concept, accepted similarities are manipulated in slightly different ways. The new paradigm or idea gains credibility not so much for its newness and its difference, but precisely because it can be seen as a reordering of the familiar, allowing one to see new potential in old concepts.

The desire to explain rupture and discontinuity are major themes not merely in the sociology of knowledge and the studies of the culture of science but more widely in western thought. This focus on change makes it almost inevitable that the incommensurable nature of old and new paradigms is emphasized. The reverse side of this same coin, where paradigms are accepted as incommensurable world views, is, however, continuity. The whole burden of Kuhnian arguments about science and the sociological insights drawn from them by Barnes is that without continuity there would be no change. When speaking of continuity and change one is not talking about discrete and distinct processes having independent relationships with an objective entity. Science, society, politics, knowledge are processes demonstrating both continuity and change at any given instance. Speaking of discontinuity or continuity is no more than the chosen emphasis of the observer and describer. More than anything else it is a function of one's vantage point, from within or without the parameters of western civilization.

There seems, however, to be a lack of terminology to keep continuity in focus while being concerned with change. Here I find the notions of the French historian Fernand Braudel most fruitful.[14] He is concerned with what he calls the *longue durée*, a term that gives a proper framework in which to understand the Kuhnian insights into science and knowledge. Braudel is speaking of history not as events but as interactive relationships between spheres of social action in their setting of time and space, a totality composed of differing rhythms and cycles. Society at any one time is the amalgam, the still frame, of the intersection of these differing spheres, each having aspects of continuity and change. There are eddies and cross currents within the fabric of society and civilization produced by the interaction of these diverse rhythms and cycles. One is looking at a retentive framework where the collective past is always available to be reworked.

Civilization is a way of looking at society in context, against the broadest set of parameters and influences, where history is part of the process. One might suggest that some of the tension between Kuhn and Barnes is that Barnes, as a sociologist, is seeking to win Kuhn, the historian, to a philosophy of science and knowledge in society, where society is an ahistorical concept. Barnes's concentration upon finitism and instrumentalism, where concept definitions are remade in each instance of use according to the utility of the time and the actors, is characteristic of the tradition of sociological thought where society is not an historical construct because the endless action of people makes history a social category. Historians are more comfortable with the concept of civilization as the wider context of time and space giving definition to the operation of society. In sociology, as in anthropology, the concept has fallen not just into disuse but disrepute for contextual historical reasons. This is no justification for permanently eradicating such a necessary vantage point, especially when it makes comprehensible the insights produced by the sociology of knowledge. Such a vantage point does not abolish the validity of the questions raised by finitism and instrumentalism but it does mean they cannot be the founding philosophic principles of enquiry.

The idea of the *longue durée*, civilization, would be the best way to approach Mary Midgley's study of the way the concept of evolution has been developed, deployed, used and abused by scientists.[15] Midgley gives a further deconstruction of the idealized, ideal-type of science by demonstrating that while maintaining that it exists, the actual practice of scientists is rooted in subjective, value-laden manipulation of information and ideas. She illuminates the way instances of concept application become the critical features of paradigm making: that the exercise of making a paradigm is indeed all about world view and is deployed in dramatized world pictures where the scientific instance gives an insight into the character of both human nature and the nature of the natural world. In creating these dramas, argues Midgley, scientists draw upon themes from philosophy and social thought, from religious and social imagery, not the 'facts' they have established. It is society of the *longue durée*, of western civilization, where today's sociobiology and selfish gene are more intimately related to Hobbes and Spencer, fallen man and original sin, than to Darwin; where the optimism of the escalator of inexorable upward progress draws upon Locke and Rousseau and alternative elements in Christian thought, where the building of the New Jerusalem is an earthly not hereafter referent.

In essence Midgley argues that the idealized notion of ideal-type science, operating through incommensurable paradigms, allows for no effective evaluative scale where even the abuse of ideal-type science can be addressed. The logic of her argument is that the actual operation of science in society, the Kuhnian science rooted in society, the perception of a *longue durée*, the perspective of western civilization, itself constitutes such an evaluative scale. When science is no longer seen as drawing on abstract essences of reason and logic outside the hurly burly of social forces then it can be recognized that scientific theories are manipulating ideas long familiar from other branches of knowledge, indeed that science is operating as part of a tradition of thought and knowledge in which a number of common and interrelated themes are being subjected to differing emphases in interpretation. Only when scientific theories are seen within the context of the values and ideas of a distinct civilization can there be any meaningful discussion of good and bad theory as it relates to the goals of society.

Ideal-type science as an objective, neutral, value-free enquiry is illusory. It is the foundation myth of science in western civilization, a myth which orders and animates anthropology as much as any other discipline. As has been cogently argued in many places, myths may be illusory in their content and not related to actual practice and yet they are real in the sense that people act and think as if they were fact. Myths encapsulate and symbolize systems of values and meaning, they are in themselves contextual dramas. Ideal-type science is myth nevertheless. Science which is claimed as the universal language and system upon which all knowledge rests is no more than the historical accumulation of choices and the working out of the properties of the specific and particular conceptual fabric of western civilization. There is nothing inevitable, inflexible, inherently necessary or compulsory about science. The myth making and confusion arise from regarding the universalizing impulse as being the same thing as the universal.

The foundation drama of modern western science is the inquisition of Galileo which is taken to demonstrate a fundamental dichotomy between science and religion. The openness of science as a system of knowing is contrasted with the rigidity supposedly characteristic of religion. Applying the perspective we have been outlining, this foundation drama demonstrates not so much any real dichotomy as attitudes shaped by an actual historical experience. The inquisition of Galileo was not a collision between two antithetical world views. It is evidence of the particular response of a powerful social institution, the Catholic Church, involved in a power struggle with a growing body of thinkers increasingly independent of that institution, and who thereby threatened its authority over ideas. This supposed demonstration of the dichotomy between religion and science is fundamental to the need for science in western civilization to be seen to be rational and value-free. It needs to be balanced against the cogent argument that the reformation of religious thought in western civilization gave a positive and constructive stimulus to the growth of science. The Protestant Reformation, it is argued, not only underlies the social formation of the modern West, but also the intellectual formation of modern western science. Here we need to examine the case put forward by Max Weber and the refinement of that argument by Hooykaas.[16]

Weber's argument is that the basic social formation upon which the political and economic dominance of the West arises, capitalism, must be seen as an outgrowth of the Protestant Reformation. While his conclusions are widely accepted, the structure of his argument is seen as problematic. Weber takes as his critical factor, his causal explanation, the doctrine of pre-destination and election particular to Calvinism. Yet the social patterns he so elegantly describes were common to the generality of Protestant groups who did not subscribe to this Calvinist doctrine. Hooykaas seems more empathetic with the climate of Protestantism when he argues that the critical factor was not election but the doctrine of the priesthood of all the believers. In this way he links the significance of the earthly 'calling' which Weber sees expressed in the social patterns generating capitalism, with the mode of enquiry giving rise to science. 'It would seem rather that the pre-ponderant influence might be the typically Protestant (perhaps even "Reformed") emphasis on the "general priesthood of all believers". This implied the right, and even the duty, for those who had the talents to study the Scripture without depending on the authority of tradition and hierarchy, together with the right and the duty to study the other book written by God, the book of nature, without regard to the authority of the fathers of natural philosophy.'[17] The Reformation then becomes a potent source of conceptual reformulation in western civilization.

Renaissance and Reformation are intimately linked movements in ideas; neither are comprehensible outside the context of the traditions and perceived abuses of late mediaeval Christianity to which they were reactions. The influx of new literary material as a stimulant to intellectual enquiry is fundamental to both Renaissance and Reformation. It was the study of ancient religious texts, early Greek sources, which led to the conclusion that the Fathers of Theology had based their formulations and doctrines upon error. In the light of these newly acquired sources there was a basic restructuring in Christian doctrine of the relationship of the individual to God, to text, and consequently to the rest of creation. Instead of this relationship being mediated by the succession of the Apostolic Church, the Protestant tradition argued that the individual believer had a direct relationship with God and His Word which was mediated by the direct action of faith and grace in the individual conscience. Mankind in its life upon earth became invested with a new significance and authority, the importance of one's 'calling' drew essentially upon the priesthood of all the believers.

The concept of authority in society was radically revised by this redefinition. It gave credence to the ability of the intellect to surpass the achievement and knowledge of the ancients and the Founding Fathers; it gave a justification for challenging instituted authority in society. The sociological significance which Hooykaas derives from this doctrine in relation to science is applicable across the whole spectrum of society. Indeed its significance can be seen to underlie the processes of modernity which, formed in the context of western civilization, have come to be global phenomena. Processes of individualization, and privatization of the individual conscience are related to the devout duty to study Scripture and maintain responsibility for a personal relationship to God. God's purpose was to be discovered in this world by the enquiry of the believer. Hence the shift from mediaeval scholasticism to modern empiricism. In the fragmentation of authority that followed the formation of Protestantism, attention inevitably focused on the quintessential human characteristic, reason, as the counterpart of faith and grace in understanding the meaning of concepts.

The Reformation with its redefined emphasis on the life of this world and the processes by which believers joined together as a community led to different patterns of thought, social formation, and new challenges to established authority in the realm of knowledge and politics.[18] Hooykaas is concerned to show how this gave rise to empirical enquiry, technological science, as demonstrated by the activity of the Royal Society in Britain. The Royal Society and the development of modern science were influenced by the political power struggles initiated by Protestantism. While Protestantism in each sect was argued as the universal meaning of the Christian message, the doctrine of the priesthood of all the believers was a charter for fragmentation. The consensus expected to arise from the action of faith and grace on the conscience never became an institutionalized embodiment of uniformity on the model of the universal Catholic Church it sought to replace. And, of course, Catholicism remained and was itself influenced by the ideas of Protestantism, as Catholic scholars were influenced by the thought of Protestant scholars, as Mandrou has demonstrated.[19]

During the course of the English Revolution, 1640–60, with the social and intellectual upheaval to enfranchise the individual conscience, the Royal Society prohibited religious debate from its proceedings. The privatization of the individual conscience seems intimately connected to the secularization of scientific enquiry in the particular historical context in which reason became an essential arbiter for the construction of a workable consensus, both in the realms of academic discourse and political power. Reason and empirical enquiry as a means of desacralizing concepts drawn from the Christian tradition was a much slower process, often not consciously intended, but practised to distance discourse from the authority of organized religion: a further working out of the priesthood of all the believers. If one looks forward in western history to the era of the Enlightenment, for example, many intellectual concepts were placed within a generalized theistic context to rescue them from errant interpretation by churchmen in a society where the Church was an established institution of power.

Where does this tour through science in western civilization leave the double-barrelled anthropologies with which we began? Indeed where does it locate anthropology in relation to science? Anthropology is that discipline established within the intellectual tradition and discourses of western civilization by which western civilization has studied and reflected upon human diversity. It takes its definition of itself as a social science from the conventional understanding of science in western civilization, and has developed and assumed its place amongst the disciplines of knowledge by being rooted in the concepts and traditions of its own civilization. This conclusion is made unequivocally by one of the few works which has applied Kuhn's insights and arguments to a study of the origins of anthropology.

Margaret Hodgen's neglected study, *Early Anthropology in the Sixteenth and Seventeenth Centuries*, traces the familiar themes and debates of anthropology back to the era of reformulation. It should not be forgotten the Renaissance and Reformation were contemporaneous with the so-called voyages of discovery to the New World, around Africa and into the Indian and Pacific Oceans. The information produced by these voyages radically altered the comprehension of the physical globe at precisely the time when the intellectual and religious spheres were being remodelled. These voyages confronted the West with a new profusion of human diversity and a need for new models to explain this diversity. There is clear evidence in Hodgen and in the intellectual history of the West that the experience of human diversity was a great stimulus to thought in a wide variety of disciplines. Yet as Hodgen shows, the questions asked, the conventions by which anthropology grew, and the way human diversity was understood rested upon theories, concepts, assumptions and generalizations particular to western civilization. We can do no better than quote Hodgen's conclusion:

> The Mind's Fidelity to the old has left its mark on anthropology as well as on other fields of thought. Modern cultural investigation has taken up its abode in a mansion of organizing ideas already designed, built and richly furnished with traditional assumptions more closely related to the early levels of Western theology and philosophy than to the data of human history. Nearly all the principles of inquiry employed by recent generations of scholars in Europe and elsewhere are of great age and antiquity. Were their genealogies consulted, it would become quickly apparent that their antecedents are to be found in the Judeo Christian Scriptures, in the classics or in the derivative Christian literature of the Middle Ages. Non-European folk have had no part in their formulation. Buddhist ideas, Muslim ideas, East Indian or Chinese ideas on cultural problems are unrepresented.[20]

Hodgen makes it clear that the significance of anthropology for the sociology of knowledge and the acceptance of the conventional nature of knowledge is not because it stands in a different relationship to western civilisation and western science but precisely because it is an integral part of the conceptual fabric of western civilization. Hodgen locates the origin and nature of the conceptual fabric underpinning the anthropology taught and practised today. Leaf's history of the subject also emphasizes this same connection by locating anthropology and its development within the history of the philosophic schools of thought of western civilization.

When we talk of double-barrelled anthropologies we are talking about the internal paradigms of what must be seen as western anthropology but all of them share common founding assumptions and arise out of a common history of intellectual enquiry and experience. The only odd one out in the list is Islamic anthropology for it is not a corollary of the internal paradigms of western anthropology. It is the corollary of western anthropology as a totality. Western anthropology is a way of knowing about the diversity of mankind based upon the conceptual fabric of western civilization; the Islamic anthropology we are proposing in the following chapters is a discourse about human diversity, the action and ideas of mankind in society, whose conceptual fabric is the world view of Islam.

Notes

1. The best overview of economic anthropology is to be found in Le Clair and Schneider, eds. *Economic Anthropology*.

2. el-Zein, *Beyond Ideology and Theology*.

3. Hodgson, *The Venture of Islam*. In particular see his introduction to volume one which deals with the nature of Islam and develops his definitions of Islamic civilization.

4. Kuhn, *The Structure of Scientific Revolutions*, *The Essential Tension*, and *The Copernican Revolution*; Foucault, *The Archaeology of Knowledge*.

5. Snow, *The Two Cultures of the Scientific Revolution*.

6. Berger, *Facing Up To Modernity*.

7. Don Cuppitt, Dean of Emmanuel College, Cambridge, is a controversial figure in Christian circles who is regarded as the arch example of what might be termed a secular theologian. The best presentation of his views relating directly to the relationship between science and religion is *Sea of Faith*.

8. For a discussion of the pitfalls of interpreting religion with a scientific perspective from a Muslim point of view see Sardar, 'Between Two Masters'.

9. Barnes, *T.S. Kuhn and the Social Sciences*.

10. Bloor, *Knowledge and Social Imagery*.

11. Evans-Pritchard, *Witchcraft, Oracles and Magic Among the Azande*.

12. Foucault, *The Order of Things*.

13. There is a vast literature on the history of western civilization; we have found particularly useful Huzinga, *The Waning of the Middle Ages*; Johnson, *A History of Christianity*; Elton, *Reformation Europe*; Dickens, *Reformation and Society in 16th century Europe*; Hay, *The Age of Renaissance*; Thomas, *Religion and the Decline of Magic* and *Man and the Natural World*.

14. Fernand Braudel *On History*; see also his monumental studies which apply the perspective of the *longue durée*, the two-volume *The Mediterranean and The Mediterranean World in the Age of Phillip II* and the even more monumental three-volume *Civilization and Capitalism 15th to 18th Century*. An interesting application of this perspective in relation to the Islamicate world is to be found in Chaudhuri, *Trade and Civilization in the Indian Ocean*.

15. Midgley, *Evolution as a Religion*.

16. Weber, *The Protestant Ethic and the Spirit of Capitalism,* and Hooykaas, *Religion and the Rise of Modern Science*; for an extension of Weber's argument to science see Merton, 'Science, Technology and Society in Seventeenth Century England', pp.471–4.

17. Hooykaas, *ibid.* p.109.

18. For a discussion of the general climate of ideas and events in the era of the English Revolution one can do no better than consult the works of Hill.

19. Mandrou, *From Humanism to Science*.

20. Hodgen, *Early Anthropology in the Sixteenth and Seventeenth Centuries*, p.478.

2

Enchained in Being

That anthropology is western can be proved entirely within its own terms of reference, and the influence of ethnocentricity upon its discourse is increasingly being recognized and discussed by its practitioners. The entire discussion so far has been couched, deliberately, within the terms of reference of western discourse. The issue is not about being western, but about the construction of reality the epithet describes. The purpose has been to emphasize that the western construction of reality must be understood as the conceptual fabric underlying the theories and practice of anthropology.

Western anthropology's sensitivity to its historical origins is in no way accidental.[1] The construction of its genealogy is a manipulation of ancestors, as sophisticated as anything to be found in its own kinship studies. It is also a highly conventional exercise in Whig history, a selective reading to make the right conceptual connections and amass an accepted body of useful analytical tools. As such, the historical reconstructions of western anthropology allow its present practitioners to avoid, or disavow, what has constituted anthropological speculation and practice in history. This obviates the need to analyse the enduring impact of the history of ideas upon current theory and practice, thereby creating a discontinuity where in reality none exists.

The 'real' history of anthropology is foreshortened: western anthropology is deemed to have commenced only when it became a profession, a recognized university discipline, in the early part of this century. For Britain genuine anthropology begins with Malinowski and Radcliffe-Brown, who enjoy a virtual monopoly in training those engaged in disseminating and doing 'real' anthropology. In America they are matched by Franz Boas, and in France one looks no further back than Durkheim. The real foundation of the discipline asserted by this construction of its history is not theory, nor concept, but practice and in the form of participant observation, the removal of anthropologists from the metropolitan armchair and colonial veranda to close association with the daily life of the studied.

This momentous shift, however, was made only as a superior method of studying a category which already existed: the 'primitive', a term lavishly used by the authorized ancestors.[2] They entered 'the field' from a world already served with concepts and theory to order their questioning of the reality they came to study. The importance of the shift in methodology, often the sole claim to originality made for western anthropology, does not alter the fact that the ancestors went out to 'the field' from the garden of an already established discourse of ideas and returned from 'the field' to tend to the cultivation of this same discourse. Whatever alteration they subsequently made amongst the flowerbeds was conditioned by the spade work, weeding, hoeing, and manuring, that had already formed the garden.

Western anthropology is not shaped out of pure description, for pure description simply does not exist. Whose description, observer or observed? From what perspective, its meaning for the observer or the observed? What is a fact, what determines the significance of a cultural or social fact and is it significant for the observer or the observed?[3] Fieldwork, ethnography, is ordered and determined by the concepts, theories and categories the worker has imbibed before encountering a living soul in some distant corner of the world. Indeed, the one thing the university discipline does not teach is fieldwork technique, and certainly not the recording and presentation of fieldwork data. What the student learns are the textbook paradigms, presented not as raw data but as that characteristic product—the ethnographic monograph—where many an intellectual, conceptual and theoretical sleight of hand constructs both the subject matter, the 'native', and the subject, anthropology, to determine the appropriate ethnographic questions and answers.[4] After examinations on the authorized tradition comes the translation to the field, a mystical *rite de passage* in which it is hardly surprising workers fall back upon the security of manipulating the categories they are familiar with in the unfamiliar setting they confront.

The objective of participant observation was to overcome the eclecticism of nineteenth-century anthropology where traits were taken out of context from widely-separated social and cultural groups and viewed as comparable and commensurate items upon which speculative theoretical schemas of human social development could be constructed. But participant observation is thereby founded upon a theoretical and conceptual proposition about the nature of society and culture already available in western discourse before it was ever tested in the field. Description in ethnography is both translation of native life into the terminology of western anthropology and simultaneous interpretation because of the existence of western anthropology. Ethnographers do ethnography to provide the context for some specific theoretical interest, such as kinship, economics or politics, related to some anthropological debate. From its conceptual, categorical and theoretical standpoint western anthropology is concerned, as Goody expresses it, in searching the world 'for positive and negative cases to confirm our ideas of the relevant factors'.[5]

Modern day anthropological euphemism requires its subject matter be termed 'the other', 'small-scale', 'non-literate' or 'peasant'. These are the current labels for the enduring concept 'primitive'. Whatever the name, the concept and its content are fundamental to western anthropology. The authorized ancestors went in search of 'the primitive' and are thereby linked to a line of genesis which commenced at the point where the 'primitive' emerged as a problem requiring intellectual attention. That watershed was Columbus's landfall in the Americas. The empirical experience of the Americas carried the

European mind beyond the confines of Greek learning and mediaeval formulae. Certain ancient notions such as barbarism and natural slavery could be manipulated, but manipulated they had to be to cover a novel application where the terms themselves acquired new meaning from contact with actual human groups. The Ancients had maintained that antipodean man was an impossibility. European man found them corporeal, requiring the formation of a policy, which is neither coterminous with nor the same thing as the more fundamental need, the construction of an intellectual structure of understanding.

It is common today to see western anthropology as the handmaiden of colonialism. This viewpoint goes hand in hand with western anthropology's historical foreshortening, as demonstrated in Talal Asad's *Anthropology and the Colonial Encounter*, where anthropology is the profession, the university based discipline, and colonialism is the full fledged jural colonialism, post the scramble for Empire. To understand even the historically foreshortened links between professional anthropology and jural colonialism the weight of history must be seen as part of the interaction. The use of historical context is not just about events and modes of action, the most significant legacy of history is in the formation and crystallization of concepts and modes of thought. Unless the history of ideas is examined as a profound influence on the action of professional anthropologists at work under jural colonialism they are caught in limbo, actors without their character notes and script, stripped of the motivation to make their responses meaningful. It is tempting to see this historical foreshortening of western anthropology, even when it is used to reveal its own shortcomings, as characteristic. A discipline that has understood its subject matter in the artificial limbo of the ethnographic present, applies the same framework to understanding its own growth as a professional discourse.

The convention of denouncing colonial anthropology, as practised by western anthropology today, serves guilty consciences only. The cases cited allow easy demolitions to be made by more sober reading of the evidence, such as those to be found in the comments of Adam Kuper.[6] Yet Kuper would hardly object to the conclusion that anthropology and colonialism are intimately connected. Rather, it is a just charge which has mistaken its mark. A charge which fails to penetrate deeply enough into the conceptual foundation of commonly accepted anthropological theory.

It is not collaboration with naked policy formulation, nor the obvious fact that the existence of Empire facilitated fieldwork that is the issue. If it were, and were accepted, the great growth industry of 'applied' anthropology, whether allied to 'development' or revolution, would constitute the real question mark. The demise of formal colonialism has not ended the dominance of western civilization over the traditional areas of anthropological involvement, rather the drive for modernization has increased the reliance on metropolitan 'experts'. Surely the original sin complained of in the link between anthropology and colonialism is that anthropology failed to generate an active and articulated critique of the metropolitan sphere, to provide the intellectual rationale to change what made western civilization colonialist. Is western anthropology today any better placed or more diligent in what Diamond has termed 'reporting back'? Does it provide the intellectual insight which challenges and seeks to change what makes western civilization neo-imperialist? For all the attitudinal shift amongst anthropologists as individuals and the activism of many in support of anti-imperialism, as a discipline of knowledge western anthropology has not yet generated new ways of thinking about the people who constitute its subject matter.

The problem of historical foreshortening in western anthropology is endemic; it falsifies and distorts on many levels. The most crucial example is its impact on anthropological understanding of non-European peoples. A belated and cogent acknowledgment of this, with profound implications for the perspectives of western anthropology, is supplied by Eric Wolf's *Europe and the People Without History*. Wolf shows that colonialism, in the sense of disruption of indigenous society by the influence and interests of European powers, has been flourishing in a variety of guises ever since Columbus touched land on Hispaniola; and even before that if we take into account Portuguese merchant venturing. To limit oneself to jural colonialism is to quibble and distort one's understanding of the processes which have been at work.

The state of tribal order that western anthropology has deemed as the starting point for its conceptualization of native life, the ideal that existed just before the anthropologist arrived, was itself the product of a long process of interaction with the influence of western expansionism that had been rippling outward. The nature of the interactions changed with the increasing proximity of colonial formation. But an intellectual schema without history must inevitably give itself a false premise for all the factors involved, the native setting, the interactions, the process and colonialism.

It is not only the experience of the colonized which is falsified, it is the very nature of colonialism itself. If we look at events at the very start of western expansionism, the domination of the Americas, an honest reading of events suggests the policy towards the American Indians was not different from the treatment meted out to inhabitants of metropolitan Europe at the same date. Thomas More's *Utopia*, the literary classic incorporating the first idealization of 'the native' written in 1516 and based on reports from the New World, saw the image of his own society in the gibbets of England.[7] Forced conversion and religiously sanctioned murder at the stake, serfdom by various legal sleights of hand, and forced clearances of land were all part of the European experience as they were being visited upon the American Indian; the only difference was one of scale, and in this bloodsoaked era of European history even that could be a moot point. The various poles of brutality, paternalism, benign and malignant neglect are always present, sometimes at the same time, sometimes shifting around in sequence. What distinguishes the Europeans in the colonial setting is not the way they acted, but the way they *thought* about the colonial setting. Indeed it was the difference in the way of thinking about the native that created the need for a category called colonial policy which was distinguished from policy in the metropolitan sphere. It was because the native was conceived as a different kind of being, inhabiting a different kind of world and circumscribed by different customs that colonial policy had to pay attention to a variety of strategies to administer and incorporate them within the framework of Empire. The perception of the difference of the native permitted discussion of their rights, and various obligations towards them were deemed to exist because of this innate difference. The effects were no less pernicious for the native than for the western labouring classes, but these two spheres were surrounded with different kinds of sophistry. One misses the point entirely if one fails to recognize that sophistry arises from categories of thought, from conventions of understanding.

The primitive, the colonial setting, the civilizing mission, the tension between the religious doctrine of dominion and its interpretation as domination are related sets of concepts which operate as European cultural constructs in the setting of historical experience. They are the ways of thought which order the policy and action of colonialism. The current critique of western anthropological complicity with colonialism rightly defines a problem but fails to identify its cause properly. It perpetuates a convention of discourse where western civilization itself provides the sole definitions of what is rational: definitions taken as non-cultural, and therefore not part of the field of study. Western powers are political agents, western people are actors but the critique does not acknowledge western civilization as a conceptual fabric which orders their thinking and therefore conditions their action.

Lynn White Jr. has taken the Christian concept of dominion as central to an understanding of the growth of western science as a culturally constructed domination of nature, both intellectually and physically.[8] The conspiracy theory of anthropology, as in Asad's collection, seems to cultivate just such an understanding, yet actually obviates the need to go back to a culturally germane notion to study its equal importance as the underpinning of colonial action and the construction of an intellectual understanding of the colonial setting. What is more, historical foreshortening would miss the obvious association of the historical experience of the ease of domination, and contingent aspects of the concept 'primitive'. It is not merely that European contact caused death, dearth and disaster for indigenous populations. These empirical realities have a conceptual referent in the notion of the fragility of the 'primitive' in the face of 'advanced' society. The nature of the 'primitive' is such that they must succumb to 'advanced' society, at which point their 'authenticity' becomes so compromised, according to this school of thought, that investigation and analysis of the interaction between 'primitive' and 'advanced' must be outside the anthropological perspective.[9] Anthropology has concerned itself with the 'primitive' as if the colonial setting did not exist. Once the fragility of the 'primitive' has been compromised by inclusion in the westernized sector of the colony or the modern state they become the province of sociology, which examines parts of a societal whole whose premises are assumed on the unanalysed model of western civilization. If authenticity can survive this transformation then it does so as a sub-cultural gloss, the point being that the questions asked of this sub-culture and its presumed functions are at best peripheral to sociological analysis. What was 'primitive' is subsumed in what is 'advanced' and what constituted the 'primitive' has no part to play in shaping and ordering the society which results, but remains a marginalized problem. The mind of the 'primitive' is bootless and rootless in a modern world to which it contributes no meaning.

The disappearing native has been both a physical reality as well as a conceptual referent. Peter Worsley's questioning of the end of anthropology because of the disappearance of its subject matter is only one example among many.[10] It would seem that Malinowski was propelled into the field by just such a sense of imminent ending. setting off to record his data before it was gone forever.[11] The concept of the 'primitive' is located in a conceptual fabric where it is intimately connected with the ways western man thinks about himself and his own society. If Divine enfranchisement of the Christian European has been ousted by a more naked assessment of power relations, it has also given way to the absolute intellectual enfranchizement of the western mind to be the recorder and interpreter of all it surveys, determining its objective reality. The strength of the western model to demand and secure the subservient inclusion of the 'primitive' to its own ways remains, the sophistry has subtly readjusted itself. The inevitability of the one-directional magnetic attraction of western civilization, for all that it structures today's studies of change, is unrecognized because it is assumed that western civilization is the natural mode because it is the conceptual fabric of the minds which make western anthropology.

Hodgen has documented the early ideas by which American Indian societies were interpreted,[12] and Anthony Pagden traces the formative debates on the proper placing of the peoples of the Americas in the European scheme of things.[13] The pervasiveness with which new models of thought were constructed upon the contemporary interpretations of ethnography can be seen from the work of Thomas More through Hobbes, Locke, and Montaigne to Montesquieu and Rousseau. While the process of conceptualization has a continuous and wide-ranging impact upon the European mind it is supposedly not until the era of the Enlightenment that the first glimmerings of their relevance to the history of western anthropology is perceived. Marvin Harris has been particularly scathing about Hodgen's thesis, treating the notion that Rousseau could be some relict of the Middle Ages as effrontery.[14] The work of Thomas Kuhn stands here as a necessary and apt riposte. Kuhn has shown that for all the consequences which stemmed from the work of Copernicus, Copernicus himself is best understood as the last Ptolemaic astronomer, a man who worked with what Hodgen terms 'old and convivial ideas'. The argument is simple: what else is there to think with but these ideas? The consequences can be understood only when the old and convivial are viewed within an empirical setting and the similarities or differences will then be apparent.

The question which looms over western anthropology is whether once the 'old and convivial' are brought into play any consequent conceptual change beyond the centrality of the 'primitive' can be demonstrated. With the American landfall a fundamental dichotomy opens in western thought between primitive and advanced, savage and civilized, we and they. This dichotomy, which created the intellectual space wherein western man thought about himself as much as he thought about 'other' people, continues to structure western anthropological thought.

The early perception of the American Indian culture and society saw it as lacking the essential constituents of European society. Discussion was based on the ideas and methods of mediaeval schoolmen both to determine what to find and to establish the conventions for the recording and analysis of information. There can be no better example of this than the treatise *On the Cannibals*, by Michel de Montaigne (1533–92), which addressed itself to what could be called the foundational anthropological question: 'To what was the partition of men into civil and uncivil to be ascribed?' In the definition of that partition lay the explanation of human nature and human culture, as well as the explanation of its development. Montaigne understood the Brazilians as

> a nation—that hath no kinde of traffike, no knowledge of Letters, no intelligence of numbers, no name of magistrate, nor of politike superioritie; no use of service, of riches, or of poverty; no contracts, no successions, no dividences, no occupation but idle; no respect of kindred, but common, no apparell but naturall, no manuring of lands, no use of wine, corne or mettle.[15]

Not very different from the earliest expression in Amerigo Vespucci's letter of 1502, *Mundus Novus* published in five European languages, this letter is the source of the terms New World and America.

> They have no laws or faith and live according to nature. They do not recognize the immortality of the soul, and they have among them no private property because everything is common, they have no boundaries or kingdoms and provinces, no king ... They obey nobody, each is lord to himself ... [They have] no justice and no gratitude, which to them is unnecessary because it is part of their code They are a very prolific people but have no heirs because they hold no property ... I fancied myself to be near the terrestrial paradise.[16]

Professional western anthropology has radically altered the terms of description by demonstrating that these were false propositions about the 'native', but it retains the structuring dynamic of Montaigne's question.

The 'primitive' differed in appearance, manners and customs, and was defined within the comparative framework of European civilization. The framework for relating peoples, manners and mores, and languages was Genesis which gave a genealogical table for humanity from Adam to the present day. Since this unitary framework informed all intellectual endeavour, the only place for the American Indian according to the available genealogical information was the era between the Fall and the Flood, or at latest the era of the fall of the Tower of Babel, prior to the reconstruction of the arts of civilization. At the time of this conceptualization history and change were very different concepts from their modern successors. As we shall see the experience of contact with the American Indian had a profound influence on these concepts. The notable point is that the definition of the concept 'primitive' occurred in an era with only a limited and particular orientation to the concept of change. As fascination with change grew in western intellectual history, how it was related to understanding the 'primitive' was already prefigured in the formation of the concept; change and the 'primitive' were indeed remote. Many different interpretations, different paradigms, were tenable within this pre-deluvian space. There was the argument between the pre-dominant orthodoxy of monogenism (that all humanity had a single origin), and polygenism (that there was more than one act of human creation and therefore the difference of the American Indians was the product of a fundamental great divide). Polygenism emerged early, in the work of Issac de le Peyrere (1594–1676), and re-emerged as an intellectual debate in the nineteenth century, when the study of human nature and human culture were directly related to the study of biological racial characteristics. The idea of the American Indians as remnants missed by the Flood, or subject to a local flood, a redefinition of the matrix, admitted a number of possibilities: that they had started with the same mental and cultural propensities, but had degenerated; that mankind had begun degenerate and Providence had caused the rise of civilization; that the natural state of mankind was an innocent primal simplicity upon which Providence had worked to give rise to civilization. The Genesis framework marked the point at which the American

Indian both entered and was sundered from the unidirectional movement of the whole of humanity.

From these ideas stem consequences in the structuring of anthropological questions. The first, association of the primitive with the primal is not disturbed by frequent discussion of American Indians as a young people, that is later additions to the ranks of humanity. Primal in the sense of original condition need have no connotations of chronology; yet it is an effortless step for this to become primal in the sense of chronologically first. What is beyond question is that American Indian society offered Europeans their first model for distinguishing not only the original condition of mankind but also the early history of mankind from contemporary European society. The concrete historical experience of contact with the American Indians started a process of conceptualization with particular historical referents. The concept once formed was widely applied; it became the familiar framework that oriented all subsequent contact with non-European peoples.

The history of western anthropology covers the era when the timescale assigned to human existence has vastly increased; the significance of this point is difficult to assimilate today. Leaf makes pertinent reference to its influence upon the history of western thought.[17] It is the essential association of time with change which distinguishes a contemporary perspective from the mediaeval historical sense. The concept of the 'primitive' was strategically located and already in place to fill the gap in European thought about the time-scale of human existence. The concept of the primitive informed the notion of the rise of civilization, and provided the models for the description of the developmental stages of that rise. It also provided the enduring question linked to time and change: the stasis of the primitive. For if the rise of civilization was a matter of transformation, then the 'primitive' had not been transformed, but provided a negative sourcebook of information for speculation about the means and nature of transformation.

The amendment of the time-scale of human existence was the culmination of a long dispute constrained by the dictum of Bishop Usher and his dating of Creation. That ethnographic information and the concept of the primitive were there to provide an explanation for a newly-emerging historical sense is best demonstrated by an example documented in Bryony Orme's *Anthropology for Archaeologists*. Thomas Harriot published in 1588 *A brief and true account of the new found land of Virginia,* a detailed account of the land, its people and their customs, illustrated by the artist John White. In 1592 the work was republished with an appendix entitled *Some picture OF THE PICTES which in the olde tyme dyd habite one part of the great Britainne.* Again the illustrations were by White who used the Virginians as models for the interpretation of classical texts to create a picture of the ancient Britons. This was in marked contrast to the conventions of his day where the practice of artists was to depict scenes from antiquity or distant lands as scenes familiar to both European artist and audience. Orme uses an illustration from Holinshed's Chronicles of 1577 to make the point. There the ancient British leader, Boadicea, is the very image of Elizabeth I and her soldiery, ready for battle with the Roman legions, are fitted out with the armour, sword and spear of the Elizabethan period.[18] The experience of America had opened a new dimension in European conceptualization, living peoples had caused a radical revision of the European past. The observed were described not only as themselves but immediately related to an analytic structure differentiating them from Europeans. Both 'we' and 'they' were then related to a developmental explanation of humanity. This has been the foundation, dynamic and lasting practice of western anthropology.

To point to the enduring importance of the 'primitive' is not to say western anthropology has not changed since the impact of Columbus's voyage on the European mind. It is rather to indicate that its changes have been structured and constrained by aspects of the concept 'primitive'. Marc Augé in *The Anthropological Circle* makes this particularly apparent. Without the concept 'primitive' the two axes of anthropology he describes, made up of two sets of mutually opposed poles, evolution-culture and symbol-function, would have little relevance. Augé demonstrates that upon these axes all the various paradigms of western anthropology can be located as different combinations of orientations. It is well recognized by western anthropologists that theoretical eclecticism is endemic, different and contending ideas are routinely brought into play to service different levels and stages of argument and explanation. One text can describe the whole circle, traverse each of the poles, for all that these poles are mutually opposed. It is also part of his thesis that the questions typical of the era of grand speculative anthropology still order the subject. The 'real' anthropological reformulations of functionalism, structural-functionalism, structuralism, and Marxist anthropology all overlay questions of explanation of culture which hinge upon origins and relationships of evolution and diffusion.

If modern anthropology describes a circle around Augé's axes then the centre of the circle is the 'primitive'. Modern students are expected to have a different attitude to the 'primitive': they are schooled with euphemism and armoured against pejorative implications and value-judgments, yet their study is dependent upon and solely about the 'primitive'. After years of being frowned upon, the term is once again being used openly by leading anthropologists. But today the 'primitive' is the fortunate possessor of an authenticity modernized mankind sacrificed in its drive for progress; the noble savage is making a comeback.

That aspects of the 'primitive' have been constructed upon European expectations is demonstrated by Arens's arresting study, *The Man Eating Myth*. Cannibalism was an aspect of barbarism according to the writers of ancient Greece. Their classical tales of cannibalism were retailed through mediaeval literature, and thus cannibalism became part of the convention Europeans used in describing peoples outside civil society.[19] Many of the early voyagers to the New World were steeped in this learning, and as Arens documents, they were soon producing elaborate narratives of the cannibalistic practices of the peoples of the Americas, lavishly supported by lurid illustrations.[20] They were of course also giving the public back home what they wanted, a good story, and more importantly just the salacious story they expected to hear. Colonial expansionism was a business needing a public image to raise funds to finance its endeavours. Western anthropology too has been long familiar with this syndrome!

Arens has investigated the earliest records of cannibalism in various parts of the world, the Americas, Africa and Melanesia and considers their 'scientific' credibility. He argues that cannibalism is best understood as an expectation of the European mind based upon the different lifestyle of indigenous peoples at a time when the gap between understanding and communication was at its greatest. Subsequent commentators who had closer associations with indigenous peoples were also products of a European education who had read the press hand-outs and been conditioned by the whole history of European literature and concepts. In Arens's submission all that participant observation and careful examination of the documentary evidence can demonstrate is that there never has been a direct eye-witness account of socially instituted cannibalism, in any of its classificatory types. The significance of Arens's study is not the question of how cannibalism got into the literature but the fact that it remains a vivid part of the continuing patrimony of western anthropology. The presumed stasis of the primitive seems here to be a function of the far stronger demonstrable stasis of the categories of western anthropology.

As Goody states in *The Domestication of the Savage Mind*: 'The trouble with the categories [of western anthropology] is that they are rooted in a we/they division which is both binary and ethnocentric, each of these features being limiting in their own way.'[21] Despite modern reformulations where difference of the 'primitive' and the 'advanced' has to be proved rather than assumed, Goody rightly points out that all anthropologists fall back upon a mode of discourse entirely composed of concepts and categories that raise the evolutionary issue, and assume the difference they claim has to be proved. The existence and rise of western science 'why did it happen "here" and nowhere else?' is today a question either avoided by a non-developmental model with no place at all for change, or by a simplistic one reifying the we/they dichotomy to a global scale.[22] The terminology of western anthropology still relies upon ideas which, as Goody says, assert nothing but a change of a more or less unidirectional kind. Western anthropology deals with its subject matter not only in terms of process but of progress too and thereby even in its most relativized form is founded upon a value element. For Goody this limited framework is easy to criticize; the important question he identifies for western anthropology, and all students of human behaviour, is how to provide an alternative.

Goody is concerned with the human mind and thought processes. This is an abiding topic of western anthropology founded upon the presumed dichotomy between irrational/rational, pre-logical/logical, magic/science.[23] These concepts have structured and underlie all enquiry, they are the framework of investigation that generates the questions. Goody's alternative is to question the technology of literacy, the actual properties of written forms, the mental manipulation entailed in the way information is written down and the purposes the written form itself creates. Instead of written lists being evidence of different forms of mentality Goody argues that they have their own potential; the permanent written record can be examined in a different way because it is a permanent written form. The technology and not the mind distinguishes the social formations made possible by writing; the technology is the basis of the types of thought to be employed. By extension his argument also suggests there should be a technology of oral communication. Goody himself, from fieldwork experience, rejects the conceptual proposition central to western anthropology that oral tradition is a fixed body of thought, a uniform tradition handed from generation to generation. But how does investigation of oral technology proceed from a framework which presumes stasis?

For all Goody's criticisms of the framework and the way his analysis shows a complexity any Grand Divide theory cannot properly accommodate or recognize; in the end his technological approach can be situated in the very framework he criticizes. Goody himself falls back upon the old mode of discourse offering merely a more complicated version, not an alternative. By emphasizing literacy as a technology he is elaborating upon one item in the list always used to create the dichotomy. Technology, after all, was one of the most obvious differences between the 'primitive' and the European, and is seen by the West as being contingent upon science and science upon mind; thus Goody is explaining the nature of the contingency. He shows the dichotomy can never be reified to the level of a global division between the West and the rest, but extending the scope does not invalidate the notion that there is a divide. There is still the mind that conceived of writing and the mind that did not, still a dichotomy to orient and structure the discipline, determine the questions, facts, and what is significant. In pushing back the frontiers of the divide, on the basis of the divide, Goody is providing complexity in default of answering questions, thus implicitly maintaining that the questions are capable of being answered even when many western anthropologists explicitly believe they cannot. The foundational questions and orientations still abide. Goody's conclusions leave him circumambulating Augé's anthropological circle. Having complicated the dividing lines Goody is seeking to claim the right to reintroduce into western anthropology the judgemental questions relativism has anathematized.

Not least Goody seems to accept the orthodox western definition of science we discussed in the first chapter. He allows science as the abandonment of intuition, imagination, and perception. We have argued that science itself relies on myth as validation in western civilization. Arthur Koestler is unusual in arguing for a place for intuition in scientific imagination and pratice.[24] Paul Hirst has shown that the rise of rationality, as a concept, went hand in hand with a belief in the existence of magic and witches; for example, the witch hunting trials of the Age of Reason depended on a new confidence in rational procedures. Belief in witches and magic as agents of the Devil was an essential and heightened aspect of the conceptual fabric of those who insisted on rational procedures. The demise of witch hunting arose from questions about the validity of evidence in proving the charges by rational means, not the lack of validity of belief in witches and magic.[25] In which case there is no shift from concrete to abstract, from signs to concepts, for intuition, imagination and perception are part of the process of forming, shaping and interpreting concepts in western civilization as elsewhere. Perhaps the most striking example for consideration is that western science is supposedly founded upon the dichotomy between religion and science, faith and experiment. The concepts and categories of science, in its most generalized understanding, are secular, materialist and reductive. Yet this does not preclude the scientist as an individual from holding religious beliefs and receiving social sanction from the culture at large. To hold that mankind is the result of a chance process of activities amongst amino acids is directly contradictory to the concept that mankind is created in God's image. Scientists with religious convictions routinely think through concepts that deny the faith which identifies their humanity as individuals.

The stasis of the 'primitive', why have 'they' not changed when 'we' have, is the long-term ordering principle of western anthropological discussion. Ethnographic description presumes a harmonious equilibrium of integrative meaning, the identification of social organization with kinship structure, the ascription of role and status, and the integration of thought and action into one, the 'style' of a culture or society. 'Other' cultures are regarded as unanimous and uniform; the task is to understand them within this convention, to produce the ideal model. The ideal type, obviously a mental construct in abstracted form, is not formulated through technique or mere procedure: conceptually for western anthropology the statement of the ideal rules of a culture is the statement of the concrete reality of 'other' cultures. Manipulation to maintain the ideal is a necessary activity of native life since, for 'them' there is only the ideal, the concrete. Interpretation. flexibility and the potential for autonomous change are the province of the 'we' pole, the style and characteristic of western civilization, whose science provides the means, the abstract but real standard of what is true and therefore tenable in thought or action.

Ethnography is about finding the form and structure of a culture or society, including the representations, signs and symbols, and meanings it maintains and operates. Culture and society as discrete and separable uniform wholes are the conceptual base of enquiry; one is seeking what makes this whole work and cohere, that is, the rules. It is recognized that rules are broken, but the investigation of how, why and the consequences are not studied. Change is assumed to be possible only by outside stimulus. Of course this is a very neat validation of the ethnographic present as the framework of study. The framework explains why one should filter out all extraneous factors to identify the primal concrete reality of any given culture or society and does not question whether this is a reductive view of culture and society.

Western anthropology is not so much about proving the moral or rational unity of mankind, since these operate as alternative assumptions and orientations, as it is about explaining culture and society. This leads to a fundamental tension, for explanation of culture cannot be detached from the search for origins, and however expressed, this gets back to posing or avoiding the question of evolution. Culture, for western anthropology, is a human creation. What in the original human condition gives rise to culture? The conventional answer, of course, is the human mind which associates cultural diversity with differences in mentality. The modern relativist revision has not abolished the question, but merely shifted the burden of proof. Instead of presuming difference, ever since Boas and Malinowksi the dominant orthodoxy has been to presume unity, making difference the entity which must be proved. Much of modern western anthropology then consists of demonstrating the culture specific rationality, the functional utility of ideas, beliefs and practices western civilization has dubbed 'primitive'. So long as what exists works to make a culture or society cohere as a whole, then it is validated. At the extreme, whatever culture is, is right within the cultural setting where it occurs. This is achieved by acceptance of a non-developmental framework, the ethnographic present. All cultures and societies are always only present, even when they have a history. History would only be expressive of the culture, history would be only events not a legacy of interpretation and conceptualization.

What then can be the basis of culture? Marshall Sahlins argues, in his *Cultural and Practical Reason*, that Malinowski is not alone in asserting that mankind responds only to the grumbling of its belly. At base western anthropology views cultural action as arising out of the need to satisfy basic needs, and basic needs are ultimately biological needs. Culture is therefore the product of practical reason, which is why culture functions, symbolizes, dialectically materializes. Sahlins shows how this conception of satisfying basic needs underpins functionalism, structuralism and Marxism in western anthropology and points out that on that premise the concept of culture, as the entity to be explained, collapses, since the premise allows no terms to explain observed cultural diversity. Because basic needs are the same everywhere in the relativist construction, all cultural action can be explained by reference back to basic needs. Therefore all cultures are equal and right within their own terms and beyond value judgement because they serve the same end, their form being nothing more than an environmentally suited other way of fulfilling the prime human directives.

Here a very important distinction has to be made. Western anthropology has battled against crude notions of biological determinism which entered into the discipline through the concept of race. Cultural performance was deemed different because of varying human potential determined by biological racial factors. In *Race, Culture and Evolution* Stocking provides an excellent analysis of these ideas, and assesses Boas's contribution in demolishing the basis for racist anthropology. But the overthrow of racist biological determinism does not necessarily mean that biology does not underlie culture, it just means it does not determine diversity. The acceptance of a unitary biological framework for all mankind is no less determinist and does not preclude evolutionary issues which are raised not by questions of culture through the evolution of mankind, but of mankind within the evolution of culture. Stocking's work has set out the cross-currents in the history of western anthropology, not least the constraints generated directly from Christian theology and sentiment. If we look at his conclusions about the polygenist/monogenist dispute of the last century we see he is pointing to the ease with which dichotomous ways of thought can relate the now supposedly abandoned error to the reformed practice.

> From a broader point of view, however, polygenism and monogenism can be regarded as specific expressions of enduring alternative attitudes towards the variety of mankind. Confronted by antipodal man, one could marvel at his fundamental likeness to oneself or one could gasp at his immediately striking differences. One could regard these differences as of degree or kind, as products of changing

environment or immutable heredity, as dynamic or static, as relative or absolute, as inconsequential or hierarchical. Considered in these terms polygenist thinking did not die with Darwin's *Origin of the Species*, nor is it entirely dead today. [26]

The concepts and categories do not go away on the basis of an attitudinal shift, they merely wash about beneath the surface of a more diffuse mode of discourse.

The secularization of social anthropological thought and the reductive consequences of believing in the biological basis of human nature cannot all be summed up in a simple inexorable rise of scientism. As Stocking's essays show, the pattern and time frame are much more complicated. He argues that it is in the work of Tylor, originator of the standard definition of culture, that one finds the conscious marrying of scientism to secularism. Tylor's concern in the scientific study of culture was, says Stocking, 'to fill the gap between Brixham Cave and European civilization without introducing the hand of God',[27] or in Tylor's own words in *Primitive Culture*: 'to escape from the rigours of transcendental philosophy and theology to start a more hopeful journey on practicable ground.'[28] That journey was about viewing culture as a natural process, in the sense in which Radcliffe-Brown sought to present western anthropology as a natural science. This certainly unites Tylor with those who came after. Yet unlike later generations he viewed the terms culture and civilization as interchangeable, denoting one evolutionary developmental movement. It is with Boas that western anthropology becomes concerned with *cultures* as a plurality. One could argue that Tylor, for all his desire for departure, was still operating within the old unitary Genesis framework on a secular natural history base. Indeed one could ask whether in western thought unity does not always have the connotation of uniformity, and whether various schools of thought have not merely moved the mechanism, cause or locus of the uniformitarian principle in searching for an answer to their foundational question. The genealogical relationship for genetic endowment, the single evolution of culture/civilization by scientific rationalism through fixed and necessary stages for a plurality of cultures motivated by the satisfaction of basic biological needs.

The concepts and categories of western anthropology are now radically secularized, with human nature being viewed as biological nature, which makes culture a human dimension explaining the nature of thought, belief and action. A standard text such as Raymond Firth's *Elements of Social Organisation* demonstrates the ways religion and ritual, kinship and political organization, economics, and technology arise as practical responses to human needs and function to service these needs. Mankind makes and mends only to give effect to the continuance of the species. The orientation of the student is implicitly assumed to be in tune with this view, the view of science in western civilization, and western anthropology is so embedded in this scientism that no student is asked to think directly about this inescapable conceptual proposition.

The dominant influence of cultural determinism apparently lifts culture-bearing mankind out of the orbit of natural phenomena and makes culture transcendent of biology. We say apparently because for Kroeber, who expounded this view in opposition to the biological determinists, culture was the product of biological evolution in being the species saltation—the great leap of mankind. The basis of this argument is of little importance, indeed hardly remembered; what is important for modern western anthropology is his view of culture as super-organic. Kroeber is in keeping with the Durkheimian tradition where the cultural or social is never individual, but super-organic and collective. Culture and society then are real entities beyond the individual which imprint themselves upon the individual who can neither change nor release himself from them. In the end, what separates mankind from the animal world is a secularized hand of God in the form of an evolutionary saltation. Within the cultural realm it is possible to relate culture to functioning for the satisfaction of biological needs because the concept of culture as super-organic makes it a different order of reality from biological determinism. Culture may then be, indeed must be, a valuation element embracing the whole of mankind. This answers the evolutionary question but still leaves open the developmental question and still operates with the categories and terminology redolent of the evolutionary frame and its valuation content. Even within the value-enhanced realm of super-organic culture western anthropology is still about and still seeking explanations of the 'primitive'.

The long quest of western anthropology has been about origins which provide explanations. The tension in the subject, now suffering a return of biological determinism in the form of socio-biological thought, arises from the relationship between individual human nature and collective culture: which explains what and to whom? Is a developmental question not always an evolutionary question? And is not diversity a fact which, with the concepts and categories of western anthropology, always raises the issue? At some point theory always gets back to an individual human tabula rasa on which culture writes, or a primal human nature which creates culture. Geertz makes the obvious assertion that there has never been any evidence of homo sapiens sapiens without attendant signs of culture.[29] It has been argued that this is a profound restructuring point for western anthropology, but there seems no reason why it is not merely Kroeber's leap in other words.

In examining the intellectual genealogy of Malinowksi, Gellner has shown how familiar ideas from the repository of European philosophy were reshuffled to make the distinctive character of the Malinowskian revolution.[30] Malinowski responded in his own way to romanticist nationalism, to produce the holistic view of functionalism in which history is merely the charter enabling the present to function. Others had previously reacted to romanticist nationalism to feed the racialist notions of western anthropology.[31] It is in the interpretations of the western conceptual fabric and not the empirical findings in foreign fields that we find what orders western anthropology and makes its revolutions. The studied people remain passive, voiceless inhabitants of the 'reserved laboratory', Gellner's chilling but apt phrase. The point to Gellner is not so much how Malinowski came to think what he did but that what he came to think failed to produce any interesting questions. The malaise, the *cul de sac*, of western anthropology is all about the search for interesting questions. The increasing interest in the history of western anthropology, in particular how it has been shaped by movements in western thought, the history of western ideas, seems geared to trying to unravel how the standard anthropological questions came to be posed in the way they were and what they mean. The motivation, as usual, is not purely historical but determined by contemporary problems. As the example of Malinowski demonstrates there are many alternatives, and much that can be manipulated by re-reading, as well as re-writing history.

Apart from the historical dimension there is also the rationalist/relativist debate which is bringing renewed importance to the discipline of western anthropology, primarily through the interest of philosophers. The rationalist/relativist debate certainly clarifies the conceptual roots of western anthropology but this new impetus seems to have locked itself more firmly than ever into a reconsideration of the terms and meanings of the dichotomy fundamental to western anthropological thought. The discussion is now concentrated on what is rational or irrational for the western anthropologist to maintain. At last western anthropologists themselves, as actors and constructors, are becoming part of the frame of reference. The debate is important and likely to be formative in the future course of western anthropology. Since the discipline itself is seen as part of western civilization, that perception determines the questions asked and how those questions should be pursued. We have yet to see whether this historical insight breaks the stranglehold of the eclectic anthropological circle.

As has been already postulated the conceptual fabric of western civilization is the frame of reference wherein we locate western anthropology and science and understand how they operate. A useful way of looking at this is provided by Peter L. Berger. 'What was previously "known" becomes at best "believed". In a further step it is an "opinion" or even a "feeling". In other words, the particular contents of consciousness that used to be taken for granted as "knowledge" are progressively deobjectivated.'[32] Berger, in setting out the levels at which discontinuity and change arguably occur, uses terms which are familiar debating grounds for western anthropology and science. Even at the extremes of the deobjectivated, the original 'knowns' are not spent forces, but wash around in the consciousness as part of the dynamic of convention, the general climate of society as well as the history of discourse. The essence of the process of deobjectification apparent in so much of Berger's work is fragmentation, a jumbling of levels and layers, in which consciousness manipulates what once were knowns, may now be believed or be merely opinions and feelings. One needs to be aware of the hierarchical relationships between these terms and that the terms are reassembled in a specific way in each argument deployed by a western anthropologist or scientist. In particular, at different stages of argument a western anthropologist may be relying upon old 'knowns' to carry the load, or be re-employing them as an opinion to be tested or be asserting them as a feeling to direct the course of general vague conclusions. This is the conviviality of civilizational consciousness; even when deobjectivated it allows new theories to fall back upon old discourses, often without the relationships being analysed or recognized. The degree to which civilizational self-awareness is absent is the degree to which problematic log-jams occur—when no question seems worth asking because it admits of no significant answers. This is the point where western anthropology falls back on the stuff of routine anthropology, enjoying the fascination of recording the weird, wonderful and diverse in mankind.

This discursive review of some of the concepts and orientations of western anthropology has been made to show just how firmly the discipline is a distinctive product of western civilization. It should be unnecessary to belabour the problems and shortcomings of western anthropology; its mythology and mystique and the characteristic ways it conceals problems are nowhere better recognized and criticized than by western anthropologists themselves. Therefore the question confronting all students and intellectuals whose world view is not derived from western civilization must be, why do they feel the need to enter upon anthropology by means of western anthropology?

The terms of reference of western anthropology are highly specific and tie it firmly to its own set of problems and intellectual dyspepsia. To do anthropology according to western anthropological concepts, categories and questions means acceptance or subservience to the propositions outlined here. To suggest, as does Akbar Ahmad, that western anthropology in its modern attitudinal structure, at least, promotes an ennobling tolerance and openness to other people and thereby justifies working through the medium of western anthropology, is most demeaning.[33] Western civilization has no monopoly upon epistemology, nor reason, nor science. Most definitely it has no monopoly upon tolerance, compassion and openness either as a base for human action or as a source of intellectual insight in understanding mankind. The science and anthropology of western civilization are the universal language of western civilization only. Other civilizations must elaborate their own ways of knowing and use them as a vantage point to observe, evaluate and enter a dialogue with the dominant western civilization. The very predicament that created western anthropology, colonialism, and its legacy as the imperialism of the mind, is behind the pervasive notion that one must think through western civilization's problematic strait-jackets in order to arrive at a better understanding of one's own distinctive concepts, civilizational identity and self.

The issue is not vilifying western anthropology, nor demanding its total rejection. The most necessary operation is to understand western anthropology within its civilizational context for the information and questions this promotes within the context of an Islamic anthropology. Most of all the issue is about clarity on the conceptual basis of Islamic anthropology. Quite simply, on the basis of Islamic concepts one cannot practise western anthropology, but one can pose essential questions about the nature of mankind, culture and society, one can produce categories to structure and order enquiry and the accumulation of data. When the Islamic conceptual base of such enquiry is elaborated and made clear one can enter a dialogue with western anthropology. Only when Islamic anthropology has refined its own ideas and understands their distinctiveness can such a dialogue have any prospect for mutual interest and stimulation. From this point onwards we have no need of a western defined frame of reference; words are employed in search of their definition and meaning within an Islamic frame of reference.

Notes

1. Until recently there were few standard histories of anthropology, and each had a slightly different focus of the relevant and important starting point. The main works are Penniman, *A Hundred Years of Anthropology;* Lowie, *The History of Ethnological Theory;* Harris, *The Rise of Anthropological Theory.* We have found invaluable Hodgen's *Early Anthropology in the Sixteenth and Seventeenth Centuries* and Stocking, *Race, Culture and Evolution.*

2. One only has to think of the titles of some of their works, especially Malinowski's pot-boilers: *Crime and Custom in Savage Society. The Sexual Life of Savages* (which often finds its way into pornographic bookshops to disappoint the clients), *Science and Superstition of Primitive Mankind,* Boas's *The Mind of Primitive Man, Primitive Art.* The text always states primitive does not mean primitive in a pejorative sense, and then proceeds to use the word without restraint in what follows.

3. See the excellent discussion of these points in Sperber, *On Anthropological Knowledge.*

4. For an insight into the ethnographic monograph see Stocking, 'The Ethnographic Magic: Fieldwork in British Anthropology from Tylor to Malinowski', *History of Anthropology* Vol. 1 and the comments by Sperber, *ibid.*

5. Goody, *The Domestication of the Savage Mind,* p.3.

6. Kuper, *Anthropology and Anthropologists.*

7. Thomas More, *Utopia,* Penguin, Harmondsworth. I have discussed More's use of ethnographic material in the context of western anthropology in 'Whose Utopia is it Anyway? *Inquiry,* Vol. 2(9) September 1985.

8. Lynn White Jr., 'The Historical Roots of our Ecological Crisis', *Science,* 155, 1203–7, 1967.

9. Authenticity is a favoured term of Levi-Strauss, see *Structural Anthropology.* This idealized virtue is also commented upon in halcyon terms by Diamond, *In Search of the Primitive.*

10. Worsley, 'The End of Anthropology'.

11. Stocking, *ibid.*

12. Hodgen, *ibid.*

13. Padgen, *The Fall of Natural Man.*

14. Harris, *The Rise of Anthropological Theory.*

15. Quoted in Hodgen, *ibid.* p.197.

16. Quoted in Hemmings, *Red Gold.* p.13–14. Both Hodgen and Hemmings include extensive quotations in similar vein from other early sources. Vespucci's letter probably provided the basis for Thomas More's *Utopia.*

17. Leaf, *Man, Mind and Science.*

18. Orme, *Anthropology for Archaeologists,* p.4–11 which includes the illustrations. For another example see the illustrated edition of the *Travels of Sir John Mandeville,* Collins, London, 1973. Mandeville was the best-selling work on the marvels of the world of the mediaeval era and still in circulation long after.

19. Mandeville as a standard reteller of Greek ethnography was a prime source of the European expectation of cannibalism.

20. For further detail see John Hemmings, *ibid.*

21. Goody, *ibid.* p.1.

22. As Goody notes, Levi-Strauss is the arch exponent of the Grand Divide.

23. Levy Bruhl is formative to the whole rationalist/relativist debate with his category of prelogical thought, or as his translator entitled his work *How Natives Think.*

24. Koestler, *The Sleepwalkers.*

25. Paul Hirst, 'Is It Rational to Reject Relativism' in Overing ed. *Reason and Morality.*

26. Stocking, *Race, Culture and Evolution,* p.45.

27. Stocking, *ibid.* pp.105–6.

28. Quoted in Stocking, *ibid.* p.101.

29. Geertz, *The Interpretation of Cultures.*

30. Gellner, 'Malinowski Go Home', *Anthropology Today,* Vol. 1(5) October 1985.

31. See the discussion of the background to racialist arguments in anthropology in Stocking, *ibid.*

32. Berger, *Facing Up To Modernity,* p. 216.

33. Ahmad, 'Defining Islamic Anthropology'.

3

Revolution, Revival and Return

The last decade has seen much discussion of Islamic revolution and revival. Behind the publicity stands a diverse movement, operating throughout the Muslim world and extending into all spheres of individual life and society. It has created a very specific response amongst Muslim intellectuals: the debate on the islamization of knowledge, a quest for the contemporary meaning of Islam amidst the complexities of the modern world. This is the context for seeking to shape an Islamic anthropology. In common with all other initiatives, however diverse, the basis of our search is the consciously acknowledged need and desire to make a return to the values and principles of Islam as the starting point and objective of action and enquiry.

There is an inevitable and necessary interaction between the knowledge base of a civilization and its intellectual disciplines; this holds true for all civilizations. Thus the sources of western civilization provide the concepts, values and categories for the study of western anthropology or any other western disciplines. Other such processes of interaction are necessary for other civilizations. What is objectionable is the argument that by virtue of their dominance the western disciplines of knowledge have defined the only means of entry into acceptable scholarship for all other people. It is vital that the activation of the link between a Muslim civilizational identity and knowledge base is established for this would offer the only genuine alternative to our present predicament.

Concepts and values are not newly made because they are employed in pursuit of 'science' but are significant because they are encrusted with civilizational meaning which relates them to all other aspects of life and thought. The redolence of concepts and values is their breadth of meaning, the associations and connections they not only express directly but subtly imply with the resonance of words and images. This redolance and resonance makes an intellectual discourse expressive of the goals and objectives, values and aspirations of its own civilization, integrates an intellectual discourse as an active agent of a world view. The western disciplines of knowledge are not without their problems and their consequences are to be seen in the endemic problems of the modern world. Developing other ways of thinking offers the only hopeful prospect for mankind. Instead of believing that humanity is necessarily reduced to the confines of our current predicament, revitalizing the concepts and values of other ways of knowing can demonstrate that mankind has the resources and capacity to make sense of its problems and resolve them. We are not dealing here with a power struggle over knowledge, we are trying to liberate ourselves from the false imposition of a faulty power structure. In that liberation there exists the possibility of offering a stimulus to western disciplines not unmindful of their own problems and in search of alternative ways of thinking within their own world view. For the Muslim world an islamization of knowledge must dedicate itself to unfolding and enabling the potential of the Muslim peoples to establish their own distinctive, humane and sustainable modernity.[1]

An intellectual structure of understanding does not arise solely from the circumstances of the moment, from a Spanish *conquistadore* confronted by an American Indian or, today, a Muslim leader seeking law and order by the re-introduction of Shariah punishments. The incident in question immediately relates to a conceptual fabric with its own characteristic ways of formulating questions to enable an intellectual understanding. This relationship has three dimensions. The first dimension obviously comprises the concepts themselves—the origin and derivation of which give them their particular definitions and their own inherent logic.

The second dimension is the history of interpretation. This is more than an intellectual history whether Whig, historicist or sound historiography. While the source of the concepts gives them definition, meaning and significance they are always apprehended through the interpretive agency of human thought and action, through their employment by people in society, both in the overtly intellectual sphere and in their more diffuse institutionalization in the organization of society. The past gives a particular specificity to concepts, establishes how they have actually been understood and manipulated, even though this may or may not be considered as exhausting the meaning of concepts. This is Foucault's archaeology of knowledge. It is history as tradition and convention, in the widest possible sense of the terms, that is always in tension with the present, a meaningful actor in contemporary debate, redefinition or reformulation.

The third dimension is the situational context of the present where understanding operates, questions are framed, and particular answers are sought by the application of concepts. This is the realm of local interests, interests distinguishing the present from the past. The contemporary perspective is always a product of history, yet it is distinctive for two vital reasons: it is a vantage point upon history; and consciously or unconsciously it has a power over the future. The present is the sphere of action where immediate interests, goals and objectives are being manipulated, even if only in slavish subservience to received convention. The contemporary perspective evaluates, determines, selects; it is a partial and particular operation rooted in the potential of both past and present, an actual ordering of a hierarchy of values and priorities determining what questions are posed in search of what desired solutions. To say this third dimension calls for a distinction between past and present is not to say one is perennially dealing with discontinuity, or newness, but to consider the features of the present as part of a process that has aspects both of continuity and change.

We must also recognize that in each dimension and in its interaction with the others hierarchical relationships are at work. In the case of islamization we must be concerned with the nature of this hierarchy, how it should be understood and how it operates. In the case of western civilization the secularization of knowledge, the deobjectivation process, has led to the assumption that hierarchy has either been abolished or is irrelevant; the present impulse and new departures are the prime directive. We have argued that this is not the case; the locus and terms of the hierarchy have merely been shifted and obscured. What deobjectivation produces is a fragmentation of the conceptual framework obfuscating the hierarchy by bringing it into play at different junctures of argument, making aspects of it operate as props to different levels of the structure of theory and debate.

In the West hierarchy operates as a cryptic hidden agenda structuring intellectual endeavour, because value-free, neutral, abstract 'science' is meant to have supplanted the original order that gave meaning to hierarchy. Yet, even this mythologized 'science' needs to reintegrate its produce with some overarching explanation and thus falls back upon the old value-laden associations in convoluted ways. As Mary Midgley has commented:

> Ethics, being patterns of incredible complexity, have to be evolved, not manufactured, and they always build on what went before. Like paradigms, they are part of the world-picture. And old ethics do not go in the dustbin. The range of moral insights possible to the human race probably does not change much, and all of them go on being needed on occasion. What does change drastically is the emphasis. Quite a small change in emphasis can make an enormous difference to life. In every age, morality has a bias. It is obvious to those who come after, but history shows us how hard even the most astute people find it to detect where the bias of their own age lies.[2]

The bias is determined by what part of the hierarchy is being operated; the manipulation of hierarchy should not obscure its existence, indeed its very manipulation is what relates past to present. In the case of western discourses of knowledge the question for islamization studies is to recognize and evaluate the manipulations as they give insights into the use and abuse of knowledge and the construction of good and bad questions.

The shaping of Islamic anthropology commences with an examination of the three dimensions which place it in the civilizational context of Islam. The concepts of Islam have a clear, unitary source of definition: the Qur'an and Sunnah. The Qur'an was revealed to the Prophet Muhammad during the course of his life at Makkah and Medina over a period of twenty-three years; it is the literal Word of God communicated to him by the Angel Gabriel. It was committed to memory and written form under the supervision of the Prophet during the course of his lifetime and has remained unchanged to the present day. The Qur'an is the completion of Prophethood because it comprises the complete Message of God to mankind, containing both specific injunctions and general principles, passages relating to particular events and circumstances of the life of the Muslim community and its Prophet and exposition of the eternal, universal, unchanging relationships of creation. It expounds both the letter and the spirit of law and understanding. As an exhortation to faith and belief the Qur'an calls upon human intuition, imagination and perception stimulated by its use of allegory and metaphor in descriptions of matters beyond direct human experience. Yet, repeatedly, the Qur'an calls upon the believer to utilize reason in seeking to understand its meaning and to recognize the significance of allegory and metaphor: reason, intuition, imagination and perception must work together if the intent of the Qur'an is to be realized. The Qur'an is the sole authority for Muslims on all matters with an institutional position in Muslim society expressive of the necessary relationship between mankind and God: submission.

It is important for the discussion that follows to make a clear distinction between concepts in the Qur'an and how those concepts have been comprehended by Muslims in history. The Qur'anic concepts are an expression of God's categories, not merely the categories with which mankind must work. They are transcendent, eternal concepts outside the temporal human realm, and underpin its specific injunctions for the regulation of human life—whether for economic behaviour, prayer, obligatory contribution to communal welfare (*zakat*) or inheritance. Without the total context of *fitrah*, created human nature; *din*, the path of religion as a total world view; *adl*, justice, equity; *adab*, culture and equilibrium; *fard*, obligation; *nafs*, individual soul; *halal*, beneficial; *haram*, destructive; *Akhirah*, hereafter; *ibadah*, worship; *zulm*, injustice; as just some examples from the extensive Qur'anic repertoire of concepts, the actual practices of an Islamic social existence would be rootless, mere isolates in search of a system rather than the natural, logical expressions of a comprehensive system. The unitary framework makes the injunctions constructive, purposive reforms for social life.

Approached in this way the Qur'anic concepts and categories stand as ideals and express values of eternal validity. The Qur'anic context is a moral and ethical domain where thought and action are structured and guided by enduring values with the goal being to integrate them with the concepts to show understanding of their comprehensiveness. As ideals and values expressing the essential nature of mankind and the definition of the reality in which mankind exists, the concepts of the Qur'an are attainable goals; mankind is perfectible as mankind. But even perfected mankind, having attained comprehension of the concepts, never becomes the possessor of their totality for mankind is finite and exists within limits of responsibility to God. The finality and totality of the concepts exists beyond the human sphere, and will only be made clear at the end of time. The tension in Islam is in the balance between the optimism of the perfectibility of mankind to operate the concepts to secure human fulfilment in the existence of this world, and humility before God.

The revelation of the Qur'an was an historical event. The emergence of Islam as a religion and the foundation of the Muslim community is more extensively documented than any other religion. However, the Qur'an itself makes it clear that the conceptual framework of Islam did not commence with the historical moment of its own revelation. The Qur'anic message is the complete version, and the same message, as the first revelation made to the first human Prophet, the first man, Adam. It is the same revelation of eternal, universal verities that has been made to all Prophets, named and unnamed in the Qur'an, which also states that no people has been left without a warner from God. While the Muslim community is defined by its allegiance to a specific historical revelation it is also conceptually related to all other human communities. Islam is not merely a universal message for all mankind from the point of the revelation of the Qur'an, but is also an expression of universal principles embedded in human experience since the creation, as historical realities. The conceptual framework of the Qur'an gives us a vantage point upon the ideals of human existence that people, throughout history, have been confronted with within the conventions of their particular society. The Qur'an's universal concepts are an evaluative scale applicable to the whole of mankind not just because they are part of the potential of humanity as created by God, but because they are part of the collective experience of mankind in history.

What is the nature of the system derived from the Qur'an, the style of the Islamic conceptual fabric? The basis of hierarchy is clear: the existence of the Absolute, God, and the nature of God is unity. All the concepts we deploy must be seen as integrative agents in search of Unity. This is why *tawhid*, unity, is today the most frequently cited Islamic concept, and for many writers everything else within the conceptual fabric of Islam can be derived from it. While this is logically true, inherent in the concept of *tawhid* itself, it is a restriction of the abundance of other Islamic concepts. *Tawhid* is the circumference wherein the other concepts and categories exist as balanced, multi-dimensional, interactive, integrative elements. What would be inimical to an Islamic outlook would be the notion of dichotomy, of mutually opposed difference. Any reduction to mutually opposed difference would be a false opposition, a reductive destruction of balance.

The Qur'anic concepts are eternal, they are givens of the Islamic perspective deriving from their source, which is Infinite. But this does not mean they constitute a closed system of enquiry. The Qur'an insistently calls for the exercise of reason and understanding because of the extensiveness, the infinite capacity, of its words. To argue otherwise would be to maintain either that the Qur'an itself has a literal exact meaning capable of being fixed by the human intellect (the literalist interpretation of religion), or that the human intellect can elevate itself to being the same as the Infinite (the deification of man as reasoning being). Both arguments are based on human assumptions and contradict the source of Islam. The accumulation of knowledge can never exhaust the meaning of concepts, but it can add to their complexity and admit of differences of human interpretation that promote debate and insight. It is impossible to conceive of anything the human intellect could prove about empirical reality that could overthrow the Islamic conceptual framework, except when interpretation has itself arbitrarily fixed meanings. The only antidote to this perennial human frailty is to keep returning to the conceptual framework and accepting error as a factor in all thought, which keeps the system open.

Islamic concepts derive from the Qur'an. But there is a secondary source of Islam to help us understand its meaning, the Sunnah, the way of the Prophet. The Qur'an makes it clear that Muhammad was a human being, and therefore fallible; the Prophet himself urged the first Muslim community to discriminate between his opinions as a human being and his teachings as a prophet. Yet as the selected Messenger of God Muhammad was an exemplary human being whose words and deeds give a living textbook through which the meaning and intention of the Quran are further explained. The Sunnah are recorded in *hadith*, the term denoting the words and deeds of the Prophet as witnessed and transmitted by members of the first Muslim community.

The *hadith* cover an immense range of activities and concerns, giving direct guidance on how the understanding of Islam is to be structured for the Muslim community in history. Here one is thinking of the *hadith* related by Mu'adh b. Jabal. When Muhammad appointed him as Governor to Yemen, making him his personal representative responsible for practical decisions in organizing the day to day life of a community, he asked him how he would judge when the occasion arose. Mu'adh b. Jabal replied that he would judge in accordance with the Qur'an. Asked what he would do if he found no direct guidance there Mu'adh replied he would act in accordance with the Sunnah. Asked what he would do if he could find no direct guidance in the Sunnah he said he would do his best to form an opinion and spare no pains, for which reply he was warmly praised by the Prophet.[3] The enduring framework of the Qur'an and Sunnah are there to form our consciousness but the only way they enter human history is by the exertion of Muslims in their daily lives.

It is through the paradigm of the Sunnah that Muslim civilization took shape. Let us take the example of *hadith*. Within a short period after the passing of the Companions of the Prophet a science of *hadith* came into being. This uniquely Muslim science was a critical methodology of sound historiography based on the study of *isnad*—the chain of narrators of hadith—which concerned itself with the probity of each link in the chain of transmission. It investigated the lives of the transmitters to establish they could actually have met, that they were people whose testimony would be acceptable in a court of law, that the chain carried the *hadith* back to a Companion of the Prophet. Further refinements were introduced to the practice of this science: for example, no hadith could be accepted if it were in contradiction to the Qur'an, if it were partisan, against reason or recognized historical fact, or avowed heavy punishment for ordinary lapses or mighty rewards for ordinary deeds. The science of *hadith* therefore created a typology of classification: *sahih* (sound) has an unbroken *isnad* resting on sound authority; *hasan* (good) has a complete *isnad* but with one weak link; *da'if* (weak) where either the *isnad* is incomplete or the authority weak. There were further categories such as *mursal* and *mudal, munkar, mudraj, maudu* which relate to the nature of the failings in the authority of the *hadith*.

The Sunnah has its own agency, *hadith*. *Hadith* spawned its own science as part of the institutionalization of *hadith* and Sunnah within the operation of Muslim civilization. It is common to read that the great compilers of *hadith*, such as Bukhari and Malik Ibn Anas, studied thousands of *hadith* but recognized only a small fraction as sound. Such a statement can give no insight into the process of a civilization unless two points are recognized: the proliferation of *hadith* indicates a desire to legitimate all action by reference back to the Prophet Muhammad as well as the Quran; the core tradition was formalized by critical inquiry distinctive to the conceptual framework of Islam. Only on the basis of these insights do the exertions of the Imams, what they accepted and what they rejected, have any civilizational and sociological significance.

Muslims regard themselves as a people of the Word, which is their Law. The formalization of *hadith* was the basis for the fluorescence of the most distinctive attribute of Muslim civilization, *fiqh* (jurisprudence). The term *fiqh*, which significantly means comprehension, is often taken to denote the body of law produced but it is better regarded as a process entailing a number of elements. It generated a distinctive system of education, a body of personnel groomed in paradigms, a system of institutional positions whose personnel had a regulatory role in the community.

The core of the education of *fuqaha* (jurists) was the Qur'an and Sunnah. Mastery of this base was characterized by two features: while the civilization and culture were literary, education and literary endeavour depended upon rote learning of text which involved oral techniques demanding prodigious feats of memory.[4] Commentaries and works of the great masters also had to be memorized. This education had its own scholastic method for distinguishing the matters considered as settled and the manipulation of 'debatable' questions. This institution of learning came to have a particular form, the *madrassa*, where students gathered but always had a personal relationship with their teacher. While the core of education was uniform, study under different masters and the collection of proof of study, the *ijaza*, could extend the qualifications of the student.[5]

On the basis of education a student could serve as a judge in a court of law, hold office in the administration of the ruler, or establish his own school. Legal training was the core of all learning and those who went on to study mathematics, physics, chemistry, medicine to become the polymaths of Muslim civilization did so on the basis of a study of law, which was the foundation of their conceptual training.

Since *fiqh* is a cornerstone of Muslim civilization it is worth noting some of its main characteristics. The study of the sources, Qur'an and Sunnah, required a detailed knowledge of the circumstances of the Revelation of each verse and the matters to which it referred. From this a distinction could be made between specific import and general principles. On the basis of this understanding a system of *qiyas* (deductive reasoning by analogy) could be used to derive pragmatic applications to questions arising in the daily life of society. We have spoken of Islam as a system with a unitary base, but it is operated and institutionalized with a minimum of formal institutions. As in education, the keynote of relationships within society are not formal institutions but networks of personal relations. There is no central priesthood, nor any authority to justify the emergence of such a body. It is scholarship and piety as personally acquired characteristics subject to their acknowledgement by society that validate institutions and their personnel. Leaders emerge, even in theology and *fiqh*. Yet there is a collective aspect the qualified can cite as authority; this is *ijma*, the consensus of the qualified, what past or present jurists agree to be the best interpretation. The ultimate bounds of *fiqh* is *ijtihad*, reasoned struggle, an individual process to be undertaken by the qualified. It has given *fiqh* a flexibility to develop and adapt.[6]

Among other major categories employed by the jurists are *halal*, the beneficial and permissible, and *haram*, the destructive and prohibited. These pervasive categories can be elucidated in any sphere of thought or action. As a total framework in search of Unity all questions pertain to Islam and an Islamic response can be debated on every topic, not because everything is written but because the challenge to unity is the essence of Muslim existence. Islam spread rapidly from its initial base in Medina and was adopted by peoples of different cultural background and social setting. The examination of *al-urf*, customary usage and practice, subject to the categories of *halal* and *haram*, was one way customs were validated and entered into the cultural body of Islam. All that was not expressly prohibited was permitted according to the framework, and since the Prophet himself had cautioned against burdensome restrictions, affirming local custom was therefore in keeping with the conceptual framework. So was *al istislah*, the unprecedented judgment motivated by the public interest, and the concept of utility, *al-maslahah*, that in each rule concerning human dealings in the Qur'an there is a conceivable point of utility which is its intention; if this point can be defined then the applicability of text should extend to every new issue where the same point of utility can be discerned.

As the principles of law were being worked out by the jurists in the early centuries of Muslim civilization they were being defined and developed through opinions on actual cases. Four main schools of law came to predominate in Sunni, orthodox Islam: the Hanbali, Shafi'i, Maliki and Hanafi. Each school of law takes its name from its founder, yet, argues Said Ramadan, they never intended to establish a tradition. They viewed their opinions as contextual, the best they could achieve for their own time and circumstances; they positively cautioned against blind following of their rulings. The clearest example is the statement by Ibn Hanbal, 'Do not imitate me or Malik or Al-Shafi'i or Al-Thawli and derive directly from where they themselves have derived.'[7] The hierarchy of Islam clearly differentiates between the opinion of jurists in operationalizing the *Shariah*; and the superior authority of the sources of the *Shariah*, the Qur'an and Sunnah. Any opinion of a jurist is subject to reformulation, argument and refutation. Each one of the subsidiary sources of *fiqh* we have mentioned has been the subject of debate and differences of opinion on its validity and definition.

The development of *fiqh* incorporated an acute sense of history and social reality. The minute attention given to the historical and social setting of Revelation by the jurists is a powerful indication of their own awareness of their place in history. Not only was it necessary to investigate the period of revelation at Makkah and Medina but accurate knowledge had also to be accumulated on pre-Islamic Arabia to assess and understand the reforms promulgated and a proper model made for the application of Islam in other cultural settings. Along with social and historical interest went the linguistic. The revelation of the Qur'an was in Arabic, a language ennobled, for many Muslims acquiring a sacredness as the vehicle for God's Word. Therefore, precision in the meaning and significance of words, a lexical and etymological fascination, became part of the intellectual procedure of Muslim civilization.

From the procedures of *fiqh* we have briefly outlined it is obvious that Muslim civilization is not monolithic, but diverse. By this we are not referring to the cleavage between Shia and Sunni, derived from differences over the succession of leadership after the Prophet and interpretation on the subject of authority within the Muslim community. The Shia take their name from their special affection for Ali, whom they believe was intended as the immediate successor of Muhammad. They have their own school of law and body of *hadith*, yet there is a commonality between Shia and Sunni on the bulk of matters. Cultural diversity can be seen not merely in differences between Sunni and Shia communities but within both sections of the Muslim world. Islam places especial value upon the family as the cornerstone of society, its system of law defines rights and obligations of family members who are given additional claims upon each other by the rules of inheritance. All these matters are uniform and socially enforceable in courts of law, yet even within the family there are differences in practice and custom between one part of the Muslim world and another. Systems of preferred marriages that build into wider family networks differ from place to place. Muslim civilization is shaped around a common core from which it diversifies according to time and space. This is as much a fact of history as part of the process envisaged by those who sought to regulate this history in conformity with the Islamic ideal, the jurists.

The Sunnah is the basic model for the institutionalization of Islam in society. So far we have considered characteristics of the intellectual system it conditioned and produced, but the process of institutionalization works in another way. The concepts and values of Qur'an and Sunnah were diffused throughout society as they formed part of the socialization of the individual Muslim. This process works alongside the formal endeavours of any *alim*, learned person. This socialization of individual behaviour within a world view forms and spreads the style of a civilization, extends beyond the sphere of their regulations.

While the process of socialization and institutionalization takes its dynamic from the Sunnah and is influenced by the social regulatory role of the *ulema* (the collective body of the learned), it goes far beyond formal matters dealt with in either Qur'an or Sunnah or the *Shariah*, the body of religious law as it has come to be understood. Religion as *din*, a total way of life, creates a hierarchy for the individual as for society. As the Source of ultimate meanings it is diffused through society by underpinning all meaning. All habits, customs, speech and behaviour are linked in some way to the meaningful realm of the *din*. The process of individual socialization works on many levels, embracing intuitive responses as well as reasoned responses, but with a value scale both explicit and implicit in the *din*. The *din* becomes the structuring point through which traditions are generated and validated, as much in the formal intellectual sphere as in popular beliefs, customary usages and interpersonal behaviour. It includes the way customs and cultural behaviour that predate the acceptance of Islam are integrated within Muslim society and are re-evaluated according to a Muslim perspective outside the orbit of the formal body of *ulema*. How Islam is institutionalized in society is not solely the work of the *ulema*, it is the work of the entire Muslim population. In this way the whole of Muslim civilization is a human interpretation of the conceptual framework of Islam, and as such is fallible, open to question and deviation from the Islamic ideal.

The flexibility of Muslim civilization with its reliance on personal networks, its concept of society, nation, supra-national community, *ummah*, and citizenship must all be viewed in terms of the Islamic framework where collective obligation and personal responsibility are both stressed. In Muslim civilization the acquiring of status and authority within society is open to all through the medium of Islam. The best among you is the most pleasing in the eyes of God: there are many formulations of this idea in Qur'an and Sunnah. This dictum not only enfranchises innovative personal action, but it also acquires conventional form and symbols in specific social settings. It does not acknowledge that whatever is right simply because it manipulates the symbols and rhetoric of Islam. Within the context of Islam, however, personal initiative would also be directed towards the establishment of a consensus, it would be argument and initiative in search of a collective expression. Human judgement must always be conditional and limited, final judgement belongs to God alone. The institutionalizing and socializing of religion in society remains always an open system interacting with and subject to the Islamic ideal.

The effect of this socialization can be traced in all Muslim conventions and cultural property. In art and stylistic forms, for example, one finds that calligraphy testifies to the centrality of the Word. The simplicity of form and intricacy of decoration to be found not only in luxury goods but also in utilitarian objects, testifies to an aesthetic sense derived from Islamic sources, the internalizing of a world view by craftsmen and women. Simplicity of form derives from balance and unity; complexity and intricacy of decoration lead the eye and the mind ever deeper to contemplate the source of balance and unity which is the infinite.

At any time or place in history the Islamic ideal will have a particular form for a specific Muslim people, but it will essentially stand above temporal reality. The Islamic ideal is a real dimension to Muslim discourse: present in whatever is done, said or thought. From inside the framework of Islam the Muslim is always conscious, however subliminally, of a distinction between Muslim society and Islam, and of the difference between her or his perception of his or her actions and how these actions might appear to God. The hierarchy generates discrete levels of criticism and social action that interact with each other. This interaction can be properly analysed only when the objective reality of the hierarchy, as well as the Muslim perception of it, are taken into account.

The ever-present sense of hierarchy is a major point of difference between the Muslim perspective and the conventions of the western disciplines that study Muslim civilization. Here we shall consider two major genres: Islamic studies and the western anthropology of Islam. Islamic studies, a discipline shaped and dominated by Orientalists,[8] has achieved a powerful influence over much Muslim discourse about Islam. While notions of an Islamic ideal are regularly discussed the discipline presents this as a closed system, derived by concentrating on culture specific historical forms of Muslim behaviour and Muslim reformers through history. It conflates the Islamic ideal with the ideals of Muslims as expressed through their actual behaviour, failing to recognize that even the most devout of reformers would have to acknowledge that they give only a partial and particular expression of the Islamic ideal.

Within western discourse, religion is viewed as the human-created response to philosophical and sociological imperatives requiring mankind to give themselves a reason and rationale for existence. Originally the western view of Islam derived from Christianity itself, and a Christian perspective could give no validity to the Revelation of Islam. From the Middle Ages onwards Islam was to the West a heresy, therefore it could be explained only in terms of human thought and action.[9] Both the conceptual fabric of Christian civilization and the rise of scientism within that civilization ensure that the Orientalist discipline can give only a distorted description of Islam. Recognition of the Islamic Revelation and its implication for the understanding and study of Muslim civilization is required to shift from a western mode of discourse, where such a level can have no validity, to an Islamic conceptual framework where it opens social reality to meaningful enquiry.

These western disciplines have spawned an apologetic school of Muslim writings, restricted to the erroneous terms of debate set by a western view of Islam as being rooted solely in the history of Muslim civilization. Their apologist literature is a potent force restricting Muslim discussion of the contemporary relevance of Islam to an agenda set by western commentators. It is the world of the five pillars of Islam: the economic system as a discrete sphere of social life: the political system as another discrete sphere; the rights of women; marriage and divorce; polygamy and slavery. This reactive body of literature diverts energy and attention from the creation of a Muslim agenda of study, enquiry and action in the modern world.

The western anthropology of Islam is a different study, being theoretically grounded in an ahistorical view of society. In this discipline Islam is the abstracted ideal description of what Muslims say and do produced by the conceptual fabric which underpins western anthropology. Western anthropologists are not slow to acknowledge that they are less interested, and often not schooled in, the literary traditions of a people, even when studying civilizations with extensive literary sources. The relevance of the literary tradition is significant only as one factor involved in social interaction in the only meaningful frame of reference, the present, analysis of which generates the portrait of the social ideal. The spiritual hierarchy acknowledged by Muslims has no reality, being valid only as self-justification and sociological rationalization of the Muslims.

Any discussion of Muslim civilization concerned with the hierarchy of distinctions between Islam and Muslims would be inadequate if it did not consider the major civilizational shift that became apparent during the thirteenth century CE. This was no single event, rather the culmination of a gradual process summed up by the acceptance by the *ulema* that the gates of *ijtihad* (intellectual struggle) were closed. The reason for this self-imposed closure of the Islamic system was a fear of *bida* (illicit innovation), resulting from the exercise of *ijtihad* by the unqualified in the context of the long-running battle between the Asharites and the Mutazilites and other contending factions. In consequence there was a redefinition of the practice of religious interpretation with the dominant mode of thought amongst the *ulema* being *taqlid*, the blind following of the authority of the early jurists on the application of *Shariah* to society. The consequences of this paradigm shift were to ramify throughout Muslim society, making Muslim civilization as a whole less able to absorb the historical challenges it had to confront.

As yet there are too few historical studies of this process within Muslim civilization to allow more than tentative generalizations about the implications of this shift. Let us consider the question of education in the light of Midgley's point that a small shift of emphasis can have major consequences for life. Once the established body of *fiqh* became the law, the *Shariah*, then education itself was re-evaluated. It became a matter of absorbing a fixed body of tradition rather than mastering a conceptual approach to the functioning of the legal system. Conceptual training for wider studies was also impaired. What had been an engine house for exploration of all branches of learning became a mechanism to assist in the withering of creative Islamic thought in many fields of enquiry.

The reliance upon rote learning became valued for its own sake. Memory retention generates its own mind set, its own critical sense where correctness of form is paramount with formal application as a logical consequence. It is no accident of history that rote learning and memory remain the core of traditional religious education. It reflects the priority given to established authority and the chosen relationship to tradition, its fixity and formal integrity. The value scholars placed upon the avoidance of *bida* resulted in generations of students being educated by distinctive means. Originality of mind was feared, for immersing students in retention of what is fixed and given is the best way to guard against innovation. The feats of memory required to assimilate an extensive body of information rest upon the assumption that questions have been settled. Memorization discourages and restricts the opportunity for the student to ask questions; it breeds a passivity of mind attuned to answering questions only in specific forms. It should not be overlooked that it has also inbred a tendency to answer questions only when they are put. When the questions appear in different guises, when the issues underlie new forms of technology and social practice, the *taqlidic* outlook is soon out of its depth. Since the *ulema's* social prominence and authority rests upon the certainty of having all the answers, deep suspicion and the rejection of modernity in any form except that which is already written is a logical consequence of the horror of *bida*.

Just as the shift to *taqlid* falsely elevated human interpretation of Islam to the status of the Divine Law, *Shariah*, so it elevated and distorted the social position and role of the *ulema*. It affected the institutionalization of Islam within Muslim civilization and those attitudes were reflected as part of individual socialization to Islam. The fixity which the learned gave to Islam as law became part of the dynamic of how the *din* was understood by the generality of Muslims. The *ulema* became the adepts of a specialized knowledge, *fiqh*, which thus lay beyond the scope of most Muslims, whose self-confidence in being able to articulate their own response to the Islamic ideal was subordinated to the special authority of the *ulema*. The *ulema* are not a unitary body, for despite the value placed upon conformity, diversity of opinion does exist. This fragmentation is obviously related to specific contextual social factors—who they are, where they come from, their connections with other power-holders such as land owners, state officials, rulers. The consequence is that the *ulema* have had a chequered history and have been able to destabilize social movements within the Muslim community seeking to put the Islamic ideal into practice.

The educational distinction between *fardu 'ayn* and *fardu kifayah* (obligatory and optional knowledge) becomes a major source of tension within Muslim civilization under the dominance of *taqlid*. Originally the two spheres distinguished religious sciences from the disciplines of the philosophical and intellectual sciences. It has become a metaphor for a socially acknowledged distinction in the understanding of religion itself. In effect this general distinction came to be understood in the restricted sense of determining between competence in *fiqh* or the lack of this competence. This emphasis went hand in hand with the curtailment of the curriculum of the *madrassa*, the confining of Islamic education to traditional religion. Muslim civilizaton has, as yet, been unable to circumvent this rupture in intellectual life. The consequence of the shift to *taqlid* has been that there is no route to the original *fardu kifayah* within the Islamic education system. For a Muslim to know the Qur'an and Sunnah is not socially validated as sufficient for the operationalizing of Islam, either in society at large or in pursuit of *fardu kifayah*. The problem solving methodology of Shariah has been appropriated and defined by the tradition-bound scholars. In this way a shift of emphasis has affected and continues to affect the dynamic of an entire civilization.

The *ulema* underwent an analogous change. Instead of applying the lessons of the past to diverse settings, they immersed themselves in a particular historical context, that of the Medina state. The depiction of the Medina state and the life of the Prophet became fixed in time and viewed only as the ancestors had understood it. This vision of the Medina state became the model; the present had always to recast itself in the mould of the past. This conformity was validated in *fiqh*. It was no longer a matter of asking new questions of the conceptual base but of using the base of *fiqh* as an imposition upon contemporary reality, with a precise list of dos and don'ts. As events have demonstrated contemporary reality will not stand still in this convenient way. Consequently, over time more and more of the actual life of Muslim civilization was handed over to forces beyond the control of Islamic redefinition. The elaborate body of *fiqh* has become truncated to deal with those aspects of social life most easily bound to tradition: personal and family behaviour.

With the rise of the paradigm of *taqlid* the dynamic of Muslim civilization changed. The timelessness of its base, the Islamic conceptual framework, was superseded by the timebound vision of the historical moment of the emergence of the Islamic model, the Medina state. Muslim civilization became reactive, responding to contemporary conditions by looking backward. Muslim civilization could no longer set its own agenda for modernity because it had come to locate its vision of the future in its own historical past. Hardly surprising then that nostalgia, imitation, stagnation, formality and inflexibility are the most frequent diagnoses of the Muslim mind made by Muslim commentators themselves. Nor that the generality of Muslims feel constrained to regard Islam as a core agenda of certain essential elements which, once restored, will automatically and with mechanical precision usher in a more righteous age.

Taqlid may be dominant but its pre-eminence has never been unquestioned. The first call for the gates of *ijtihad* to be opened came with Ibn Taymiya in the fourteenth century CE.[10] Reform movements—Islamic revival and revolution in today's terminology—have been constant factors in the history of Muslim civilization. One could even argue that the *taqlid–ijtihad* axis that all such initiatives have been grounded in has been part of the problem of revival within Muslim civilization. *Fiqh* is accepted as part of the system itself and this imposes a restriction on any reforms. Often the question is limited to what *fiqh* means today, rather than to what the mechanism of recognizing and generating *fiqh* allows one to do beyond the bounds of historical *fiqh*. The recognition that *fiqh* and Shariah are two distinct entities, closely related and interactive but not coterminous, has been blocked. Reform movements cannot be amalgamated under the term fundamentalism: each movement or initiative has its own programme and agenda of specific concerns beyond the common call for a return to *ijtihad*. Each can and should be analysed in terms of its declared aspirations and for the purpose it envisages for *ijtihad* in society. The history of these initiatives cannot be examined in purely social terms; the nature of the adherents they attract, how the movement and its followers interact with and cross cut the *ulema* itself, the nature of their relationship to rulers and other movements and organizations within Muslim society are factors necessary for a proper assessment. However, the role of revival movements in Muslim civilization can be evaluated only when the hierarchy of Islam is shown to be central to their analysis.

The various revival and reform movements have had one major impact upon Muslim civilization: they have given practical and specific expression to the distinction between Islam, the Islamic ideal, and the actual state of Muslim society in history. They have pointed to the conceptual openness of the Islamic system and have provided a counterbalance to the dominance of *taqlid*. They have been a reminder that Islam is not and never can be the sum total of what Muslims say, do or think, and that no one group within Muslim society, no matter how learned, can define Islam according to their dictates for all time.

Civilization includes contacts beyond its own frontiers; the environment is affected by interactions with other civilizations. In looking at changes in the intellectual system we have given indicators of how decline in the vitality of Muslim civilization was a self-inflicted process. In looking at the wider fate of Muslim civilization one observes that the intellectual decline acted in conjunction with the major historical challenge faced by Muslim civilization: the rise of the colonial, commercial, economic and industrial power of the West. Even those areas that escaped direct formal colonization were affected by this process.

The geographical extent of Muslim civilization placed it in the middle of a network of routes. The Muslim world has had links with and a presence in Europe, China, the Indian subcontinent, the South East Asian Archipelago, and sub-Saharan Africa.[11] The Muslim trans-Saharan trade provided the gold that underpinned European currency in the Middle Ages; the wealth generated by this trade maintained the urban and intellectual life of the Maghrib. The knowledge, skill and innovativeness of cartographers, geographers and travellers of this region was eagerly sought by their European neighbours and provided the stimulus to the European voyages of discovery.

The mercantile expansion of Europe undercut a major source of the economic vitality of the Muslim world which had been an entrepôt of global trade. As these networks passed under the domination of European traders Muslim trade diminished and wealth generation became more dependent upon the extraction of surplus from the land. Quite obviously we are talking in gross terms of regional and local processes over a long period of time. The growth of the western challenge to Muslim civilization from 1400–1800 CE covered the era when the core tradition of the Muslim world was reshaping itself according to a preservationist and conservationist frame of mind. The hold of *taqlid* was strengthening and consequently the educational system was retreating into a traditionalist redoubt. How far and in what ways the two processes were interlinked would again be a topic worthy of further attention.

The opening years of the nineteenth century provide a convenient watershed for looking at the history of the interaction of the Muslim world and the West. It opened with Napolean's expeditionary adventure into Egypt from which many trace the birth of Orientalism, the creation of the reformulated western model for understanding the Muslim world. The repercussions of the French Revolution inspired the growth of idealism and romanticism that in various ways encouraged the nationalist movements across Europe which had much to do with the destabilization of the Balkan region and decline of Muslim life in Eastern Europe. This particular rolling back of Muslim frontiers, coupled with the submersion of a Muslim population within the fabric of Europe was a major influence upon Ottoman attitudes to the modernity of the West. From 1800 the form of colonial rule in the Indian subcontinent began to change, producing the British model of how Islam was to be incorporated within the framework of Empire.

It is instructive, however, to note Hobsbawm's comments on the social and economic state of Europe as this era opened.[12] France itself was hardly more materially advanced than the Muslim world when the expeditionary adventure was launched. In Britain the foundations of industrial growth had been taking shape since around 1750, but the impact of these developments as a major social transformation was not felt until well after 1800. It was less the actual material might of Europe that impinged upon Muslim civilization than the fruits of an ideological disparity. The ideological vitality of Europe enabled it to take advantage of the opportunities of its history, to operate a political, educational and scientific system which serves its own purposes and answers its own value system, even when problems are raised within a western perspective.

From 1800 onwards the ideological framework of the West had developed its modern form. Progress as an ideology linked endeavours in various spheres, economic, commercial, social, intellectual and scientific. It produced a self-confident expansionist outlook that assumed the prerogative of dominance over all other modes of thought and action, which in turn was confirmed by the reaction of the peoples subject to its influence. Based upon the material benefits mercantile colonialism had extracted up to 1800, the expansion of western dominance gradually hardened into the colonial civilizing mission characteristic of the nineteenth century, and whose legacy is with us today.

Within the Muslim world colonialism produced a great blow to self-esteem which heightened nostalgia for the past; Muslims looked back to a time when they regarded themselves as the predominant world civilization. In many ways this confirmed the Muslim perception of seeing their own integrity and autonomy only in the past. Alien domination had the further consequence of making religious sentiment wish to maintain a religious purity at all costs. The preservationist tendencies of *taqlid* became a focus of defiance against domination. The drive to get out of the intractable problems of colonial domination was not merely a matter of ejecting the colonial rulers. The other necessity was to match their capacity for control by acquiring their superior skills. The obvious route was to seek to domesticate the power of the Imperium, the West, within Muslim society by copying the techniques of the West in education, social system, and most of all science and technology. Since imitation in conformity to a fixed and given model had become part of the tone of Muslim civilization in its interpretation of Islam it was perhaps inevitable that imitation of the perceived sources of western power should become characteristic of the Muslim response.

The era of colonialism introduced a set of alien boundaries and demarcations into the Muslim world, with different nations acquiring different characteristics according to whose sphere of influence they belonged. This determined which European language became their *lingua franca* of modernity, and hence which set of ideologies and western schools of thought exerted most influence. Similarly, the type of economic infrastructure serving the interests of the colonial powers was also determined by the power itself. The exploitative infrastructures of colonialism became the economic, industrial, social and intellectual legacy of emergent independent Muslim states. This legacy has created lines of communication and non-communication within the modern Muslim world, within nations as well as between nations. It has been a potent force in destabilizing Muslim civilization as a whole, creating the very barriers the ideal of the *ummah*, as expressed by Muslims, seeks to surmount. The concept of *ummah*, in the sense of the community of believers, is the civilizational communal identity of the Muslim. Today it is not merely intellectually difficult to think on the level of the *ummah*, its existence is practically and pragmatically fraught with pitfalls and problems. The emotional pull of *ummatic* thought has been distorted for many Muslims by other lesser panistic movements and ideologies. The Muslim world is interlinked and integrated into an international economic order created and dominated by the West. But each Muslim state is individually incorporated into this global network by links that dominate any collective Muslim identity. So far, this has prevented Muslim identity of interests developing beyond the lowest common denominators in uncontentious spheres of activity. The only real thing operating beyond this minimal sphere is rhetoric and hyperbole with no practical referrants.

The Muslim reaction to colonialism was expressed in the drive to modernization. This was both a distinct Muslim reaction, as in Turkey and Egypt, as well as an acquired reaction under the tutelage of a resident colonial administration, as in the Indian sub-continent. The results have been summed up in an aptly termed syndrome: occi-dentosis, which sounds about as pernicious as have been its consequences.[13] The drive for modernization and the specific nature of the colonial experience in each part of the Muslim world have opened cleavages within Muslim society. It is too simplistic to speak of a modern sector and a traditional sector as if these were two easily distinguished and discrete aspects of society as a whole, or as referents on an international scale. The cleavages exist within individual Muslims and are a form of multiple schizophrenia affecting the socialization of the individual differentially in different spheres of their life in Muslim society, and affecting individuals in disparate ways. The breaches are complex, operating on all levels: conceptual, individual and collective. They originate with attempts to make a compromise between a Muslim identity and western modernity, according to western definitions.

If we return to the educational sphere we can examine some of the complexities associated with modernization. At one level one could point to the creation of a system of schools based on western models using European teaching materials in the Muslim world, beginning with the military academies established in Turkey in the nineteenth century. The modern sector schools have been centres for spreading western values, both implicitly as embedded in the intellectual content of education, and explicitly through the socially validated priority these schools and the system of education give to things western. However potent the occidentosis within the schools, the individual student is not automatically precluded from maintaining a traditional Muslim outlook, for many who pass through this system maintain an allegiance to Islam central to their being. But home and school are two discrete spheres that do not interact at any level; neither has the authority nor validity to provide a critique of the other.

Increasingly more people in the Muslim world have received their education entirely within the confines of the modern sector where attitudes towards Islam and Muslim history are generated by Orientalist and Islamicist studies. From the predicament of their societies as well as the overt and implicit western values of their education they may easily identify Islam, as institutionalized in Muslim society, as a conservative, reactionary force out of touch with contemporary reality. Yet, Islam can have an influence even on the most secularized modernist. Because Islam as practised and embodied in the traditional patterns of society is deemed part of the problem of backwardness does not therefore mean that this is the totality of Islam. People who accept the modernizing ideologies of the West, such as socialism or feminism, do not have to abandon being Muslims. There are numerous attempts at syncretism, such as the Islamic socialism of Bhutto or the liberated stance of the Egyptian writer and doctor, Nawal el-Saadawi. The Islamic ideal, the set of universal values that stand beyond any specific institutionalization in Muslim society, can continue to have a validity that is far more than cultural gloss, and may even penetrate deeper than political expediency, to provide a vantage point upon modernity and western ideas that cannot be characterized as traditional.

Colonialism certainly curtailed the operation of Islam within Muslim society and restricted traditional Islamic education. Muslim nations, of their own volition or under colonial tutelage, imported European codes of law to modernize the state. Islamic law was not abolished, nor did it cease to function but it was relegated to the areas of personal and family law. The traditional Islamic education system continued to function to produce the scholars who serviced these courts and who worked in the administration of the mosque and its attendant social organizations. These were positions of social authority and power, but held within a different system nestling within the modern state. While traditional scholars are viewed by some as an anachronism, for the majority of Muslims they still wield a potent authenticity.

This rupture has generated an active competition and antagonism between the spheres of society. Definite choices have to be made involving values and priorities about life chances in choosing which sphere of education a child enters. For the student within the traditional Islamic education system the objective is still the mastery of *fiqh*. Very few areas of Islamic law will have any operational social relevance, since the framework for decision-making within the state is based on western codes of law. Since the student will be entering upon a career where the knowledge acquired can be operationalized only in limited matters, there is a predisposition to passivity towards the other topics in the educational system.

It could be argued that the contemporary social setting exaggerates all the problems we have discussed above in connection with *taqlid*. A scholar who is marginalized because of his traditional education is likely to be suspicious of the modern state, associating modernity with the denigration of Islam. He is likely to exist in a curtailed and encapsulated Islamic space within the modern state, the world of the mosque. The role of *ulema* as islamizing agents in contemporary Muslim society is conditioned by all these factors. Although their opinions are sought on a whole range of modern problems, their competence to comment and the nature of their response are conditioned by their background. The *ulema* themselves are part of the predicament of Islam in Muslim civilization today. They are far more secure with a conventional model of Islam as personal piety than with Islam as providing the conceptual and structural referents of a total social system. They strenuously and rightly maintain that that is the nature of Islam, but how to proceed beyond rhetoric and exhortation remains an undefined, indefinite question to which they have no practical solutions.

When the *ulema* are appealed to for an opinion they are employed by Muslim society in a purely reactive role. They are asked to comment and issue *fatwa*, legal opinions, on the end product, but the problems of modernity reside not merely in the finished result but also in the interrelated processes: industrial practices, scientific techniques of enquiry and experiment, the risks of accident and pollution, the costs of social and physical change in the environment. Making

formal judgements does not help to generate an autonomous, indigenous model for creating goods and services compatible and consonant
with an Islamic set of values. Three applications to the Saudi *ulema*
before they sanctioned the introduction of the telephone—and then
because it might be used to spread word of Islam—is not merely an
amusing apocryphal tale. It is an all too accurate metaphor of the vision of how Islam operates within the Muslim world today. It is more
a product of the history of Muslim interpretation of Islam and the experience of Muslim civilization in history, than it is the functioning of
the conceptual framework of Islam. All that it betokens is an enduring
attachment to an Islamic ideal, without any operational dynamism.

Recent decades have seen the ending of formal colonialism with
the independence of the Muslim world and the subsequent era of 'development'. The acknowledged problems of 'development', all defined
on western models, remain acute, even for the richest Muslim nations.
The overriding awareness is of a cycle of dependency upon the West
as provider and purveyor, dominant market, and perennial source of
the choices that can or ought to be made. Increasingly it is being seen
that the terms of 'development' inevitably entail dependency, and that
westernization in a host of guises involves an enduring imperialism of
the mind. 'Development', as presently defined, cannot genuinely be
internalized without eradication of an autonomous Muslim identity.
Even the acceptance of such a 'development' would produce only second class westerners.

Peter Berger has argued that the processes which make up 'development' engender a condition he calls the homeless mind.[14] As more
and more cherished values of Muslim society have been threatened
by the scramble for 'development', as various projects and initiatives
have produced social pressures and human misery, a deep process of
re-evaluation has got underway. The prospect of homelessness, which
Berger defines as the loss of overarching significance which integrates
all aspects of life into a unitary system of values, is a price more and
more Muslims are coming to perceive as entirely opposed to the
Islamic viewpoint. Increasingly it is a price Muslims are unwilling to
pay for the market version of modernity: westernization. The antidote

to homelessness for Muslims is to make the return to one's true home, the *dar al Islam*, an aspiration which unites a vast and various cross-section of Muslims throughout the world despite the diversity of approaches and the conditions of contemporary reality. Most of all it is a return instinctively motivated by the basic sources of Islam: the Qur'an and Sunnah.

Our specific interest is in the islamization of knowledge. It is just one aspect of the movement for return but it is crucial for the future and solidity of the entire venture. As Sardar has pointed out, revival without an intellectual structure of understanding is merely ferment in search of a focus.[15] Unless Muslim civilization can recapture the ability to think islamically about problems and generate Islamic methodologies for solving its problems, it must be fated to be dependent on the thought of others. It must remain reactive rather than constructively active. This is the difference between picking your way along a highway laid down by others and proceeding with one's own road building programme for the future.

There are two dominant approaches to the present islamization of knowledge that need brief consideration here. The first begins with the formal referents of the Islamic system as defined in *fiqh*, the second concerns a methodology for constructing the project of islamization of knowledge. The first approach is most evident in Islamic economics where the increasing number of Islamic banks and investment agencies being established fuels the claim that this is now an intellectual and operational field of Islam.

The writings of Islamic economists, however, reveals that these claims may be premature. The majority of works outline a vision of Islam as a totality and then commence their economics with formal propositions from the Qur'an and Sunnah on production and exchange relations. The objective of study is to devise an economic policy that abolishes *riba*, usury, and incorporates the various categories of contractual arrangements such as *mudabara*. The description of the Islamic framework is a rhetorical device with economists seeking to graft the formal Islamic propositions upon a definition of economics based on western terminology.[16]

Of those who have adopted a more thorough-going approach Naqvi is notable for seeking to define economic man based upon Islamic concepts.[17] Stimulating comments on Islamic economics have been made by Sardar, perhaps because he is not a trained economist and is thereby not constrained by ready-made definitions.[18] He argues that we need not just a conceptual redefinition of economic man which relies on four cardinal Islamic referents but a redefinition of what constitutes the economic process within a social context that incorporates the whole range of Islamic conceptual referents. He points to the lack of a rigorous Islamic terminology for discussing society and social processes. Thus Islamic economists fall back upon the only available language, the terminology of western economics and social science which circumscribes the parameters of Islamic economics.[19] There is criticism of western economic performance but no Islamic critique of western economics.

Another strand that has found its way into Islamic economics can be seen in the work of Khurshid Ahmad, but it is pervasive in many other fields too.[20] The arch exponent of this view is Maulana Mawdudi whose extensive writings are widely available and who was also the founder of the Jamaat-i-Islami of Pakistan.[21] The essence of this approach, which is grounded in the formal propositions of *fiqh sharia*,[22] is not altered by Mawdudi's recognition of the need for a return to *ijtihad* to overhaul Shariah. *Ijtihad* is not intended to be a generalized approach, but will be applied in certain limited cases which are not, or perhaps cannot be, specified. His fulsome defence of *purdah*, the seclusion of women, along with his general understanding of the role of women in society, is based upon the most restrictive and particular of *fiqh* interpretations: the bulk of *fiqh* remains despite awkward questions being raised by contemporary reality. Along with this mechanical model of the Islamic system generated from a limited set of formal propositions goes a very particular view of transformation in society. Islamization is a process of stripping away all foreign importations until only the core of pure Islamic items remains. It is less a matter of conscious thought, critical awareness, careful policy making and planned change than a reactive response. This notion, that islamization is what is left over when everything else has been removed, is pervasive within contemporary Muslim studies. It is hardly surprising then that scholars such as Islamic economists, who are anxious to produce a body of work, fall back upon a system such as western economics to fill their conceptual void.

The most coherent schema for the islamization of knowledge is that produced by the late Ismail al-Faruqi which is specifically directed to the social sciences since they express and translate epistemology, philosophy and ideology into structures of understanding and methodologies of enquiry.[23] His critique of western social sciences and their relation to the western conceptual fabric is pertinent and exemplary; as the most noted expounder of the concept of *tawhid*, his depiction of the Islamic framework is also unexceptional. But neither critique nor elaboration of *tawhid* are islamization of knowledge. Only an elaborate, laborious civilizational project will produce islamization of knowledge at some date in the future, for it requires institutionalization by gradual steps in order to exist. The first stage outlined is mastery of the western disciplines of knowledge; then the scholar liaises with traditional Islamic scholars whose knowledge will be arbitrated by the masters of western learning. The effect of the interaction would temper the influence of western knowledge and further clarify the conceptual referents of Islamic knowledge. This would be assisted by a study of the works of past Muslim thinkers on the subject matter of western disciplines.

In revising the schema Faruqi seems to have taken note of the powerful arguments put forward for islamization as a conceptual procedure. But even in revision the established body of western learning is a powerful constraint through which islamization is effected. The call for a conceptual approach has been made by a number of commentators, dating back to the early work of Jaffar Sheikh Idris.[24] Sardar's approach is the most stimulating because he stresses the operational process as being the embodiment of islamization now, just as it was in the foundation of Muslim civilization. In essence we are challenged to see that islamization begins in a mental shift, a paradigm shift, within the consciousness of the Muslim thinker. It commences with a return to the basic sources of conceptual meaning, Qur'an and Sunnah, and proceeds upon their logic and dynamic as an ongoing, unfolding process constantly open for debate, questioning, reformulation and amendment. What he is pointing to is a distinctive method of solving problems, where definition and description of the problems, their analysis and solution are conditioned and shaped by the conceptual fabric of Islam.

Arbitration of how to think Islamically cannot be handed over in ready-made packages, the western disciplines of knowledge, and still enable the Muslim thinker to maintain the proper relationship with Islamic sources. The nature of Islam requires that islamization be seen as an active process, a means of walking along a specific pathway, a means of thinking and doing. To embark upon that journey, to get Muslim civilization on the move again, requires us to work out the meaning and implications of the signposts of our route, the concepts of Islam. The subject matter of islamization concerns itself with developing a terminology which expresses and utilizes these signposts as the only meaningful indicators.

Notes

1. Sardar, ed. *The Touch of Midas*.
2. Midgley, *Evolution as a Religion*, p.139–40.
3. Mishkat al-Masabih, Book XVII, chapter 3.
4. There is now a growing literature on the book in Muslim civilization, see Sardar, *Information and the Muslim World*.
5. For an excellent discussion of the institutions of learning in the Muslim world see Makdisi, *The Rise of the Colleges*.
6. For a general discussion of Islamic law see Ramadan, *Islamic Law*; for a fascinating discussion of the institutionalizing processes of early Islam see Rahman, *Islamic Methodology in History*.
7. Ramadan, *ibid*. p.213.
8. The classic study is *Orientalism* by Said; see also *Orientalism, Islam and Islamists* edited by Husain, Olson, and Qureshi.
9. For a discussion of the formation of a Christian response to Islam in the Middle Ages see the excellent studies of Daniel, *Islam and the West* and *The Arabs and Mediaeval Europe;* also Southern, *Western Views of Islam in the Middle Ages*.
10. Ibn Taymiya, *Public Duties in Islam*.
11. Bovill, *The Golden Trade of the Moors*.
12. Hobsbawn, *The Age of Revolution*.
13. The full pathology is set out in *Occidentosis* by Jalal Al-i Ahmad.
14. Berger, *The Homeless Mind*.
15. See Sardar, 'Is there an Islamic resurgence?' and his detailed study *Islamic Futures*.
16. For a general guide to the literature of Islamic economics see Siddiqui, *Islamic Economics*.
17. Naqvi, *Ethics and Economics*.
18. Sardar, *Islamic Futures*.
19. See also Asaria, 'Constructing the Edifice of Homo Islamicus'.
20. Khurshid Ahmad, 'Economic Development in an Islamic Framework' in *Studies in Islamic Economics*.
21. Maulana Mawdudi's extensive publications are widely available. They include *Islamic Law and Constitution, Birth Control, Islamic Way of Life, The Economic Problem of Man and Its Islamic Solution, Purdah and the Status of Women, Fundamentals of Faith*.
22. For a further discussion of Mawdudi see Davies, 'The Legacy of Mawdudi and Shariati'.
23. Al-Faruqi, *Islamization of Knowledge*; and 'A conceptual framework for the islamization of knowledge'.
24. Idris, *The Islamization of Knowledge*.

4

Islamic Anthropology in
Words and Meanings

The best Muslim scholarship pays particular attention to words and their meanings and the significance that stems from their roots. The insight, understanding and images embodied in their study are demonstrated by al-Attas's elegant exposition of *din*.[1] This lexical and etymological concern stems from the expression of revelation in a specific language, Arabic. A re-examination of the felicity and fecundity of words is vital for modern Muslim scholarship: without precision in the definition of terms discourse is unintelligible. Without meaningful terminology further enquiry will be fruitless. Islamic anthropology must have its own meaningful terminology if its purpose and structure are to be understood, and if it is to be relevant to our present needs.

Islamic anthropology is the study of mankind in society from the premises and according to the conceptual orientations of Islam. We must begin with the terms of reference of our conception of mankind and this requires going to the Source of Islam itself, the Qur'an.[2] The Qur'an makes it abundantly clear that the founding premise of Islamic anthropology should be that mankind is a unitary creation. We read in Surah An Nisa, 4:1.

> O mankind! Be conscious of your Sustainer, who has cre-
> ated you out of one living entity, and out of it created its
> mate and out of the two spread abroad a multitude of men
> and women. And remain conscious of God, in whose name
> you demand [your rights] from one another, and of those
> ties of kinship. Verily God is ever watchful over you!

All of humanity derives from a single 'living entity', for which the
term is *nafs*. The word *nafs* has many connotations: soul, spirit, mind,
animate being, living entity, human being, person, self, mankind, life
essence, humankind, vital principle. None of these implications are
in contention with each other, rather they extend our comprehension
of the significance of the word. The cardinal pointers are the bringing
together of individual and collective implications: it is explanation of
mankind as a generality, emphasized by the unequivocal universal cast
of the verse, and of the self as personal identity. There is no juxtaposi-
tion between the individual and the group but rather they are bound
together for understanding. So too are the spiritual and material implications of the term: mankind is mind and soul, spirit and animate
human being.

From the single entity, *nafs*, derives a pair: man and woman. The
term used is *zawhaja*, signifying its mate, from *zawj*, a pair, one of a
pair. The term has no specific gender connotations implying equally
a woman's mate or a man's mate. While there is no priority mentioned in the creation of men or women it is obvious they have been
intentionally created for a necessary relationship with each other, and
through this relationship the existence and survival of the human race
is secured. As with all relationships, that between man and woman has
many facets, being based not only on biological ties, but extending
into the social, moral and spiritual spheres. All these different facets of
interconnection are inherent in the purpose of creation itself and from
which instruction on how relationships should be operated in daily life
is derived. This is made clear in Surah Ar Rum, 30:21:

> And of His signs is this: He created for you helpmeets from
> yourselves that ye might find rest in them, and He ordained

between you love and mercy. Lo, herein indeed are portents
for folk who reflect.

Each additional dimension of definition adds to our comprehension
of the beneficent purpose of creation. In the ordering of creation there
are signs, *ayat*, for mankind to reflect upon and which generate a proper understanding. The signs are amenable to rational and conceptual
understanding, but they are also, as in this specific case, valuational
referents for the conduct of the relationships inherent in creation.

The full parameters of the Qur'anic framework for understanding
the relations between man and woman are given in Surah At Tawbah,
9:71, where they are a logical consequence of the equality of their origin in a single entity:

> And [as for] the believers, both men and women—they are
> close (*awliya*) unto one another: they [all] enjoin the doing
> of what is right and forbid the doing of what is wrong, and
> are constant in prayer, and render the purifying dues, and
> pay heed unto God and His Apostle. It is they upon whom
> God will bestow His grace: verily, God is almighty, wise!

The term *awliya*, rendered here as close, more usually has the connotation of men and women being the protectors of one another, with the
added significance of their being guides or in charge of one another.
There is a mutuality in the relationship which should be characterized
by love and mercy; it has a moral and spiritual basis to be expressed in
actions that cover the whole spectrum of existence. It is only when the
whole spectrum is considered that male-female relationships can be
properly subjected to analysis and question.

Both men and women derive a basic common nature from their
origin in a single source, the *nafs*. This commonality applies to the
entirety of humankind. The implications of Surah 4:1 go further: the
unitary creation of mankind by God is a source of rights possessed
by all human beings that validates their recognition in human relations, again as a universal principle. These rights must be understood
as arising from ties of kinship between the whole of humanity. The

universality of the Islamic frame of reference is allied to the most central metaphor for understanding personal Muslim existence, the family.

There are three elementary dimensions running through the Qur'anic references to the creation of humankind. When we refer to humankind we are discussing implications that apply equally to men and women as the consequence of the common orgin in the *nafs*. First, there are frequent references to the formation of mankind out of clay (Surah Al Hijr, 15:26):

> And indeed, We have created mankind out of sounding clay, out of dark slime transmuted—whereas the invisible beings We had created, [long] before that, out of the fire of scorching winds. And lo! Thy Sustainer said unto the angels: 'Behold, I am about to create mortal man out of sounding clay, out of dark slime transmuted; and when I have formed him fully and breathed into him of My Spirit, fall down before him in prostration.'

The term used here is *salsal*, which the philological authorities predominantly agree denotes dried clay which emits a sound. In the Qur'an the term is used exclusively with reference to the creation of mankind. We follow Asad in seeing this as an allusion to the power of articulate speech as a defining characteristic in mankind. The *salsal* derives out of dark slime, fetid mud, and has been taken by commentators to stress the humble origins of mankind's biological form which this verse states as being *masnun*—altered, brought into shape, or transmuted by God in the act of creation.

The second dimension concerns the full forming of mankind, the link between the act of divine creation and the processes of human procreation. In Surah Al Mu'minun 23:12 we read:

> Now, indeed, we create man out of the essence of clay,
> And then We cause him to remain a drop of sperm in
> [the womb's] firm keeping, and then We create out of the
> drop of sperm a germ-cell, and then We create out of the

> germ-cell an embryonic lump, and then We create within
> the embryonic lump bones, and then We clothe the bones
> with flesh—and then We bring [all] this into being as a new
> creation: hallowed, therefore, is God, the best of artisans.

The creation of mankind is out of humble organic and inorganic substances of the earth; the process of procreation, apparent to mankind as the beginning of actual existence, is also a divine creation. Two levels of understanding and analysis are brought together to demonstrate the consonance between biological origin and procreative process. Evolution is purposive creation, not random amalgamation, out of the properties of the created physical universe. It brings forth distinct orders of creation with definite attributes and potential as species, as well as differentiation between male and female. The distinct orders of creation are sustained through time by inherent processes of procreation, and each creation is a discrete sustainable process according to the rules of its origination in the Divine Will.

The third and most essential dimension recurs in Surah Al Sajdah 32:6, where all three elements are brought together within a conceptual framework of understanding:

> Such is He who knows all that is beyond the reach of a created being's perception, as well as all that can be witnessed by a creature's senses or mind: the Almighty, the Dispenser of Grace, who makes most excellent everything that He creates. Thus He begins the creation of man out of clay, then He causes him to be begotten out of the essence of humble fluid: and then He forms him in accordance with what he is meant to be, and breathes into him of His spirit: and [thus O men] He endows you with hearing, and sight, and feelings as well as minds: [yet] how seldom are you grateful.

The element of completion of mankind, the derivation of human potentialities and conscious self-awareness, our senses, intuition and reason, is the breathing of the spirit of God into each human being. The consonance of the entire procedure is found again in this third element. It adds a higher spiritual dimension and potential to human existence, which is the purpose of the divine will.

In mankind's creation by God there is no distinction between derivation, evolution; generation, procreative process; and endowments, the physical, mental and spiritual capabilities. Human abilities—hearing, sight, feelings and mind—enable mankind to study perceptible matters concerning our origin, but we are not confronted by three discrete analytical frameworks but by three integrated dimensions of one and the same matter. Our approach to understanding the unitary creation of mankind is through the Unity of God which opens up the consonance of all the dimensions of human nature and existence for our scrutiny. Within the conceptual framework of *tawhid*, unity, there are various dimensions which all contribute to the unitary nature of mankind. The origin of life in fetid mud can never diminish mankind's identity as recipient of the spirit of God. Neither can mankind be viewed solely as a spiritual being for organic and inorganic constituents of the physical form are inextricably part of existence and purposeful creation. It is only when the various dimensions and levels of analysis of mankind and the processes of human operations are integrated that we can unravel genuine significance. If any of the dimensions is seen as a discrete and separable area of knowledge then a distorted, reductive view of humanity must result. Purposeful ordered creation by God is the founding *a priori* of the Islamic perspective. As Surah Sad 38:27, states:

> And [thus it is] We have not created heaven and earth and
> all that is between them without meaning and purpose, as
> is the surmise of those who are bent on denying the truth:
> but then woe from the fire [of hell] unto all who are bent
> on denying the truth.

This Qur'anic frame of reference is the definition of the question of origins in Islamic anthropology—it provides the dynamic of our intellectual endeavour.

In his translation, *The Message of the Quran*, Asad characteristically uses the present tense to denote the continual processes of creation.

He argues that the past tense used in the Arabic is to demonstrate that processes such as procreation, which we experience now, were the same at the origin of human creation and the use of the present tense in English conveys the same significant implication. Whatever linguistic form is used, the understanding we derive is of a conceptual consonance in the dimensions of human creation established at the beginning, extending over the past, operating in the present, and stretching on into the future. When dealing with conceptual matters a lineal time frame is a simplification of the complex relationships being described. All of time and space, all temporality and corporeality, pertains to God whether in its origins, present perceptible operation or future potential, because by virtue of purposeful creation all time and space have a spiritual dimension necessary for their meaningful comprehension (Surah Al An'am, 6:95):

> Verily, God is the One, who cleaves the grain and the fruit kernel asunder, bringing forth the living out of that which is dead, and He is the One who brings forth the dead out of that which is alive. This, then is God: and yet, how perverted are your minds! [He is] the One who causes the dawn to break; and he has made the night to be [a source of] stillness, and the sun and the moon to run their appointed courses: [all] this is laid down by the will of the Almighty, the All Knowing.

In this framework one cannot say 'God began the universe' and then proceed to investigate and accumulate information about mankind or the universe without further reference to the Creator. The essence of the conceptual framework of Islam is that the consequence of creation by God is a necessary enduring relationship that structures all activity and intellectual endeavour. Creation entails more than mankind's possession of a common origin, common biological form and common nature: it requires that all knowledge, enquiry and speculation be structured by a relationship with God. As creation cannot be understood as a single event but is rather a process involving the unfolding of inherent characteristics which all relate to God, so the application of sense and reason to the accumulation of knowledge must be a constant dynamic balanced by reintegration with its source, God, if it is to be meaningful and fulfil its purpose and objective.

To understand what is entailed in the creation of mankind we need to examine three connected concepts: *fitrah*, *khilafah*, and *din*, for these concepts lead us to a definition of mankind in a social context. In common with the pattern already outlined these three concepts deploy connected consonant dimensions to define the full implications of human existence. These concepts are so closely connected that most of the quotations used here relate to all three at the same time. While we use the verses to discuss only one concept at a time, in fact additional layers of implication and connotation are being added to the interconnections of all three concepts. *Fitrah*, the inherent nature or natural disposition of mankind, we see as the dimension of capacities and endowments; *khilafah*, human trusteeship as God's vice-regent on earth, we see as the dimension defining human status and rights: and *din*, the concept of religion as a total way of life in the widest possible sense of the term, we see as the dimension of operational process. These are a mutually defining set of concepts making the various dimensions of human existence a consonant conceptual totality.

Fitrah is endowed upon all mankind by God. From our point of view creation is not only purposive in a generalized sense as it relates to God's intention, but also by a human acknowledgement that precedes our physical existence. Mankind begins with a covenant between God and every created individual, and hence mankind is a collectivity. This covenant is referred to in Surah Al A'raf, 7:172:

> And whenever thy Sustainer brings forth their offspring from the loins of the children of Adam, He thus calls upon them to bear witness about themselves: 'Am I not your Sustainer?'—to which they answer: 'Yea, indeed, we do bear witness thereto!' [Of this We remind you,] lest you say on the Day of Resurrection, 'Verily, we were unaware of this.'

The *fitrah* is the natural disposition to be aware of our origin as the purposeful creation of God and the indebtedness this betokens. It is an awareness of God as *Rabb*, here translated as Sustainer. The term *Rabb* is often rendered as Lord; it also signifies nourisher, cherisher, the fosterer of a thing in such a manner as to make it attain one condition after another until it reaches its goal of completion. The *fitrah* is aware of its own existence as a process capable of completion, that completion being the fulfilling of its debt to its Lord and Creator, and its ultimate return to God. It is conscious of a necessary, inescapable relationship, between mankind and God. Other relationships are also comprehended by it. In Surah Al Baqarah, 2:30 we read:

> And lo! The Sustainer said unto the angels: 'Behold, I am about to establish upon earth one who shall inherit it' (*khilafah*). They said: 'Wilt Thou place on it such as will spread corruption therein and shed blood—whereas it is we who extol Thy limitless glory, and praise Thee, and hallow Thy name?' [God] answered: 'Verily, I know that which you do not know.' And He imparted unto Adam the name of all things; then He brought them within the ken of the angels and said: 'Declare unto Me the names of these [things], if what you say is true.' They replied: 'Limitless art Thou in Thy glory! No knowledge have we save that which Thou hast imparted to us. Verily, Thou alone are all-knowing, truly wise.' Said He: 'O Adam convey unto them the names of these [things].' And as soon as [Adam] had conveyed unto them the names, [God] said: 'Did I not say unto you, verily, I alone know the hidden reality of the heavens and the earth, and know all that you bring into the open and all that you would conceal?'

The allegory of Adam is used throughout the Qur'an to refer to the collective origin of all humankind. The verse speaks of Adam literally learning 'all the names'. The term *ism*, name, according to the philologists, implies an expression conveying knowledge of a thing, its substance or attribute for the purpose of definition. For al-Attas this signifies the knowledge of perceptible, tangible relationships. Asad takes it to mean the capacity for logical definition and thus conceptual thought.[3]

The *fitrah* is created as a faculty, a disposition, with inherent knowledge. This knowledge encompasses, in conventional Islamic terms, both the seen and the unseen. The *fitrah* knows that it has covenanted with God and knows about the physical world wherein it exists. The knowledge possessed by the *fitrah* is a capacity not merely for sensate existence, sight, hearing, touch and taste, but also a capacity for cultural existence with the power of articulate speech, language, conceptual thought and reasoning, intuition and imagination. What is being made clear in the exposition of these concepts is the general disposition of the whole of humankind for cultural and social existence as the inherent consequence of the relationships of purposeful creation. The general disposition defines the parameters of human cultural and social existence, but not the specific details of how the cultural and social capacity are institutionalized into specific forms. Or rather it defines the characteristics that underlie all form, no matter how diverse. As we have already mentioned the Qur'anic conceptual framework relates the individual to the collective for the purpose of understanding. The capacities of the *fitrah* as culture-bearing traits again emphasize this link. The natural disposition of human beings is to join together in groups to express their aptitude for culture and social existence. There is no vantage point within this context where the individual becomes an analytical isolate in distinction to the group. The logical implication of the conceptual framework is that the ideal setting for the individual is in a grouping where his inherent cultural and social capacity finds specific formal expression.

The function of the *fitrah* is referred to a number of times in the Qur'an:

> And on earth there are signs [of God's existence, visible] to all who are endowed with inner certainty, just as [there are signs thereof] within your own selves: can you not, then. see? (Surah Adh Dhariyat, 51:20)

and

> Behold, in the heavens as well as on earth there are indeed messages for all who [are willing to] believe. And in your

own nature, and in [that of] all the animals which He scatters [over the earth] there are messages for people who are endowed with inner certainty. (Surah Al Jathiyah, 45:3)

Most completely it is set out in Surah Ar Rum, 30:30:

And so, set thy face steadfastly towards the [one ever-true] faith (*din*), turning away from all that is false, in accordance with the natural disposition (*fitrah*) which God has instilled into man: [for] not to allow any change to corrupt what God has thus created—this is the [purpose of the one] ever-true faith (*din*); but most people know it not.

The *fitrah*, through the potentialities of sense, reason, intuition and spiritual awareness, is an instrument of discernment between right and wrong, between true and false. Its highest dimension is the discernment of the existence and Unity of God. The exercise of this faculty can operate in many ways and generate a number of analytical levels, each level being part of the same revelation. It is the innate ability of mankind to read the signs, *ayat*, inherent in the order of creation; understanding these signs leads to an understanding of the origin of all existence in the Unity of God—they are evidence of one level of revelation. Another level of revelation is contained within mankind itself, in the *fitrah*, itself a sign and a message to the self-aware, self-reflecting person. The third level of revelation is the specific and most usual sense of the term, the direct messages from God granted to the various prophets throughout human history. The *fitrah* is the faculty through which these various consonant analytical levels and their mutually reinforcing implications and consequences are articulated to generate understanding and insight. Since the *fitrah* is an innate reasoning, moral and ethical sense possessed by all human beings, when it is exercised in full consciousness, it enables mankind to organize the social and cultural facets of life into a harmonious balance based upon a proper recognition of necessary relationships. In addition it entails the notion of a discretionary power to order social and cultural existence in consonance with the purpose of creation. There is an inevitable relationship between the faculty of discernment and its expression through an operational process, the *din*; they are inseparable dimensions of the Islamic conceptual view of life.

The *fitrah*, the capacity for self-awareness, is facilitated by the endowments it received in creation. Its highest self-awareness is the recognition of its origin in a covenant between mankind and God. There is one fundamental essential in understanding the nature of this covenant that binds mankind: it endows mankind with, can only be repaid, fulfilled or completed with, free will. The central tenet of Islam is expressed as follows:

> There shall be no coercion in matters of faith. Distinct has now become the right way from [the way of] error: hence, he who rejects the powers of evil and believes in God has indeed taken hold of a support most unfailing, which shall never give way: for God is all-hearing, all-knowing. (Surah Al Baqarah, 2:256)

In his exposition of *din* al-Attas has elaborated the various connotations of the concept of indebtedness and the imagery of a bargain, a transaction, a loan, used throughout the Qur'an to express mankind's covenant with God. The purpose and function of the *fitrah* is to prompt a willing acknowledgement of this convenanted indebtedness. God, who intentionally created humankind and our capacities, could have compelled our subservience and the form this should take in living, but as the Qur'an repeatedly makes clear, it is God who enjoined free will upon us as the highest challenge of existence.

From the attribute of free will stems mankind's capacity to rise higher than the angels or to sink lower than brute beasts. Mankind can heed the promptings of the *fitrah* that predispose them to recognition and fulfilment of their covenant with God, or reject this covenant. The notion of free will is not just a spiritual referent, it has major consequences for how we understand the operation of mankind in history by establishing the parameters within which humanity can operate. There are no imposed constraints on what mankind can achieve, either for good or bad, apart from the voluntary acknowledgement by the *fitrah* in the application of the moral and ethical choices. As al-Attas so pithily points out, true freedom consists in acting in accordance with the demands of one's nature: this will give definite formal attributes to the exercise of freedom, it will give definition to the social and cultural institutionalization of modes of existence, it will have consequences detectable in action, but it is freedom because it is subject to no constraint other than awareness of one's own inherent nature. It is in this sense that Islam, meaning submission, is spoken of as the natural religion of mankind.

The two dimensions of mankind as a biological entity but also as a cultural and social entity are entirely consonant and inextricably linked, yet neither has precedence over, nor is the causal explanation for, the other. Both biology and culture are the generalized potential with which human history commences. Mankind originates in biology with its distinctive generative processes and needs and a human nature with knowledge, awareness of origins, relationships and the capacity to formulate knowledge about mankind and the world at large. The entire argument over origins within western anthropology is subsumed within the definitional terms of the Qur'an's exposition of the origin of mankind. From an Islamic perspective mankind does not acquire civilization or refinement, in the sense of seeking something additional and superior to their original endowments. Civilization and refinement are the products of employing the endowments of mankind's origins and are therefore conditions subject to evaluation as expressions of mankind's origin and nature.

Within the distinct and discrete orders of creation mankind has a particular status, this is not an absolute station but one defined by relationships and having consequences for the operation of the network of relationships that is the setting of human existence. The status of all mankind, men and women, is as the *khilafah*, the vice-regent of God upon earth.[4] We have already seen in Surah 2:30 that the status of *khilafah* is ascribed to mankind by God. The term derives from the verb *khilafah*, signifying that he succeeded another. Commentators have argued that this has a dual implication: that of mankind in general succeeding, according to God's will, to the inheritance of the earth; as well as the implication that each generation of mankind succeeds the other in assuming the obligations of the status of *khilafah*. The word itself makes it clear it is a relational term. It is the defining of these relations we need to examine.

First, the substance of mankind's vice-regency over the earth is a trust; in Surah Al Ahzab, 33:72 we read:

> Verily, We did offer the trust [of reason and volition] to the heavens and the earth, and the mountains: but they refused to bear it because they were afraid of it. Yet man took it up—for, verily, he has always been prone to be most wicked, most foolish.

The trust, *ammanah*, has been variously interpreted by commentators. Here it is given as reason and volition, a most satisfying interpretation since it refers back to the capacities of the *fitrah*, and the linkage made between them in Surah 2:30. The ending of the verse has been interpolated by commentators in the sense of the whole passage in which it occurs: human groups turning away from the terms of the trust. Zamakhshari sees the meaning of the end of the verse as 'Yet mankind took it [the trust] up and then failed to measure up to the moral responsibility arising from the reason and comparative free will with which he has been endowed—for, he has always been prone to be most wicked, most foolish.'⁵ Al-Attas has paid particular attention to this point. He notes the word for man in Arabic, *insan*, has the basic connotation of one prone to forgetfulness. What mankind forgets, he says, is its covenant with and accepted trust from God. This implication of the term for man generates an integrative understanding of the repeated Qur'anic calls for mankind to reflect, for there is frequent reference to the negligence of spiritual truths as one of the recurrent human characteristics; it is one of the elements in its narration about Adam, who was not merely the first man, but metaphorically and allegorically stands for the whole of the human race.

The concept of a trust, *ammanah*, logically entails responsibility and the notion of rights and duties implicit in the terms of the trust. The *khilafah* has been entrusted to inherit the earth, to have the use of all the bounties for the sustenance and enrichment of mankind's life on it. The capacities of the *fitrah* are the means to be employed so that the status and role of the *khilafah* can be enjoyed. There is a right to fulfilment of the biological, material, social, cultural and spiritual dimensions of human existence upon earth, and to that end the whole of created nature can be husbanded and employed. Since all men and women are *khilafah* there is a basic equality in their rights of access to and enjoyment of the bounties of earthly existence.

The capacities of the *fitrah* and the status of *khilafah* make mankind pre-eminent within the created universe. The Qur'an repeatedly makes it clear that the trust expressing these facts is an entitlement balanced by duties, and not an absolute right of ownership, usage and disposal of the physical environment and all it contains. *Khilafah*, as a relational term, is the definition of a stewardship, a usufruct, on two levels: as between man as steward, *khilafah*, and God the Absolute Owner; and as amongst mankind who bear responsibility within and between each generation. Since all mankind is heir to the status of *khilafah* one group can have no absolute right to alienate and monopolize what is the patrimony of all people on a conditional basis.

The status of *khilafah* does not make mankind independent of God but rather creates a permanent on-going relationship. This is made clear in Surah An Naml, 27:61:

> Nay—Who is it that has made the earth a fitting abode [for living things], and has caused running waters [to flow] in its midst, and has set upon it mountains firm, and has placed a barrier between the two great bodies of water? Could there be any divine power besides God? Nay, most of those [who think so] do not know [what they are saying]! Nay—who is it that responds to the distressed when he calls out to Him, and who removes the ill [that caused the distress], and has made you inherit the earth (*khilafah*)? Could there be any divine power besides God? How seldom do you keep this in mind!

God the Creator is the Owner of all things, the All-Powerful: the counterbalance of mankind's status as *khilafah* is to remain the *abd*, the slave of their Lord, *Rabb*, subservient to the terms of the trust established by God.

The other element contained in the concept of *khilafah* is accountability which is again interlinked with the connotation of *fitrah* and *din*. It is reiterated throughout Surah At Taghabun: 64. The Surah opens:

> All that is in the heavens and all that is on earth extols God's limitless glory: He is all dominion, and to Him all praise is due; and He has the power to will anything. He it is who has created you: and among you are such as deny the truth, and among you are such as believe [in it]. And God sees all that you do. He has created the heavens and the earth in accordance with [an inner] truth and has formed you—and formed you so well; and with Him is your journey's end. He knows all that you keep secret as well as all that you bring into the open: for God has full knowledge of what is in the hearts [of men].

To God alone belongs dominion, everything else has been created and derives from God. The inner truth is taken by commentators to mean the establishment of all creation in fulfilment of a definite purpose in consonance with God's planning wisdom—the return to God. The end of existence is not physical death in this world, our existence extends into the spiritual realm of the Hereafter, *Akhirah*. So in Surah 64:7 we read:

> They who are bent on denying the truth claim that they will never be raised from the dead! Say, Yea, by my Sustainer, most surely will you be raised from the dead, and then, most surely, will you be made to understand what you did [in this life]! For, easy is this for God! Believe, then [O men] in God and His Apostle and the light [of revelation] which We have bestowed [on you] from on high. And God is fully aware of all that you do. [Think of] the time

when He shall gather you all together unto the Day of the [Last] Gathering—the Day of Loss and Gain! For as for him who shall have believed in God and done what is just and right, He will [on that Day] efface his bad deeds, and will admit him into gardens through which running waters flow, therein to abide beyond count of time: that will be a triumph supreme! But as for those who are bent on denying the truth and on giving the lie to Our messages—they are destined for the fire, therein to abide: and how vile a journey's end.

The status of mankind as *khilafah* includes the return to God. That is the occasion when the terms of mankind's covenant, the use of their faculties, *fitrah*, the exercise of the trusted status, *khilafah*, the living out of the operational process, the *din*, will be evaluated. The metaphor of a bargain, a contractual relationship, is repeated in reference to the Day of Judgement as the Day of Loss and Gain. God is All-Knowing and All-Aware of mankind's activities, open and secret. This is a conceptual referent to what we openly acknowledge as well as our intentions, the overt form of action and word and the inherent implications of the processes by which we form things, organize systems of action and devise structures of thought. Just as the inner truth of creation is its purposive intent so the substance of mankind's judgement will be the purposive content, intent and effect of human thought and action. The substance of ultimate Judgement is how mankind in the business of living integrated the principles of their relationship to God, their rights and duties to other human beings and their rights and duties to the rest of created nature, the physical environment and its flora and fauna, into a coherent and rightly-guided way of life consonant with the Unity of God.

There is no contradiction between mankind as *abd*, one subservient to God, and mankind with the unique status and role as *khilafah*, vice-regent of God upon earth. They are the consonant layers by which the terms of mankind's trust and its implications are made comprehensible. The responsibility and accountability of mankind is unfolded for understanding only by the integration of the two dimensions within the concept of *khilafah*. What must circumscribe the exercise of role of *khilafah* and make meaningful restraints to thought and action is the awareness of the absolute dominion of God, the continuance and relevance of the status of *abd*, while the rights of pre-eminence are being enjoyed in earthly existence. It is only when earthly existence is balanced by its spiritual dimension, its completion in the return to God, that the full parameters constraining the responsibility of living have been taken into consideration.

Neither the concept of *fitrah* nor of *khilafah* can be understood without the context of *din*, religion as a total way of life. The basis of *din* is made clear in Surah Al Imran, 3:19:

> Behold, the only [true] religion (*din*) in the sight of God is [man's] self-surrender (*al-islam*) unto Him; and those who were vouchsafed revelation aforetime took, out of mutual jealousy, to divergent views [on this point] only after knowledge [thereof] had come unto them. But as for him who denies the truth of God's messages—behold, God is swift in reckoning!

Al-Attas gives the implications of the word from the Arabic root *dyn*, as indebtedness, submissiveness, judicious power and custom and habit, all with the connotations of an operational system and referring not only to the individual human being, but also the group an individual belongs to and mankind as a whole. He also relates the understanding of the term to *dayn*, meaning obligation, as well as being conceptually linked to the verb *maddana*, to build, to civilize, to humanize, or refine; and from *maddana* to the word *medina*, meaning town or city.[6]

Al-Attas's approach has been to subsume the concepts of *fitrah* and *khilafah* within the framework of *din*. Most certainly the concepts are overlapping because the implications of indebtedness, submissiveness, judicious power and custom and habit are common and necessary for the understanding of each concept. However, we have taken a different approach, and feel that by examining each concept as a significant dimension in its own right, with important distinguishing characteristics, we have gained an important insight into the integrative nature of the Qur'anic perspective. Rather than one concept being subsumed within another, as with the over-reliance on the study of *tawhid* where the definition of each particular concept is obscured by being merged, this approach enables the framework of *tawhid* to be seen as a setting wherein the articulation of concepts occurs with each concept adding to the multi-dimensional nature of the whole. If we focus on the articulation of concepts rather than their analogous nature, their being another way of expressing the same general idea, then we raise questions that give direction to our intellectual endeavour. We are suggesting that by this approach we become aware of a series of analytical levels as fruitful points of reference for further enquiry. The overlapping, integrative and consonant nature of the dimensions and levels we recognize obviously derives from there being a unitary framework wherein all the concepts interact with each other, where they belong in harmonious balance; in Al-Attas's words they are 'in their right place'. We are merely pointing out that it is the profundity of this simplicity that makes an Islamic intellectual approach so stimulating. It is the density and complexity of relationships within this simplicity we should be seeking to unravel to generate ways of studying and lines of enquiry.

The prime definitional connotation of *din* is as an operational process of social and cultural life, a total way of life. It is the term denoting the system where the capacities of the *fitrah* are given particular expression and the status and rights of the *khilafah* are incorporated and institutionalized as the routine practice of human interrelationships. The foundation of *din* arises out of mankind's enduring relationship with the Creator, as we have seen in Surah 3:19. This relates to indebtedness and submission as is made clear in Surah Al An'am 6:161:

> Say: 'Behold, my Sustainer has guided me unto a straight way through an ever-true faith (*din*)—the way of Abraham, who turned from all that is false, and was not of those who ascribe divinity to aught beside Him.' Say: 'Behold, my prayer, and [all] my acts of worship, and my living and my dying are for God [alone], the Sustainer of all the worlds, in whose divinity none has a share: for thus have I been

bidden—and I shall always be foremost among those who surrender themselves to Him.'

The surrender to God is a process involving all aspects of life, and continuing into the Hereafter. The term for worship, *ibadah*, signifies an act of servitude, the action of an *abd*, slave, in serving his master. In the context of this verse it is clear that *ibadah* is every right action taken in consciousness of mankind's servitude to God, in consonance with the truth of the creation of the universe and the order that maintains the universe, within mankind's especial status, employing his distinctive endowments. Worship is an entire pattern of human existence, it is the entirety of social and cultural existence that constitutes the straight path of religion, the *din*.

In the Qur'anic context *din* is consistently referred to in connection with two factors: guidance and messages. Just as mankind enters worldly existence with self-awareness by virtue of created endowments derived from a covenant with God, and a pre-eminent status derived from a trust from God, so the *din* originates in a guidance from God incorporated in the act of creation. We read in Surah Ta Ha, 20:122:

> Thereafter, [however] His Sustainer elected him [for His grace], and accepted his repentance, and bestowed His guidance upon him, saying: 'Down with you all from this [state of innocence, and be henceforth] enemies unto one another! Nonetheless, there shall most certainly come unto you guidance from Me: and he who follows My guidance will not go astray, and neither will he be unhappy. But as for him who shall turn away from remembering Me—his shall be a life of narrow scope; and on the Day of Resurrection We shall raise him up blind.'

This verse is the culmination of the account of the fall of Adam and Eve. After they had been tempted and deceived by *Iblis* (Satan), and thus become conscious of the need to recognize moral choice and exercise moral discernment, they repented and were forgiven by God. After repentance came the granting of guidance on how to live in the world, which was to be their abode as a consequence of their disobedience. The guidance concerned the exercise of discernment in the recognition of a proper balance in the necessary relationships of creation. Adam is therefore regarded as the first man and the first prophet, for the message he brought was the message of Islam. Furthermore the verse affirms that guidance from God in the institution of prophethood, *risalah*, will be recurrent in human history, just as the Qur'an affirms that the institution is completed in its own revelation to Prophet Muhammad. We gain an insight into the nature of guidance in Surah Al Ma'idah, 5:3:

> Forbidden to you are carrion, and blood, and the flesh of swine, and that over which any name other than God's has been invoked, and the animal that has been strangled, or beaten to death, or killed by a fall, or gored to death, or savaged by a beast of prey, save that which you [yourselves] may have slaughtered while it was still alive; and [forbidden to you is] all that has been slaughtered on idolatrous altars. And [you are forbidden] to seek to learn through divination what the future may hold in store for you: that is sinful conduct. Today, those who are bent on denying the truth have lost all hope of [your ever forsaking] your religion: do not, then, hold them in awe, but stand in awe of Me! Today I have perfected your religious law for you and have bestowed upon you the full measure of My blessings, and willed that self-surrender unto Me shall be your religion. As for him, however, who is driven [to what is forbidden] by dire necessity and not by an inclination to sinning—behold, God is much-forgiving, a dispenser of grace.

This single verse covers the full parameters of guidance to *din*. It joins together injunctions for matters that structure social life derived from the exigencies of human history. In the conjuction of practical action with spiritual import is the completion of religion, the totality of the message of God to mankind, the *din* that has been selected for us and bestowed upon us as a universal principle.

This verse was revealed to Prophet Muhammad at Arafat on the afternoon of Friday, the ninth of Dhu'l-Hijjah AH 10, some eighty-two days before his death. It contains the last legal injunction revealed to the Prophet. Religion, *din*, is a way of life where the conceptual totality of existence is translated into an ongoing process. A way of doing needs structural referents, but these are meaningful only because of their conceptual significance. The specific injunctions of the Qur'an are given as a reformative process so that a community of believers caught in the web of human history can realign themselves with the inherent and conceptual truth of existence and thereby equip themselves to establish a dynamic system of social existence, that is a diachronic system moving through time, incorporating and consonant with all the dimensions of reality, including the spiritual. It is in this sense that the truth has been made clear and distinguished from the way of error. In the survival of the Qur'an intact, unchanged from the time of Muhammad to the present, we have a sourcebook that relates the choices and decisions of daily living to their purpose, meaning and significance. The level where the message is unchanging is that of conceptual relationships. It is the conceptual relationship of a mode of operation to its enduring point of reference that must be maintained, rather than the *din* being seen purely as a matter of a precise, and limited number of definite instructions.

The basis and foundation of *din* is guidance from God on how to organize the whole of earthly life in consonance with the true reality of existence: purposeful creation that is both corporeal and spiritual by the one, absolute, unitary God. Life based upon this principle generates felicity, it promotes the flourishing of all human capacities and potentials in a constructive balance that secures the enjoyment of all the benefits of life and the earth within their natural limits, without corruption or injustice. This submission and self-surrender, *islam*, creates the balance and is the balance. In this connection it is instructive to note Asad's rendering of those who turn away from God's guidance, *man asrafa*, as 'those who waste their own self, logically it would be related to the narrowing of the scope of life referred to in Surah 20:122. He considers a number of words deriving from the same root: *musrif,* one who is given to excesses or commits excesses, one who is wasteful; *israf,* which literally means wastefulness or lack of moderation in one's doings. *Israf,* he points out, is synonymous with the term *tuqhyan,* meaning overweening arrogance.[7] These terms are used in the Qur'an in connection with those oblivious of the guidance contained in God's messages to mankind or of their enduring reliance upon God. Asad sees this as denoting excess in the sense of violation of the moral imperative to recognize the natural limits inherent in all things. What is referred to is not merely the wasting of the self in an abstract sense but the wasting and withering of the human potential within a pattern of social existence, a *din,* that should be grounded in balancing the natural limits of the truth and order of creation. Turning away from the right guidance that should be the substance of the organization of *din,* opens the path for waste, corruption, and hence injustice in social existence. This should be seen in connection with the way some Muslim writers have examined the concept of *zulm,* which also signifies tyranny, waste, corruption and injustice, as a way of examining contemporary ecological problems.[8]

Attaining a balance between a recognition of natural limits and the avoidance of excess should be the dynamic of the organization of an entire way of life. This mode of living extends the scope of existence, gives positive benefits and reinforces constructive gains for humanity, not as abstract, purely spiritual matters but as powerful, pragmatic social, cultural, ecological, scientific and technical intellectual referents. The objective and potential of the *din* is achieving an ideal society as a system of practical action that allows the individual security, contentment and fulfilment of all the dimensions of his being without harmful conflicting pressures. In Surah An Nur, 24:55 we read:

> God has promised those who have attained to faith and do righteous deeds that, of a certainty, He will cause them to accede to power on earth [literally cause them to be successors on earth], even as he caused [some of] those who lived before them to accede to it; and that, of a certainty, He will firmly establish for them the religion which He has been pleased to bestow on them; and that of a certainty, He will

cause their erstwhile state of fear to be replaced by a sense of security—[seeing that] they worship Me [alone], not ascribing divine powers to aught beside Me. But all who, after [having understood] this, choose to deny the truth—it is they, they who are truly iniquitous!

Guidance to *din* is contained in messages from God. We have seen that at one level *fitrah* constitutes a message from God, at another level these messages are contained in signs, *ayat*, in the order of the universe, upon which mankind is called to reflect. This leads to the implication of *din* as a natural, universal religion or pattern of life embedded in creation that the human intellect can recognize by reflecting upon all aspects of creation. There is another level of guidance to mankind, these are specific messages from God transmitted by selected human beings designated in the Qur'an as prophets, messengers and warners. The important distinction is that the messages they bear have two analytical levels: the basis of the message is always the same, it is the *din* of *islam*, that is the natural, universal religion of living, it is guidance to a total way of life founded upon recognition of mankind's creation by God and servitude to God to be repaid in self-surrender to God. The second analytical level is the specifics of the message and this level opens up the whole of the Qur'anic perspective for understanding human life in social existence.

The way the specific messages generate an understanding of mankind is set out in Surah Al Ma'idah, 5:48:

> And unto thee [O Prophet] have We vouchsafed this divine writ, setting forth the truth, confirming the truth of whatever there still remains of earlier revelations and determining what is true therein. Judge, then, between the followers of earlier revelation in accordance with what God has bestowed from on high, and do not follow their errant views, forsaking the truth that has come unto thee. Unto every one of you have We appointed a [different] law and way of life. And if God had so willed, He could surely have made you all one single community: but [He willed it otherwise] in order to test you by means of what He has

vouchsafed unto you. Vie, then, with one another in doing good works! Unto God you all must return; and then He will make you truly understand all that on which you were wont to differ.

Here we have a whole complex of implications and significances for Islamic social thought. This message to Muhammad is a confirmation of the truth which was also the basis of all previous messages to mankind, although, not all previous massages have survived intact. As we have seen in other verses human interpretation as well as human forgetfulness and wilful disavowal of God's messages have become mingled with and distorted the purity of previous messages that have been part of human experience. There is a distinction to be made between the effects of human interpretation and human culpable fallibility, though they both generate errant views. This verse makes it unequivocally clear that the specific message of revelation granted to Muhammad, Islam, must be the basis of all understanding for all Muslims. It reiterates the essence of previous revelations and through its specific entailments embodies all the conceptual principles as a way of life. 'Judge, then, between the followers of earlier revelations' can then be seen as an invitation and guidance to an Islamic conceptual approach to knowledge. In accordance with all the Qur'an contains we have a specific guidance to a means of judgement, that is discernment, definition and distinction as it applies to intellectual, moral, ethical, social as well as legal matters. In the context of the passage where this verse occurs the earlier revelations referred to are the Torah and Gospels, and hence the Jewish and Christian communities. In other Qur'anic verses the same exercise of Islamic discernment is related to the understanding of all creation and mankind.

The second major implication contained in this verse is that human diversity, the division of mankind into different communities is part of the order of creation. If God had so willed he could have made one single community. In this verse we are called upon to recognize that God has appointed diversity within mankind with two referents: a difference of laws, *shariah*, and way of life, *minhaj*. *Shariah* signifies literally the way to a watering place and is used in the Qur'an to denote a system of law necessary for a community's social and spiritual welfare. *Minhaj* denotes an open road in an abstract sense, and signifies a way of life. Both terms have connotations of direction and movement, that is, both imply the understanding of social existence, living, as a process. Both these terms are more restricted but contingent aspects of *din*. The particular laws (*shariah*) promulgated through the various specific guidances granted by God, and the particular way of life (*minhaj*) recommended in them, are therefore contextual attributes of *din*. This makes *din* a conceptual vantage for the study of the unity in diversity and the diversity in unity of mankind. Through the guidance of the Qur'anic framework we can strive to comprehend the consonance that exists within and behind all human diversity, and originates in the same source as the specific *din*, *shariah* and *minhaj* of the Muslim community. Furthermore we must recognize that guidance and messages engage a process that operates through time, and is subject to the exigencies of history, human interpretation and fallibility. To study human diversity is therefore to study ways of life subject to change and deviation. Just as there is a consonance which underlies diversity so there is a consonance in the processes that can affect the course and direction of change in all societies in history.

In this verse we are told the manner whereby diverse communities should relate to one another is in vying to do good works, although our understanding of what constitutes good works would be shaped by our own specific laws and way of life. But these are consonant systems, as this verse makes clear, through them we are tested by God in our earthly existence. All communities are composed of Muslims, in the original sense of the term that all people have been created by God, have a common biological form and substance and possess a common nature and common endowments. All peoples of all communities will ultimately return to God for judgement when all will be subject to the same judgement concerning the same matters: their actions and intentions in conducting their earthly existence. Therefore the basis of our relations with other peoples should reflect the consonance of our existence. The only meaningful realm where this insight can be operated in human life is the doing of good works, in the widest application and understanding of that term. In connection with other verses it would seem to imply a dialogue about the translation or eternal verities into pragmatic modes of life that are righteous and good for all human beings. It is a relationship concerned with the consequences of ways of living, not fruitless disputations about matters of dogma.

Having opened up the field for social thought upon an Islamic foundation, we need to add to our understanding of it by considering other Qur'anic referents. First, let us consider some of the points relating to the creative intention of human diversity. In Surah Ar Rum, 30:22 we read:

> And among His wonders is the creation of the heavens and the earth, and the diversity of your tongues and colours: for in this, behold, there are message indeed for all who are possessed of [innate] knowledge!

The diversity of mankind contains a message from God that is instructive and requires study by reasoning intellectual beings. The study of the multiformity of tongues and colours instructs us in the single purpose of existence, the recognition of the Unity of God and the understanding of our proper relationship to God through a *din* of submission. In the context of this verse we should remember that by definition all mankind possesses innate knowledge, that is the condition of our birth into this world.

In Surah Al Hujurat, 49:13 it is written:

> O men! Behold, We have created you all out of a male and female, and have made you into nations and tribes, so that you might know one another. Verily, the noblest of you in the sight of God is the one who is most deeply conscious of Him. Behold, God is all-knowing, all-aware.

The common origin of all mankind is in a single entity from which derive male and female. This ordering of the biological form of mankind creates necessary relationships concerned with the procreative survival of mankind, and by this process a multitude of men and women have spread over the earth forming themselves into nations and tribes. This is a conceptual referent that leads to the recognition of various categories, such as nation and tribe, by which the heterogeneity of mankind can be described and analysed. The purpose of the organization of mankind into categories such as nations and tribes is to give them all, in their own distinct ways, a sense of identity.

This sense of identity is a necessary facet of human make-up. By virtue of creation mankind is involved in a network of relationships stemming from our biological, cultural and spiritual nature. As we have seen these relationships call for understanding and application on a variety of levels. Human organization into definable groupings is one of the levels where we acquire a sense of identity as individuals which relates us to other members of our group, and to a set of established social and cultural rules. Life as an isolate individual is impossible from an Islamic perspective, life is a relational term that connects us both to other human beings and to God. The fulfilment of life requires *din*, *shariah*, and *minhaj*, which define people as nations and tribes in time and space. It is through the specifics of our sense of identity in one human group, our nation or tribe, that we come to recognize our relation to universals and are helped to reflect upon the true significance of what is universal.

Al-Attas finds that the link between the root meaning of *din* traced through *maddana* to *medina* defines mankind as a social being. He sees this theme repeated in the imagery of a bargain or transaction used in the Qur'an to express mankind's covenant with God, as it is a form of social behaviour he reckons to be characteristic of life in towns and cities. That the full implications of *din* can be achieved only in society is a potent metaphor for the social dimension of human life. Unfortunately, al-Attas seems to imply that *din* can be achieved only in towns and cities. He seems to be confusing categories of human organization, such as cities or towns, nations or tribes, for the wider principle we take to be the inescapable meaning and connotation of *din*. The *din* can be fully realized only in society; it is the settled rules of social existence, the ongoing system of social organization that constitutes the meaning of *din*. Such organization can as easily be demonstrated by any analytical category, be it nations or tribes, cities or towns, pastoralist, agriculturalist or industrial, or any other.

It is the possession of settled rules of social interaction and relationships that makes us human. They can be demonstrated by a multitude of forms of organization and association such as nations, tribes, towns, cities, which are categories of analysis, not definitional terms for our human social nature. We make the point because in the minds of the unwary linking *din* to towns and cities, with the Muslim penchant for seeing these as the glories of their historic achievement, could lead to a school of social analysis that destroys the very universality that is the essence of the meaning of *din*. We should not forget it was the identification of what is natural in social life with the form of their own way of life that led Europeans to describe erroneously the American Indians as having no settled rules of social life. The Europeans' faulty ethnography was not pure prejudice, nor simple ignorance: it was a consequence of their limited conceptual view of civilization. They excluded diversity from a definition of mankind and have had to wrestle with a way to include it ever since.

From an Islamic standpoint it is logically impossible to conceive of a group of people that do not have a system of social organization, for that is inherent in our definition of mankind. Similarly the definition admits of analytical levels that can be used to distinguish between the general possession of a set of rules, social organization and culture, and the specific attributes and form these possess. In this Islamic frame of reference there can be no logical opposites, no description of a society as the negative of a Muslim one. There can only be categories of analysis distinctive in the nature and substance of their diversity. The formal difference of the rules of social organization operated by each group or category admit of analysis because they are composed of consonant spheres of activity. Our sense of identity should foster rather than diminish our desire to understand and appreciate other nations and tribes, it should encourage us to look outwards from our own group, knowing that to exist in such human groups is a common necessity shared by all of humanity. It should also condemn all racial, national or tribal prejudice, *asabiyyah*, which denies the dignity and rights of others.

The existence of human diversity and the process of knowing one another through this multiformity is a universal frame of reference. This is further elaborated in Surah An Nahl, 16:36:

> And indeed, within every community have we raised up an apostle [entrusted with this message]: 'Worship God, and shun the powers of evil!' And among those [past generations] were people whom God graced with His guidance, just as there was among them [many a one] who inevitably fell prey to grievous error: go, then, about the earth and behold what happened in the end to those who gave the lie to the truth!

The universality of the Islamic frame of reference is both that the *din* relates to universal unchanging verities embedded in creation and that the guidance to *din* has occurred in every community as an historical experience. It is a *din*, of *al-islam*, that has been followed in the past as well as having been rejected, forgotten and neglected. The specific *din* of Islam revealed in the Qur'an gives definite characteristics to Muslim civilization, but it does not set the Muslim community apart from other peoples who quite clearly have been confronted by the same challenge. The *din* of Islam is a call to a way of life based upon understanding that recognizes the harmony between the specific message granted to Muhammad and the common experience of all other peoples and thereby informs our ability to exercise discernment and right judgement, not only within the life of the Muslim community but in its relations with all other communities. As a way of understanding it enables us to accumulate relevant knowledge which enhances the maintenance of this *din* through Muslim history. As a way of coming to know other people it enables the Muslim to care for the state of all humanity.

This verse is one of many that invites us to study history to refine our understanding of the significance of human existence in all its dimensions. To question why obviously sophisticated, materially affluent and powerful civilizations are now buried in the sand prompts us to recognize that the essential attributes that make up the concepts of *din*, *shariah* and *minhaj* are not confined to material power. If the understanding of these dimensions of social existence have not been properly balanced, or if the emphasis has been placed on one aspect of existence to the distortion and detriment of others, no amount of wealth, power or splendour can maintain and sustain a civilization.

Essentially the Qur'anic message is that social and cultural life is a moral and ethical domain. The message defines essential relationships that integrate the biological with the spiritual, the material with the moral, the individual with the collective, the collective with the transcendent. The reality of human existence finds its earthly expression in the rules mankind employs to organize itself. Without a means to understand the inescapable domain of our existence, the social and cultural realm, we are unable to comprehend and make sense of that other inescapable dimension of human life, the spiritual. Without a system of social thought and analysis consonant with the spiritual dimension that defines human existence, we are unfitted to translate the spiritual promptings of our innate nature into a constructive, balanced pattern of social life.

Another aspect of this verse is that it states that all communities have received a warner. The term *ummah* primarily denotes a group having certain characteristics or circumstances in common. It is used to express a community, a people, a nation, and also a civilization. In the Qur'anic context it is clear that what a people share in common is their system of social organization, their *shariah* and *minhaj* as specific expression of *din*. Since *din* is essentially an operational process wherein human capacities are refined, civilized, according to the needs of our inherent nature and in light of the objective of human existence, then we can take the term *ummah* to denote civilization in a very significant way. Civilization is a qualitative term referring to the inherent capacity of all mankind to refine themselves in relation to the truth of their origin and existence, to recognize the significance of the completion of human life in the Hereafter. Therefore the condition of civilization is an analytic dimension of every community, and as a group of people having common rules that pertain to achieving and fulfilling this condition, every community is a civilization.

A system of social thought should ask relevant questions about human organization based upon this proposition. We can define the various categories of rules employed by a community but the relevance lies within an evaluation of whether they promote or waste the potential for human fulfilment. The Qur'anic perspective on civilization, in this sense, is thoroughly inclusive for no amount of classification can be employed to say this society is civilized while that one is not. The familiar employment of this kind of typological classification in western anthropology and western social thought rested upon the concept of the primitive. It was not the result of seeing social life solely in material terms, it also involved defining some forms of spiritual awareness as primitive, and therefore seeing some human beings as unqualified or unable to recognize higher spiritual truths.

The general sense in which the term *ummah* is used is in no way contradicted by the use of the term to denote Muslims as one single, international community of believers, a civilization in the sense of peoples of many societies and cultures sharing common characteristics. In Surah Al Anbiya, 21:92 we read:

> Verily, [O you who believe in Me,] this community of yours
> is one single community, since I am the Sustainer of you all:
> worship then Me [alone].

By the very definition of the term *ummah* Muslims who all hold to a common *Shariah* must be one community, called upon to refine and civilize themselves within the specific terms of the guidance granted to them and to which they give allegiance. Yet the essential basis that defines the existence of the Muslim *ummah*, belief in one God alone, makes them conceptually consonant with all other communities in the world today, or in the history of mankind. God is the sustainer of all communities, all human life must return to God for judgement. There is no special superiority granted to a Muslim by virtue of self-proclamation as a Muslim: the *kalimah shahhadah*, avowal of faith, is the recognition of the universal challenge all mankind is engaged upon. Ali Shariati has suggested that this is more a matter of Muslims assuming an onerous and perilous responsibility than a superior status over the rest of mankind.[9]

The manner in which to approach other people, based on Qur'anic concepts, has already been referred to in discussion of 49:13 above. It is further defined in Surah Al An'am, 6:105 where we read:

> And thus do We give many facets to Our messages. And to the end that they might say, 'Thou has taken [all this] well to heart' (literally thou hast learned [it well], i.e. God's message) and that We might make it clear unto people of [innate] knowledge, follow thou what has been revealed unto thee by thy Sustainer—save whom there is no deity— and turn thy back upon all who ascribe divinity to aught beside Him. Yet if God had so willed, they would not have ascribed divinity to aught beside Him; hence, We have not made thee their keeper, and neither art thou responsible for their conduct. But do not revile those [beings] whom they invoke instead of God, lest they verily revile God out of spite, and in ignorance: for goodly indeed have We made their own doings appear unto every community. In time, [however] unto their Sustainer they must return: and then He will make them [truly] understand all that they were doing.

The Qur'an calls upon all believers to hold to its many-faceted message that reveals the true significance of life which is both a way of living and a way of understanding about life. The clear basis of the message is the oneness of God. Believers are told to turn their back upon all who ascribe divinity to aught beside God, yet this clear call does not mean there should and can be no form of relations with other peoples. On the contrary, a necessary frame of reference and style for such relations is clearly outlined. The beliefs of other people, even when they diametrically oppose those of Islam, are not to be reviled, since such a course of action could have damaging consequences. There should be tolerance towards all societies despite the most fundamental of differences, and even what would seem to be the most intrinsic rupture has important lessons and is integrated within the Islamic framework.

Our preference for our own patterns of language, culture and society is part of our sense of identity and is part of the inherent order created in human social existence. Within the context of the Qur'an, where it is stated all people have received a warner from God, the existence of beliefs other than in the Unity of God must result from impulses within human society, connected with the operation of human free will. The injunction not to revile the beliefs of others then must be part of the call to study the history of mankind to gain a better understanding of how human free will operates. Not even disbelief in the Unity of God takes any people outside the framework of Islam. One cannot study mankind from an Islamic perspective if one begins by denigrating the beliefs that structure and order the system of life of another people, for a study of others has a positive import for understanding the implications and entailments of an Islamic way of life. We must always include ourselves, as Muslims, and Muslim society as part of the subject matter of enquiry. Studying the ways of non-Muslim peoples is a means of reflecting upon Muslim society. Studying all society is a way of reflecting on the universal frame of reference of Islam.

In this chapter we have set out the Qur'anic referents that give the general parameters for an Islamic anthropology, and demonstrate the necessity for such a study to exist within Muslim intellectual endeavour. We have given the outlines of this study by looking at verses pertaining to necessary definitions that structure enquiry. We have seen Qur'anic definitions open up categories and analytical structures that enable enquiry to be conducted, and suggest lines of questioning relevant to and distinctive of an Islamic anthropology. Our concern has been with the broad framework and while we have mentioned the significant analytical distinction between *din* and *shariah* we have not examined the way the Qur'an's *shariah* also contributes to and generates further definitions and analytical categories for Islamic anthropology. It is important to recognize the significance of *shariah* in this connection. The conceptual totality of the Qur'an underpins and gives meaning to its specific injunctions. The injunctions have both specific form and general implication and must be studied and analysed for their contribution to shaping an Islamic anthropology. Such central areas of social analysis as the family are primarily dealt with in the context of *shariah*; the same is true of economic behaviour and political organization. By this we mean that the general referents of an Islamic perspective as a conceptual frame of reference are unfolded through the context and meaning of specific injunctions.

More than anything else we have been concerned to establish the way one can approach the Qur'an to derive the shape and structure, content and style of Islamic anthropology. We have concentrated on the general outlines only since Hammudah Abd al-Ati's work, *The Family Structure in Islam*, deals comprehensively and masterfully with the Qur'an and its *Shariah* concerning the family as an institution of social process. By examination of the Qur'anic framework Abd al-Ati offers a conceptual approach to analysing the processes that make up any social system. His examination of the significance of the specific *shariah* injunctions of the Qur'an, and therefore the contextual dimension of its *din*, generates propositions of general import for Islamic social thought.

The most important proposition advanced by Abd al-Ati is his definition of the permissible structures encompassed in *halal* and *haram*. Abd al-Ati argues this characteristic of the *shariah*, actually defines spheres of social action, parameters within which various forms of organization and institutionalization can fulfil the requirements of the *shariah*. The *shariah* contextualises Islam for the Muslim community but it still allows diversity and a whole variety of factors of regional significance to be incorporated harmoniously within its structure. There are many ways of embodying the same meaning, purpose and objective within a system of social organization, and many diverse systems of organization can be formed upon the same set of principles and still fulfil their meaning. Not only is Abd al-Ati giving us a way of approaching the Qur'an and its *shariah*, he is also giving us an Islamic way of understanding social process, a new way of thinking about social rules and norms that can be applied in the study of any society.

Social rules and normative behaviour are usually regarded as precisely definable, impositional instruments that express the ideal pattern of a society. Islam, as revealed in the Qur'an, is quintessentially and axiomatically intended to define an ideal pattern of life. And yet, its specific injunctions consist not of precise impositional norms with definite form but of permissible structures, parameters wherein various forms of action can be accommodated without violating the maintenance of the structure itself. We see this as a genuinely demanding insight for it opens up not merely a way of analysing social process on the level of a society and culture as a whole but also provides a way of looking at individual action within the context of a particular society. The incorporation of the individual within his social setting is just as multi-dimensional as the Islamic definition of the general framework of society and culture. It is important to question how the organization of society facilitates the integration of the individual, how variation in individual behaviour is distinguished from deviance. Furthermore there are collective responsibilities that must be organized at the level of society as a whole, but implemented by the action of individuals and directed to the needs and concerns of individuals. Our concern in study must be both to understand how society organizes itself, and how it operates harmoniously for the individual in society.

In this chapter we have been concerned with the Qur'an's narration of the nature of mankind, the origin, organization and purpose of human existence. The Qur'an is the source of the Muslim's ultimate reality definitions, its statements define the foundation of understanding and give us the conceptual propositions that compose our framework for coming to terms with and studying the world around us. It unlocks the gate to a pathway of knowledge, exhorts us to travel along it and gives us the signposts that mark out the route. The style and spirit of the Qur'an help us to keep in mind the objective that should animate and motivate all our questions, and it should be a constant encouragement to keep the aims of our enquiry as broad and as bold as possible. The outlook of the Qur'an is uncompromisingly universal and inclusive; scholarship often requires attention to matters of detail. As we examine these necessary small distinctions we need to remember the breadth of meaning they relate to and we must be aware that unless we can fit our small footprints of knowledge into that broader pathway we will have missed the point of the whole journey.

Notes

1. Al-Attas, *Islam, Secularism and the Philosophy of the Future*; this volume thankfully incorporates and makes widely available his earlier study of the concept of *din*, *Islam, the Concept of Religion and the Foundation of Ethics and Morality.*

2. In this chapter I have taken all translations of the Qur'an from Asad's *The Message of the Qur'an*. No single translation can fully capture the quality of the Qur'an, however; for lucid explanation and stimulating analysis I have found Asad's translation the best source. There may of course be questions arising from the particularity of this translation at certain points but since such questions would only multiply by using a number of different translations the argument for consistency seemed overwhelming. I have also followed throughout the practice of quoting verses in their entirety or continuing a quotation to the end of a verse. This may seem pedantic, but I can only note that when I was first coming to terms with Muslim scholarship I found it the most helpful practice in the works of others and have therefore employed it myself.

3. See al-Attas, *ibid*. pp.75-9 and Asad, *ibid*. p.9, note 23.

4. For discussion of the concept of *khalifah* see the writings of Haider, 'Heritage and Harmony', 'The City Never Lies', 'The City of Learning', and 'Man and Nature', and 'Habitat and Values in Islam: a conceptual formulation of an Islamic city' in *The Touch of Midas*, ed. Sardar.

5. Quoted in Asad, *ibid*. p.653, note 88.

6. Al-Attas, *ibid*. p.58.

7. Asad, *ibid*. p.485, note 110 and p.290, note 21.

8. Here I am particularly thinking of the various contributions to Sardar, ed. *The Touch of Midas*, where this theme is clearly brought out.

9. Shariati, *On the Sociology of Islam.*

5

Consonance, Concepts and Context

In the last chapter we examined the Qur'anic conception of human life and its entailments. While this provides the inescapable foundation for Islamic anthropology it is not of itself a science of social thought and analysis. What the Qur'an provides is the conceptual framework wherein such a science can be shaped, developed and operated by Muslim thinkers. The conceptual framework supports an Islamic anthropology when anthropologists utilize its terms of reference, definitions and categories as the basis of their theories and hypotheses. The conceptual framework remains an enduring scale for the evaluation of the paradigms and insights generated by such a discourse. Most of all the Islamic perspective makes Islamic anthropology distinctive when the Qur'an's style of exposition of the nature of human existence becomes the dynamic of enquiry. A genuine Islamic anthropology endeavours to generate relevant questions to open the sphere of social existence as lived and experienced by men and women now and throughout history.

The understanding of Islamic anthropology advanced here is that it is the study of consonance. The dictionary definition of consonance is being in agreement with, being consistent with, making concord, harmonious. We maintain that the aim of Islamic anthropology should be understanding the nature, conditions, meaning and implications of consonance in the study of all mankind in their communal existence. Islamic anthropology is a social science, concerned with studying mankind in its social communal relations in the diversity of social and cultural settings that exist around the world today and have existed in the past. The focus of its attention is human action, its diversity of form and institutionalization; it seeks to understand the principles that order, organize and give it meaning. We do not conceive of Islamic anthropology as a descriptive but as an explicatory science: concerned to unfold the meaning and implications of communal existence by the comparative study of the principles that generate diverse action and maintain the diversity of societies and cultures. The objective of explication has practical and pragmatic significance. We regard this study as the search for information, insight and knowledge that will promote discernment and understanding of how communal existence can be organized to the best advantage of the citizen. Such knowledge is essential to facilitate informed judgement in the decisions confronting societies in their internal affairs or in their relations with other societies.

The obvious question we must answer is, if Islamic anthropology is a study of human diversity on what basis can it be comparative, and how can it be described as a study of consonance? What distinguishes Islamic anthropology is that it bases itself upon the concepts and values of Islam. There is nothing peculiar in this, for as we have noted in preceding chapters, all analysis of observed reality is rooted in concepts and values which invest information with relevance and significance; the implicit logic and reasoning of the linking generalizations of one's conceptual framework define what is relevant and important to question and seek to uncover about reality. Most of all the value structure of one's conceptual framework determines how knowledge can be utilized and the objectives to which it should be applied. It is axiomatic of Islam that it is based on universal principles which Islamic anthropology is seeking to unfold in the study of human communal diversity.

If existence is accepted as a universal system capable of being comprehended through its entailed complex of conceptual principles and values, then consonance must be a quality of that system. It is an *a priori* of a universal system that everything belongs and relates to that system. What an Islamic anthropology is striving for is an understanding of how consonance operates, what this necessary presumption of its conceptual framework can possibly mean and imply in relation to the observed action of humanity in their diverse communities, how it is demonstrated, the conditions it is capable of generating. Diversity and consonance, instead of being irreconcilable, inimical conditions, are presumed to have a necessary interrelationship and interaction. From such a perspective the study of observed human diversity, the nature of the differences between peoples and the boundaries these differences create admit of having purposeful meaning, constructive functions, of making a positive contribution to the existence and maintenance of the whole of humanity—it is the task of Islamic anthropology to investigate and understand these matters. Such a study would have pragmatic significance enabling relations between peoples, societies, and cultures to be conducted to their best advantage. There is a great difference between accepting that consonance must be a quality of human existence and being able to point at a demonstration of it; this is how the meaning of consonance can be understood, this is what it implies. We maintain that Islamic anthropology should endeavour to fill this gap.

Here we are concerned to explore a set of ideas arising from the conceptual premises and values of Islam and see what their implications are for anthropology. What we hope to convey is the quality of thought about mankind in community that we feel should characterize Islamic anthropology, the methodology it should employ and the kinds of questions it should ask. Our interest here is to grasp the central themes of Islamic anthropology rather than to compare it with the western anthropology taught today. However, since western anthropology is such a dominant presence there are a number of key areas where it will be necessary to emphasize the difference in perspectives. In outlining our view of Islamic anthropology as a study of consonance we have already addressed one of the major distinctions: there is no place for the concept of 'otherness' as in western anthropology.

To recognize diversity is not the same as recognizing the members of different social and cultural groups as 'other'. The standpoint of Islamic anthropology is not analogous to the rationalist pole of western anthropology because both are founded upon the assumption there are absolutes which are universal. Nor is Islamic anthropology analogous to the relativist pole of western anthropology because it accepts diversity as fundamental and as causing real difference in the beliefs and practices of human groups, in terms of which their action and operation in history must be understood. Both poles of western anthropology incorporate and generate propositions revolving around the status and meaning of the 'otherness' of the peoples who are the object of their study.

Islamic anthropology embraces aspects of both the rationalist and relativist poles in a distinctive synthesis, using the basic definitions of human nature and community and the definition of universal principles intrinsic to Islam. By virtue of its founding axioms and assumptions Islamic anthropology can never be a study that seeks to describe or compare 'other' societies in Muslim terms, for the societies of Muslim civilization are all, if you will, as 'other' as any non-Muslim society. Or, to put it another way, all societies are equivalent, consonant entities within a universal system. It is the basis of Islam that all societies and all human beings stand in the same necessary ongoing relationship to the source of Islam, the source of the concepts and values of Islam and Islamic anthropology. Therefore even diversity can be analysed from the standpoint of these concepts and values.

The Islamic concept that expresses this view of existence is *tawhid*, unity.[1] We have argued that there has been a tendency to subsume the definition and implications of the multiplicity of other Islamic concepts and values within expositions of *tawhid*. Yet despite all the attention given to it, we feel there are aspects of this Islamic paradigm par excellence that have been sorely neglected. *Tawhid* is the concept expressing the nature of Creator and creation. This proposition is far more extensive than the familiar statement that Islam views all of existence as a unity by virtue of all things having a common origin in the purposeful and intentional will of the sole creator, God. The *tawhidic* conception of creation is dynamic and integral; it expresses unity by integrating and relating origin to the ongoing processes of existence, constantly being unfolded in necessary relationships, and the objective of existence where both origin and processes achieve their completion. In the Islamic perspective creation is a teleologic, interrelated and interactive, processual, systemic whole; the centre and circumference of the system of creation is *tawhid*, which encompasses and transcends time and space.

What is essential to *tawhid* is the idea of system it brings into being, a system dependent upon *tawhid* and in perpetual relationship and interaction with it. Definition is given to the nature of the unitary system through the multiplicity of other Islamic concepts and values. It is for this reason we argue Muslim scholarship should shift its attention to studying the entailed concepts and values. Its interest should be in developing and expanding its ideas about system and process.

Tawhid is a multi-dimensional, interactive, dynamic, relational concept. These characteristics are the cardinal referents upon which the Islamic intellectual perspective should be built and are also applicable to all the other concepts and values defining the system. The inherent teleology of the system makes the Islamic view of existence one of moral purpose where every action has a moral and ethical dimension. This essential characteristic of the Islamic world view implies that all our disciplines and discourses of knowledge should be evaluative studies concerned not merely with description that unfolds understanding of actual relationships, but also concerned with questions of implications and consequences: the could, should or ought to be of actual relationships.

The supreme function of the *tawhidic* paradigm is to generate a balanced understanding. The concept of unity requires all the multiplex dimensions of existence to be seen as integrated and interactive and this necessarily entails the concept of balance. The various dimensions and capacities of the system are consonant, purposeful, intentionally created attributes designed for relationship and interaction with each other. Therefore, they cannot be viewed as contending and competing elements each seeking to distort the others' operation and function.

Their teleologic purpose and intention is compatible with unity, with achieving a balance that enhances the fulfilment and completion of the created, processual systemic existence.

From this it is easy to see that an Islamic intellectual approach is holistic. This should not be understood to mean just the disposition to regard all communities as having the need and capacity to form themselves into wholes that offer their individual members an integrated world of meaning, the conventional use of the term in western anthropology where it has long had currency. The Islamic holistic perspective is universal, the communal whole is itself part of a universal whole which is also a realm of meaning, interaction and integration; the universal level also demonstrates the disposition to holism. What this implies for anthropology is a radical departure in topics of study, for such a universal conception of holism would require the study of relations between communities, not as a minor subsidiary of understanding how a community operates internally but as a prime focus of attention in its own right. Intercommunity relations are themselves a necessary dimension of human action in communal existence; they bring diverse communities into a substantive wider realm of operation with a distinctive nature, mechanisms, dynamics, principles, and conditions of their own. The manner whereby relations between diverse communities are formed, sustained and maintained through time and space, the principles such relations demonstrate, the needs they fulfil, the potentials they offer, the effect they have upon the individual communities involved are therefore investigated not as an extension of the conceptual analysis of compartmentalized communities but as a dimension subject to conceptual analysis and formulation in its own right. It is a presumption of an Islamic holistic approach that the universal system includes the tendency of constituent wholes to build into greater wholes; this creates distinctive categories and vantage points for analysis of human behaviour. This would include not merely the study of international relations but also the study of empires, colonialism, civilizations, panistic movements and belief systems—their meaning, dynamics, implications and consequences, natures, modes of operation, incorporation and institutionalization as particular phenomena that cannot be adequately understood from the vantage point of society as the single holistic entity. This arena of human behaviour has been badly neglected until now—which might perhaps suggest that the reason why international relations are so appalling is the lack of informed knowledge behind them.

The Islamic universal and holistic understanding means communities cannot in themselves be viewed as the limit of system. The Islamic definition of community or society is more complex and multidimensional than that found in either western anthropology or western sociology. The arguments in western anthropology about boundary formation and maintenance, most particularly about the difficulty in recognizing and defining them in study, we take as an indication of the limitation of their definition of society as a bounded systemic whole. From the Islamic perspective of universal holism it would be perfectly possible to expect a range of categories and conditions of boundary formation to exist and operate, each answering to diverse functions and needs that, far from working for the closure of a society, are designed in fact to maintain flexible, adaptive boundaries. The existence of different kinds of community boundaries, the operation of flexibility or closure through different boundary mechanisms may well be related to ecological, historical or cultural factors. These factors need not feed only into the area of relations between different communities but could be indicators of important features of beliefs and ideas as well as ecological and historical influences operating within different communities. If one presumes society to be a watertight compartment these constraints and ideas operating within and between societies would never be open properly for study. Different ideas about the scope and meaning of communal boundary formation may well affect the action of a community in its response to change. It is just these kinds of questions that Muslim social scientists should be addressing. This kind of approach to questioning is part of the wider ramifications of the Islamic conception of system and a principal reason for our arguing for greater concentration on the study of the multiplicity of Islamic concepts and values. In this way more intellectual attention is focused upon processes of interaction thus generating a more complex conception of system. The more multivariate our conceptual analysis, the more it is consonant with and employs the spirit of the multidimensional reality of the cardinal concept, *tawhid*. This concept expresses a unity which is infinite and illimitable; it unifies an infinitely complex system and must constantly seek to expand its understanding of system.

The shift of emphasis to multivariate conceptual analysis would have additional advantages in that it would enable us to distinguish more categories and levels of analysis, generate new questions, and expand our knowledge. It may indeed be comforting to the human mind to impose form and limitation upon observed reality to create a sense of order and control—to fix reality into watertight compartments with precise formal meaning and institutional implications. The desire to make reality manageable may be both laudable and essentially human, but unfortunately it usually proceeds by means of cutting reality down to the limits of human frailty by imposing an arbitrary closed certainty upon a reality which, irrespective of human will, remains open. Intellectual history and the experience of mankind has shown that whatever temporary consolation such limitations offer they are nevertheless arbitrary, conventional limitations rooted in the mind of man rather than in the nature of reality. They are a decidedly inadequate way to contemplate God since they fail to capture the most essential attributes of His nature as the Infinite, the Omnipotent, the Eternal who has initiated and ordered creation, nourishes and sustains creation according to His capacities and not those of mankind.

Existence, observed reality, is a dynamic process that entails the notion of change. The failure to devise ways of thinking about and understanding reality that are multivariate and multi-dimensional as well as processually dynamic has consequences for human action. Our action in community is a consequence of our belief systems, which are the basis of incorporation and institutionalization of systems from kinship and marriage, to political systems, to our modes of economic activity and means of exploitation of our environment, to our science and technology and all the branches of artistic and intellectual endeavour. There can be little doubt human institutions and patterns of action are incorporated for regularity, order, maintenance, balance and control, to be stable systems for the delivery of well-being and value, in the widest understanding of the terms. Yet it is demonstrably true that instability can be generated by a rigid observance of those patterns that previously delivered stability. In other words by doing not only what is believed and intended to be good but by doing what has previously been known to have been good, action may generate harmful consequences not previously experienced. The failure of formal systems to comprehend and encompass change within their fabric has been observable throughout history. It is precisely the desire of human systems to regard and seek to incorporate balance as a static condition to be maintained by continuation of the same form that causes decay. Such a view of human action, of the potential of observed reality, has been a hard won idea that western anthropology is still wrestling to incorporate. We argue it should be a basic axiom of Islamic social thought; it is the logical meaning of the Qur'an's references to the decay of civilizations, although as we shall see it has not always been integral to the thought and action of Muslims in history.

In *Islamic Methodology in History*, Fazlur Rahman presents an excellent examination of the early institutionalization of Islam in Muslim society, arguing that in the earliest phase interpretive thought predominated. This enabled the first Muslims to do things differently from the model of Prophetic behaviour, precisely in order to fulfil the model. Rahman calls this the *living sunnah*, an interpretive process. He then examines the formation of the characteristic institutions of Muslim civilization that crystallized around a number of concepts, *sunnah*, *ijma*, *ijtihad*, *hadith*, that affected social institutions, and shows how the dynamic aspects of these concepts were negated in the process of institutionalization. The search for regularity and order imposed a falsification upon certain aspects of the concepts in their incorporation into institutions. While the institutionalization of these concepts in forms of action and thought gave rise to the classical flowering of Muslim civilization, they also contained in their mode of incorporation a rationale nurturing the seeds of stultification that was bound to generate their stultification and ossification in time. The *taqlidic* paradigm of blind following of historical precedent was an implicit consequence of the way the institutions were incorporated. Rahman sees this as a denial of the inherent logic of an Islamic understanding. Its consequence for the operation of Muslim civilization has been to make it backward looking, in the sense of seeing its future as modelled only in its past.

Rahman's historical study not only brings into focus the general argument we have been making, but also indicates a distinctive way of analysing institutions. The argument has important implications for the way an Islamic anthropology should question the formal incorporation of human action and thought: how it should view institutionalization. The central proposition of this approach is to regard all human thought and action as interpretive, a response to the substantive factors that lie behind them. Institutionalization is a process engendered by a network of interactive relationships between concepts and values in a situational context, enabled by a specific form, having a set of functions and operated by a personnel whose roles and responsibilities are defined. But institutionalization is also a logic, a rationale produced by the community's comprehension of the network of interactive relationships defining the sphere of action where the formal institution is to operate to fulfil both its functions and its purpose. The crucial questions about the intentional purpose for this primarily concerns the value load an institution is designed to regulate, order and maintain. The nature of the logic and rationale employed by a community in incorporating a formal institution is a dimension of institutionalization open to analysis and that must be analysed. As Rahman's study demonstrates, the logic and rationale of institutionalization becomes part of the interactive context of the operation of the institution and is capable of generating a variety of conditions that affect the regulation, ordering and maintenance of its value load. The most important consequence of this way of thinking about institutions is that it makes adaptive capacity a necessary dimension of both the operation of an institution and of our analysis of them. It generates a set of questions seldom posed in this way and suggests the elements that would be involved in an evaluative analysis of the teleology of institutions. Institutions should necessarily be viewed as evaluative structures and as having a teleology; this seems to us axiomatic of Islamic thought.

We have suggested that the study of system and process are central to an understanding of Islamic concepts and values. What does this shift of emphasis mean? It does not mean seeking to define the meaning of each and every concept and value in isolation, although we certainly have to strive to perceive the various dimensions of each concept. Rather, Islamic scholarship should be seeking to grasp their relational definition, for their true significance exists only in relation to their interaction with the system as a whole.

Let us take a simple example of two concepts we considered in the last chapter, *khilafah* and *abudiyyah* (human vice-regency upon earth, and servitude). Taken in isolation these concepts generate diametrically opposed views of mankind. *Khilafah*, while it contains the notion of responsibility, nevertheless focuses upon the pre-eminent place of mankind in the creative order by virtue of the possession of free will. *Abudiyyah* is the servitude of a slave perpetually subject to his master; it betokens one who is impotent, without the power to determine action. The appropriate and only action available to a slave is to serve as instructed, according to an existing and original pattern set down by his master. Taken in isolation both concepts are multidimensional. It is possible from a consideration of either *khilafah* or *abudiyyah* to recognize the positive and negative conditions they can generate, or the balanced and imbalanced modes of operation they can demonstrate: the good *khilafah* and the tyrannical *khilafah*, the loyal, virtuous slave or the resentful, grudging one. Each concept is inherently evaluative, with a moral and ethical dimension.

Viewed in isolation as part of a system these two concepts would suggest alternative ways of looking at reality. They certainly would lead to the system being seen as multi-dimensional. The crucial point is that the conception of system that would result from seeing these concepts as self-contained isolates would be of one operating by antithesis, by the antagonism of competing elements, rather than one with an harmonious balance to which all dimensions are contributory.

From isolating concepts it is possible to conceive of a system, but the nature of that system would be fragmentary. The quality of the whole may be conceived as unified and balanced, but these qualities are de-linked from its constituent parts: the constituent parts can be related to unity, balance and harmony only at the level of the whole and not in their mutual relations within the system. To define Islamic concepts and values in isolation then effectively violates cardinal principles of the *tawhidic* paradigm and results in an unIslamic outlook. Unity, balance and harmony are not merely dimensions of the system as a whole but of the processual interactive operation of the constituent parts of the system.

The definition of *khilafah* or *abudiyyah* in their own terms is only part of their proper definition which is manifest when they are brought into interactive relationship; this mutual definition arises from the points where aspects of their individual definition impinge upon the definition and content of another concept. Vice-regents can interpret their role as the assumption of the powers of regency, self-determining slaves have a clearer idea of where the limits occur in the employment of their powers, the instances where responsible, that is restrained, action is inevitable and necessary. The sphere of proper action is more harmoniously defined. As the multiplicity of concepts and values are brought into relation with each other as mutually defining dimensions their evaluative aspects gain in precision. The points of articulation between concepts and values can be seen to focus on action, to define its implications and consequences and thereby clarify what is or ought to be right action. We should make the point that the Qur'an is constantly calling attention to the fact that the predominant arena for human discernment is that of action: this is the only matter for human determination, judgement on it being exercised between themselves, as well as being the subject of final Judgement. Islam is action-orientated, its purpose is to promote the understanding of action.

It is often argued that mulivariate analysis leads to a greater sense of the complexity of systems and processes which only compounds confusion. The more variables one can see in a given situation, it is said, the more difficult it becomes to make decisions, to balance and give due accord to each of the factors. From an Islamic perspective this confusion is more apparent than real. For while we perceive the complexity of the system through the multiplicity of its dimensions, all the interrelations and interactions are purposeful and intentional, sharing the same teleology. System and process are not only matters of internal interaction, they are perpetually in interaction with, and held in place by, the centre and circumference. No consideration of interaction can be complete unless it views all the complex workings of system as integrated with *tawhid*, and having the function of harmoniously balancing a unity within a unity.

The idea that understanding of the complexity of systems involves moral dilemmas is a peculiarly western syndrome. The more that is understood in western scholarship the harder it becomes to make a judgement. The more aspects to an individual's action in community, the more difficult it has become for the western student of human society to advance opinions, or to feel he or she has the right to judge. Nowhere is this syndrome more clearly demonstrated than in fully relativist western anthropology. Essentially this predicament, for it is a predicament when one can identify problems but not resolve them, has arisen because western scholarship has shunned overarching explanations that integrate complexity or integrate the observer with the observed in a shared frame of reference that allows for evaluative judgement. Explanations in western social science are based on moral neutrality, and inevitably general moral inertia in the application of knowledge. Specifically in the case of western anthropology we have suggested that moral neutrality is based on the fact that despite arguments for a biologically unitary mankind there is no overarching framework of social and cultural analysis where observer and observed can be unified for a mutual dialogue.

As we have sought to make clear, the Islamic vantage point is significantly different for complexity is conceived as central to unity. The dynamic of questioning of complexity itself is distinctive since one is seeking to discover how complexity harmonizes and allows for morally responsible action. The overarching unity and all its entailed assumptions are open to discussion between observer and observed because they are accepted as part of a shared framework despite all apparent and real diversity; how it is shared is part of the concern of Islamic anthropology. Limits are defined within which harmonious relationships can be instituted as constructive integrations of complexity to promote action to fulfil the potential of human abilities. That is in essence the optimism of the Islamic view of mankind.

From the foregoing it might seem that Islamic social thought must be inextricably wedded to the ideal type, but we would argue it is precisely because of the optimism of the Islamic view of mankind that an ideal state is attainable, that makes ideal type analysis unnecessary. There is a pragmatic approach about what actually constitutes human action in community. Given the predominance of the ideal type in western social science this point needs some elaboration. In chapter three we made the point that Qur'anic concepts and values are God's and not man's, that they are intentional and purposefully communicated to enable comprehension of the meaning of reality, and thus generate right relationships and action. However, the meaning of concepts and values is more extensive than any single or multiple meaning attributed to them by people. The only ideal type for Islamic social thought would be a conceptual definition of the meaning and implications of concepts and values in interaction. Conceptual analysis is about understanding the principles that define permissible structures, not impositional structures. The notion of the ideal type is an analytical or evaluative tool for the examination of observed reality, but observed reality does not generate the fullness and completion of concepts and values. In an Islamic perspective we are always dealing with created concepts and values, and their partial interpretation in human action.

It is logically possible that negative interpretations of concepts and values can be made, and decisions reached which emphasize certain values at the expense of others. In interpretive human action where the elements of choice are exercised by the actors, it is not necessary that an ideal pattern should occur. That the concepts and values have the capacity for harmonious operation does not guarantee that they are used to this end by humanity, for Islam does not impose; there is no compulsion in religion precisely because mankind has choice and the capacity to discern what is right. That is the challenge and purpose of human life. Revelation of the concepts and values is given to make this knowledge available to enable the challenge to be met.

For Muslim thinkers then the ideal type is a mental construct in the sense of being a contemplation of the potential conditions of concepts and values that enables observed reality to be analysed. The problem arising from the use of ideal types in western scholarship is they have been used to generate a view of human action as answering to rules, but these rules have been very specific, being geared to a notion of the pattern of action people think they ought to be following, whether or not they actually do. Ideal patterns of action then become human creations, in a view of existence that is man-centred and man-defined. The actual assumptions of ideal types, as defined in western scholarship, make it hard to see human community as dynamic; its ideal is itself static and should work to maintain society as it is. Change can then be only a rupture of meaning where a new ideal type is constructed out of human circumstances, by human actors to give themselves meaning in the midst of an uncontrollable bewildering reality that, in T.S. Eliot's words, will not stay still, will not stay in place.

It is a founding proposition of the Islamic outlook that human action in history has usually fallen short of the ideal, and that is precisely what we are interested in studying. It is a pragmatic view of human community acknowledging the fallibility of human systems, their ability to be unstable, unjust, and to limit human potential, as well as their ability to devise systems that promote justice, well-being and the fulfilment of human potential. Islamic anthropology is concerned with the meaning and implications of human communal behaviour, the systems and processes that are institutionalized with the objective of an ideal, but without that ideal being an attained state identified with what people do. In such a viewpoint change is not only an integral part of the process but a necessary focus of behavioural investigation. Change is not an extraneous ingredient to be considered only after it has occurred; it is an integral dynamic in any act of choice by an individual or community. The Islamic social science perspective admits of a lack of fit, the recognition of partial fit, and the potential for perfect fit between the ideal and the reality. Its conception of ideal types, being non-formally specific, actually enables more diverse conditions of reality to be recognized and analysed.

So far we have been dealing with the orientations of study produced by Islam, its concepts and values, and we have recognized certain propositions about mankind in community and the nature of existence. The Islamic worldview makes reality familiar and orders the real world into the categories and relationships about which the Islamic anthropologist asks questions. In the process of study we look for similarities and differences in what we observe according to our conceptual terms of reference and refine our understanding accordingly. The Islamic basis of our study does not take us outside the Kuhnian argument for the conventional nature of knowledge and the means of knowledge accumulation—it defines the terms of that convention. It does not mean our minds are closed or that we have predetermined notions about human behaviour. The base in Islamic concepts and values does not obviate but rather heightens the necessity for intellectual rigour, vitality of debate, and a wide perspective. Islamic anthropology does not seek to impose a pattern on reality but to study the pattern to which it believes reality inherently fits.

So what are the concepts and values that form the basis of Islamic anthropology? The source of the concepts and values is the Qur'an, and a number of them have been dealt with in previous chapters. However, we now have to face a stark realization. Islam offers a multiplicity of concepts and values but there is nowhere we can turn to find a comprehensive intellectual elaboration and full list of them as the starting point of enquiry. The best available source is the list of some ninety concepts cited as requiring urgent intellectual attention by Sardar in *Islamic Futures*.[2] This thought-provoking work on Islamic conceptual analysis points out that modern Muslim scholarship has yet to formulate the concepts and values that will be the starting point of enquiry.

This is not an insuperable impediment, as Sardar's own work ably demonstrates, but it is a cautionary note. Even when we deal with the multiplicity represented by the most familiar of the concepts—*tawhid, ijma, adl, ijtihad, istislah, sunnah, fitrah, khilafah, din, shariah, shura, ilm*—we have not begun to tap the rich vein of available concepts. Indeed, in his list Sardar includes a number of items many Muslim thinkers might not even recognize as concepts requiring analysis. We take this to be an indication of the intellectual predicament of Muslim civilization today. Most contemporary Muslim thinkers outline a few key Islamic concepts and rely upon dominant western disciplines to complete the conceptual gaps.

Muslim scholarship is re-awakening to the need for reconstruction after being dominated for centuries by western intellectual paradigms. This most potent of all colonial legacies, the imperialism of the mind, underlies all Muslim problems, whether they be economic, political, social or cultural, because it requires that they be defined and resolved within the terms of reference of western intellectual disciplines. Yet these very disciplines have been an intrinsic part of the development of their predicaments. What the imperialism of the mind offers is not the notion that the patient must get worse before it can get better but rather that for the patient, the Muslim world, there is only permanent disease. If modernity means submission to the intellectual premises of western scholarship, then Muslim society can look forward only to becoming a subservient branch of western modernity. In this state an Islamic intellectual approach is alien, just as western-defined modernity is a state of permanent alienation for the Muslim. We reject the notion this is a valid choice, or that it is the only choice, unlike many commentators on the islamization of knowledge who believe that one can work through western intellectual disciplines to achieve the synthesis resulting in contemporary Muslim scholarship. This is the timid man's option, the desire to sugarcoat the bitter pill, to offer a palliative rather than a genuine remedy.

We have detailed the context, dynamics and background of an Islamic way of thought precisely for this reason. This way of thought should be the clear and conscious choice of Muslim intellectuals who must begin constructing modern disciplines of Islamic scholarship by being aware of what their own way of thought entails. This is the only valid option that will enable Islamic disciplines to investigate the problems of modernity, or of history, so that they can think their way to genuine Islamic remedies for the human condition. Modern Muslim scholarship can find true meaning only within the parameters of Islam. When we properly apprehend the context of our conceptual fabric we can then move ahead to delineate our intellectual disciplines. Only when the Islamic discipline has been formed can it begin to explore the ideas and methodology of western knowledge and engage in a necessary, and potentially mutually beneficial, dialogue of ideas.

Unless we are clear about the context in which the categories of Islamic anthropology and social analysis are to be operated and investigated, a discussion of the categories themselves will have little significance and there will be plenty of space for mental inertia and force of habit to regard what is offered as merely a gloss upon conventional western anthropology. It is not just the categories but the entire way of thinking about them and manipulating them that must be Islamic. From the standpoint of the Islamic conception of system and process we now turn to the categories and terms of reference of the Islamic anthropology we are proposing. Here we will examine the basic units of investigation, the implications of our categories, what they are assumed to contain and entail, and the relevant questions they raise.

Islamic anthropology is concerned to study all mankind as *ummah*. *Ummah* can denote a range of units of community formation: it can imply a people, a society, a nation, a tribe, a culture, or a multi-social, multi-cultural community in the sense it is used to describe Muslim civilization. The precise application of the term *ummah* to the single community of Muslim believers bound by definite obligations is a distinct but consonant aspect of the conceptual import of the term *ummah* as a way of looking at mankind in society. *Ummah* is the basic category of investigation for Islamic anthropology since it is an *a priori* of the Islamic perspective that mankind is created as a culture-bearing, social being who must necessarily exist in community. Without community the inherent capacities of mankind could not be employed or fulfilled. Mankind is composed of individuals with innate social needs;

the existence and survival of mankind as a biological, social, cultural and spiritual being is secured through the ordering of relationships that are part of purposive creation; they not only connect individuals but they also assume the need for collective action, that is, action undertaken by some individuals on behalf of all the members of a group. The concept of *ummah* includes the idea of a diversity of communities, that mankind necessarily forms itself into a plurality of communities.

The prime significance of *ummah* is a group of people sharing common characteristics. However, the main effect of the concept of *ummah* as a way of looking at human communities is the emphasis it throws on relationships. *Ummah* is the context where the relationships necessary to human beings are organized according to a pattern, given routine expression through networks of associations between individuals who hold common beliefs as the basis of their mode of existence and incorporation into processes of social life within a community. What defines *ummah* as the context for human social existence is *din*. From an Islamic perspective every *ummah* possesses a *din*; a people's *din* makes their community a realm of meaning, being their distinctive way of knowing the world, themselves and other communities. *Ummah* is the category where all the endowments, capacities and needs that comprise human nature and make us human are given specific expression through an operative process that invests all the dimensions of life with coherence and meaning. The *din* is a people's means of relating themselves to the Universal. The word *din* is often rendered as religion, but we have seen that its conceptual import is far wider. It is the conceptual realm of a community, the means of relating to the Universal by which the consequences of universals are translated into a meaningful process of living in the widest possible terms. The *din* is the pinnacle of hierarchy within a community, the body of the ultimate definitions of reality that, as an operative process, orders and gives meaning to the routine of community life, its organization, maintenance and change.

The concepts of *ummah* and *din* are mutually defining and they give distinctive characteristics to the Islamic view of communal existence. For Islamic anthropology all communities are equivalent entities, consonant units not merely because all human beings have social and cultural capacities that must be given expression in organized relationships, or biological needs that must be ordered and maintained through networks of relationships, but because they are moral domains. The existence of the individual presupposes the existence of a community, and they are teleologically unified in the exercise of human endowments, rights and obligations, duties and responsibilities in all spheres of human behaviour. It is the total context of the Islamic perspective, the *tawhidic* paradigm that generates the definition of community as a moral entity, and thereby defines the orientation of the questions and concerns of Islamic anthropology. We seek to explore how a community functions as a system that facilitates the harmonious embodiment of moral values as a constructive environment for right action, or hinders or deforms the purposive intent of moral values within a way of life and therefore impairs the ability or opportunity for right action.

Ummah is the sphere of thought, organization and action where the relationships of human life are actualized as system and process. One quality the conceptual definition of community gives to Islamic anthropology is an essentially open view of the nature of community, for it includes no notion of form or determinate boundaries, no definite list of items that must be present. The purpose of a community is to achieve moral balance within and between a network of relationships, to keep these relationships from corruption; this objective can be attained in many ways, partially or in full, but how it is attained is determined by the action of the people in community. While the network of relationships are known and exist for all mankind, how they are translated into a particular pattern of living is the function of a *din* in an *ummah*. The nature and boundaries of a community are determined essentially by relationships, the interaction and articulation of a number of conceptual propositions all concerned with the operation of moral values. How these relationships are organized within the terms of its *din* gives specific form to a community and determines how it recognizes its boundaries. The very openness of the conceptual definition of *ummah* demands that Islamic anthropology investigates and studies carefully the network of factors that can affect the actual form and processes of a given community.

While the study of the factors impinging upon the form and organization of a community can be viewed as an explanation of communal diversity, this is not the dynamic or objective of Islamic anthropology. The concern is not to understand how communities have developed through human action in a given physical environment, but how the form and operative process of a community embodies and fulfils the moral purpose common to all human existence. This perspective creates the equivalence and consonance of all communities. Within the confines of the specific form and organization of a community according to its *din,* an Islamic anthropologist is interested in questioning how the size, scope, technical repertoire, system of beliefs, processes of social organization, systems of authority, economic organization and relationship to the physical environment operate as a coherent moral structure for the fulfilment of values that are the purpose and challenge of all human existence.

Even though the Islamic anthropologist must obviously engage in careful investigation of particular forms and types of community, the classification and typology of communities can never imply any evaluative ranking of communities according to size, scale, organization or any other attributes. Classification and typology are the means of recording the enabling mechanisms employed by a particular society to fulfil its overarching objective of facilitating right action by both individual and community in pursuit of their joint moral purpose. While this makes all communities evaluative structures, both as systems of human incorporation and action and from the analytical perspective of Islamic anthropology, the only superiority or inferiority that has any meaning is in the moral actions of a community. Superior moral action in any instance is the product of a community's achieving a balanced integration of all the dimensions of life enabling the harmonious fulfilment of the capabilities of human beings in their relationships. Moral action results from a system that encourages individual and group abilities and the relationships necessary for human existence; those with other people, their physical environment and with God. Superior moral action can be achieved as easily in a small-scale society with limited technical expertise as in a complex large-scale society with a rich profusion of technical resources at its disposal. The technical and material resources of a community certainly have moral implications since they can be used to further moral action but they are not in themselves a comprehensive definition of the moral purpose of a community.

Within the Islamic perspective there is a distinctive definition of progress that does not reduce the operations, opportunities and potential of human communal life to an assessment of material conditions. Material conditions are not ends in themselves, but the result of choices in the balancing and integration of values. They are also enabling mechanisms through which values are delivered, enjoyed and employed in a community. Progress is not an assessment of wealth but an evaluation of the integration and harmonious balance of a system of values, including the ability of material conditions to fulfil the spiritual dimension.

It should be obvious from this that the concept of the 'primitive' not only has no place but has no meaning whatsoever within Islamic anthropology. 'Primitive' can never be an assessment of the actual material condition, beliefs, ideas and form of organization of a people, nor can any set of characteristics of a community simply by virtue of their presence classify it as 'primitive'. The only possible application of the term 'primitive' would be to a system that prevented individuals and the group from engaging in right action. As such, 'primitive' behaviour could occur in any type of community. Indeed within an Islamic perspective 'primitive' behaviour is a constant, ever present possibility and potential of all human beings. In the classic Islamic formulation all mankind can rise to be higher than the angels or fall to be lower than the beasts.[3] We can think of no reason why the term 'primitive', even within the Islamic definition we have given, should ever be employed in Islamic anthropology. There are many other ways of expressing this quality of action so avoidance of the term would ensure there could never be any confusion between the orientations of Islamic anthropology and the use of the term in western anthropology.

As we stated earlier Islamic anthropology makes a distinctive synthesis between rationalism, in the sense of recognizing universal principles applicable to the study of all communities, and relativism, in the sense of maintaining that any community can be understood only in terms of its own identity. The synthesizing concept for both is *din*. Within the *tawhidic* paradigm there is only one absolute, God, and the *din* of any community is their means of relating to this absolute. Every community possesses a *din* expressing universal and enduring relationships that define the moral purpose of existence. People of all communities therefore can engage in discussing the organization of right action. Even though the unit of investigation for Islamic anthropology is an *ummah*, behaviour can be understood and analysed only when it is seen through the specifics of the *din* it embodies. The entry point for Islamic anthropological enquiry is the study of a community's *din* and its contextual elements of *shariah* and *minhaj*. By definition community is integrated through the possession of a *din*, whose distinguishing features and interpretation are seen in the institutionalization of its *shariah* and *minhaj*. The basis for any comparative analysis must be through studying the *din* of a community as it is understood by the members of that community.

Shariah and *minhaj* we have previously mentioned as the contextual aspects of *din*; we must now consider their implications for Islamic anthropology. In the last chapter we considered the root meaning of the terms, both related to a path and therefore have the connotation of a process, a movement directed towards an objective. The term *shariah* is instantly familiar as the religious law of Islam, the body of specific injunctions contained in the Qur'an that structure the way of life of a Muslim community. For Islamic anthropology the *shariah* is a community's specific body of normative rules derived from and expressing the structural referents of its *din*. The important point to note is that we carefully select the term normative rules, rather than law. Law is a term implying both rules and a system of administration, processes of institutionalization with the attendant processes of training, selecting, appointing of a personnel to operate and maintain them and their authority, duties and obligations within a community. Even in the Muslim system there are aspects of the Qur'anic *shariah*, such as the detail of prayer and ablution, that, while being undisputably *shariah* and clear normative rules that structure modes of behaviour and the routines of community life, are not law in this restrictive definite sense. We feel the significance lies in the distinction between normative rules that are the responsibility of the individual and normative rules that require a system of administration. Within Islam people congregate together for prayer but only the individual can pray, only on an individual basis will their prayer be accepted from them or their individual motivation or state of mind invalidate their prayer. There is no compulsion in religion so while the community can emphasize the importance of prayer to the individual, or operate a sanction, a law, to encourage the observance of prayer, the enforcement of that law can be achieved only by the individual. The nature of the normative rule, what it contains and applies to must be understood, for not all normative rules by their very definition can be part of an administration of law in the restricted sense of the term.

Studying the *shariah* of a community then means examining its body of normative rules. These give specific definition to relationships within the community: how they must be effected, the kinds of behaviour appropriate to these relationships, the rights and duties in a relationship, and the sanctions that can be applied to ensure compliance with the normative rules. It is important to distinguish between those matters involving personal responsibilities and those involving the collective organization of the community. From the conceptual point of view the way in which the normative rules are institutionalized is a matter for a community; and the diversity of means employed by different communities would be an interesting aspect of study within Islamic anthropology. The *shariah* has been given institutional form not by the Qur'an but through Muslim interpretation.

We have stressed the emphasis an Islamic perspective places on interpretive thought and action. In investigating the *shariah* of a community the Islamic anthropologist is clearly examining community structures evident in the specific normative rules that define the system of land holding, the economic systems, the available sanctions to enforce economic rights, and the specific institutions that control right action in this sphere. The political relations of a community would constitute another sphere encompassing the sources of authority recognized by a community. their organization, duties and functions, the administration of justice, exercised either by the political authority in a community or by a separate process of administration. In examining these spheres of action what the Islamic anthropologist is considering is a process of interpretation wherein the normative rule is translated into a system and processes of action by means of a rationale, the rationale being the product of the interaction between the *din* and its *shariah*.

Since institutionalization in a community is a process of interpretation the Islamic anthropologist must be concerned to study systems of thought and belief, as understood by members of a community. In particular the manipulations of thought and belief condition the interpretation given to *din* and *shariah* and underpin the system of institutionalization. The thought and belief system determines how constraints, whether arising from the individual, the idea of community, the definition of the natural environment or relations with other communities, are recognized and incorporated into the institutional pattern of a community. The consideration given to the rationale of interpretation—how wide a scope is recognized, whether a community considers its normative base as fixed and therefore a form given for all time, or whether there is authority for change in the normative base and how this is defined, organized and operated—all relate to how change is conceptualized by a community, how they adapt to it and how it can be incorporated within the institutional framework of a community.

Shariah is a concept of normative rules that defines permissible structures within a society. Within these permissible structures systems and processes of institutionalization take place that routinize the maintenance and control of behaviour. The *shariah* as a direct expression of *din* is a body of normative rules with superior authority; it can give rise to dependent bodies that devise laws and routines of action. Important distinctions need to be made and understood in the ways these two spheres interact, especially the rationale upon which their interaction is based. Continuity and change are processes in all aspects of individual and communal life; how they are understood, how they can be incorporated, whether change is always conceived as a threat or only some kinds of change, are all part of the interaction between institutions, the *shariah* and the *din* of a community. How change affects a community is related to the nature of the permissible structures recognized by a community and how they are operated. At the limits of the permissible structure are the articulation points that determine the view of change. Every community has a history, as well as its own distinctive means of recording it. Studying what a community records as history and how it manipulates history within the present is a powerful indicator for the Islamic anthropologist, of the conception of interaction between the hierarchy of spheres of meaning of a community.

Minhaj is also a contextualization of *din*—in the last chapter we referred to it as the way of life of a community in a general sense. *Minhaj* as an interpretation of *din* must also be normative, a translation of ultimate reality definitions into patterns of routine action and behaviour. We take *minhaj* to signify the diffused socialization processes of a community that give form to its cultural behaviour, in the specific sense of acquired behaviour in community, and attach all manners, customs and products of the individual and community to the meaningful realm of their *din*. Again one is seeking to understand *minhaj* as an interpretive rendition through permissible structures that controls the cultural property and behaviour of a community. In studying *minhaj* one is looking at the signs and symbols and systems of communication through which ultimate meanings are diffused throughout a community. An important aspect of *minhaj* would be to investigate how it interacts with the institutions derived from *shariah*. While both relate to *din* and contextualize the *din* according to the circumstances of the community, as a realm of more diffuse meaning *minhaj* contains sources of ideas and principles of action that can be critical of the operation of the institutional forms of the *shariah*. The socialization of behaviour patterns is normative, concerned with values and related to the ultimate sources of meaning of a community, and can pose challenges to instituted authority and generate alternative ideas about appropriate behaviour. How the realms of *shariah* and *minhaj* interact is an important dynamic of a community and a potential source of autonomous change. The *minhaj* focuses attention on how the *din* collectively shared by a community is internalized in the individual to generate common patterns of action. But it is essentially the sphere where one can investigate the mechanism of incorporation of the individual into community, the manner of behaviour deemed appropriate by the community as a whole and that actually results in the action of the individual. It is also important to consider the scope for individual flexibility and differentiation within the norms of a community. The content of *minhaj* will be important when one tries to understand the ease with which dissension can arise in a community, the extent of tolerance, what sanction and authority these have, what response they will occasion and how they are incorporated into the community or seen as a threat. *Minhaj* is also a sphere of institutionalization, but the diffuse institutionalization of patterns of individual action and behaviour within the community.

The concepts and orientations we have outlined, *ummah*, *din*, *shariah* and *minhaj* are the foundation of ethnography in Islamic anthropology, but ethnography is not and can never be pure description since pure description does not exist. The ethnography of Islamic anthropology is ordered by the objectives of enquiry we have set out above. To outline the approach of Islamic anthropology to ethnography we will suppose an Islamic anthropologist has materialized in the midst of a community and discuss how he/she would set about asking questions to learn the *din* of that community in all its contextual specifics. Our anthropologist would begin by seeking to identify the *shariah* and *minhaj* as formulated and understood in that community. This would involve trying to understand how values have been actualized in the specific circumstances applicable to that community. What constitutes values such as justice, *adl*; communal wellbeing, *istislah*; knowledge, *ilm*; limits or parameters, *hadd*; permissible, *halal*; prohibited, *haram*; peace, *aman*; formal allegiance to authority, *bai'ah*; consensus, *ijma*; reform and setting things to right, *islah*; reality and 'true' facts, *haqiqah*; order and rule, *hukm*; waste and profligacy, *israf*; moral review, *istihsab*; custom and practice, *istihsan*; and communal autonomy, *istiqlal*, can be understood only through social mechanisms. The actualization is both an interpretation and itself a process of balancing and integrating specific limits, recognizing that the importance of some interactions and articulations require definite institutional form, while others are subsidiary, to be effected as a consequence of the operation of defined institutions.

Having learnt the specifics of a community, the Islamic anthropologist would be keen to study the implications and consequences arising from the system and process of that community: what constraints affect the operation of values; are there constraints in the institutionalization that would generate problems; what conditions within the environment or in relationship to other communities would occasion these problems; could one resolve these problems within the institutional form of a community; are there mechanisms which could fulfil this function, or would problems occasion crisis; what effect would crisis have on the community; what range of responses would they have to crisis or be able to justify and effect in such a case. It should be clear that the Islamic anthropologist must be interested in ethnography not as a static reportage upon community but to learn about community as a dynamic process, a process that must be adaptive because it must confront and integrate change, or at least be able to absorb and respond to change. How change occurs, what constitutes change and the impact of change is seen as directly related to the institutional form given in interpretation of the community's *din*, *shariah*, and *minhaj*.

The ideas, questions and evaluations of the Islamic anthropologist are informed in a dialogue with the people they study; the members of the community must be active participants in research. The Islamic anthropologist, like any other anthropologist, is influenced by his own social and cultural background. The most sensitive part of the ethnographic exercise is precisely in the anthropologist's own assumptions, and it is here that ethnography must involve an active learning from the people and dialogue of ideas if he is ever to get beyond an in-built ethnocentrism to attain the objective of Islamic anthropology. Unless dialogue is involved, ethnography would merely become a way of confirming the limited and partial understanding of the meaning of concepts and values within Muslim civilization in time and space. Instead of expanding understanding as the objective of enquiry, differences of opinion would inevitably lead to people of other communities being seen as 'other'. The essence of dialogue is the founding proposition that values have meaning shared by both the observer and observed through their difference of approach to actualizing these values in a way of life. The abstract conceptual meaning of concepts and values have significance only when they are realized in human action, where both observer and observed stand in the same relation to the intention and purpose of those concepts and values.

This particular understanding of ethnography obviously implies the broad outlines of methodology: questioning based upon identifying the values actualized and operationalized through systems of process. It also should make it clear that participant observation must be the principal technique. The literary sources of a literate society must also be studied; they are part of the network of interactions that are the community in time and space. It is precisely because *din*, *shariah* and *minhaj* are taken as hierarchical principles standing behind observed action and interpreted in observed action that ultimately the nature and parameters of human interpretive interactions can be understood only by participant observation. The basis of community and human action is by definition for Islamic anthropology qualitative and evaluative; discernment and understanding can therefore be achieved only by incorporating a qualitative and evaluative element. From the standpoint of knowledge within an Islamic perspective there is no way a subjective element can be removed. The important question is recognizing and integrating it as a constructive part of the process of study. Ethnography would also essentially rely upon learning the language of a community in an association with the community that is conducted over an extended period of time. The techniques of sample and survey, the collecting of statistical information, is an important part of ethnography, and of recording ethnographic data. However, without the exercise of participant observation, what to sample and survey, what statistical information to collect, would always rely upon the ethnocentric notions of the anthropologist and therefore be questionable items of limited utility for study.

The dialogue of ethnography we have outlined is one part of Islamic anthropology. In itself it promotes a breed of social scientists fitted to reflect upon the nature of their own community, their civilization of origin. There is a second dimension of the discipline where this is a direct and necessary part of the discourse of Islamic anthropology. We have said the subject is a comparative social science; on the basis of its own ethnography Islamic anthropologists can engage upon analysis, cross-communal comparisons. Here Muslim communities and civilization are involved as consonant equivalent sources of comparative data, and must necessarily be included. Muslim civilization and the diversity of Muslim communities are not matters to be assumed and left as unanalysed baselines for comparison; they are proper subjects for ethnography as much as any non-Muslim community. By definition Muslim communities and civilization are themselves only interpretive renditions in time and space of the concepts and values of Islam that Islamic anthropology is trying to understand.

By looking at the diverse ways communities have been structured and how they function, comparative analysis is seeking insight into the opportunities and potential that can be incorporated into the activity of any community to enhance the delivery and fulfilment of values. It also examines the constraints that generate problems in communal existence, so that a community can be better informed and better able to avoid or resolve these predicaments. As an explicatory social science Islamic anthropology is concerned to accumulate knowledge that informs practical policy making.

The relationships between conceptual objectives and their embodiment in different patterns of institutionalization is also an aspect of the study. It is concerned with questions such as whether there is a carrying capacity for certain institutions, whether certain values can best be fulfilled only by small units, either by small-scale communities or at the level of small units within a community. Does an increase in the population pose a challenge to institutions in their ability to fulfil their value load; what consequences would this have in terms of the operation of the institution, the pattern of relationships within the community and attitudes to institutional and individual behaviour? How can institutions adapt to different kinds of change; are some kinds of institutions inherently better able to adapt; what characteristics facilitate this process; and does it occur at the expense of any aspects of its value load? Are there certain types of institutions which are better at achieving and preserving values in community; and what general principles does this indicate for our understanding of the operation of community as a moral domain? Community as a moral domain is a product of interaction; material conditions are part of the system of interaction impinging upon all the other dimensions of human existence. How a community employs and evaluates material concerns is related to the exercise of choice and decision governed by values.

Comparative analysis is a process that works through classification and typology. Within the context of Islamic anthropology, as we have already discussed, these are not ranking procedures. We can extend this. Islamic anthropology is concerned with the diversity of community, studying archaeology, history and the communal forms of the present day to acquire information. It regards community as a dynamic form that must encounter and integrate change, or respond to or be affected by change in a variety of ways. History is an important aspect of any community; there can be no community without history. The record of interpretation of *din*, *shariah*, and *minhaj* in history conditions the interactions that constitute community in the present, and how its processes and institutions are understood and operated.

Community as a system of interaction confronts and encounters change and is a system for the accumulation of knowledge, but accumulation of knowledge that enables the manipulations of either the social, cultural, intellectual, scientific, material or even the spiritual spheres is always a contextual progress, subject to question from the same standpoint that renders all communities equivalent. For western anthropology in its modern Malinowskian reformulation all societies are always only present, history has been collapsed. For Islamic anthropology all communities are always presently engaged, dynamically related to a notion of progress and reformative developmental procedure that is common for all communities through all time and space. There may indeed be communities that were or are superior, but that is not a function of their classification through institutional forms, material conditions, ideas or beliefs; their superiority would be evaluated and recognized in the right action undertaken by people in that community and by the community as a whole. The challenge to human betterment is ever present in all communities. The accumulation of knowledge and refinement of our understanding on how human betterment can be instituted is the objective of Islamic anthropology. Such insight can be derived from any and all communities.

In this broad review of how Islamic anthropology would go about its business we have conceived of Islamic anthropology as a unitary social science of mankind in community. We can think of no valid justification for making any division analogous to the distinction between western anthropology and western sociology. Western anthropology has concerned itself with 'primitive' societies, or in modern parlance, small-scale, non-literate societies. Western sociology has concerned itself with 'advanced' society which is complex, large-scale. The only meaningful distinction between these two western disciplines arises from the nature of the comparisons they make with the model of western civilization, or which they seek to pretend they do not make. Quite simply, for Islamic anthropology all communities as moral domains are equivalent and are subject to the same set of conceptual principles, are all presently engaged upon the same challenge, whenever they existed or wherever they exist, they all enable one to reflect upon the implications and consequences of values, and the same values will be differentially embodied and expressed by them all. There are no meaningful dividing lines between some kinds of community and other kinds of community, most definitely not between Muslim communities and non-Muslim communities. Any attempt to create dividing lines would be more likely to generate false intellectual propositions than insight. One can advance any name one likes for the discourse of study outlined here, the only significant point about naming is that what is named remains a unitary study of mankind in community. The unitary nature of the discipline is, we maintain, the distinctive Islamic imperative.

On the basis that the discourse we call Islamic anthropology is a unitary study of mankind in community, we accept it is a vast and wide-ranging discourse of knowledge. This is not quite as alarming as might at first sight appear. What we feel we have been shaping is a discourse that gives the disciplinary framework for many associated fields of specialization, which is quite a different matter from distinguishing disciplines such as western anthropology and western sociology. Within the disciplinary framework we call Islamic anthropology, multi-disciplinary studies would need to be undertaken by the anthropologist. Economics, political studies, international relations, law, ecology, environmental studies, social policy studies, administrative studies, history and archaeology all contribute to and can take from it. Perhaps just as much as we have been shaping an Islamic anthropology we have been reflecting upon the orientations and themes that must be common to all Islamic social sciences. That we cannot assume those orientions to be well known and refine a small space within them for anthropology is a function of the current state of Muslim scholarship, a bench mark of how far the islamization of knowledge has yet to go. It is to a consideration of what presently constitutes the discourse of Islamic social science that we turn next.

Notes

1. Modern discussions of *tawhid* are Faruqi, *Tawhid* and Kotb, *The Characteristics of the Islamic Concept.*

2. Sardar, *Islamic Futures.*

3. This is used as the basis of an exposition of Islamic anthropology by Shariati, *On the Sociology of Islam.*

6

Discourse and Dialogue

The distinguishing characteristics of the Islamic anthropology we have outlined are its concept of man, and its concept of community. These concepts are taken directly from the source of Islam, the Qur'an, and provide the basic building blocks for a discourse of social science. It is on the basis of these two Islamic concepts and their entailments, as well as their integration and interrelationship with the whole repertoire of other Islamic concepts, that Islamic anthropology is a distinct and different discourse of knowledge from western anthropology.

Disciplinary boundaries are an outgrowth of particular conceptual propositions; the naming and ordering of things is never merely a matter of convenience but a convenient expression of the logic of conceptual implications. The labels applied to disciplines describe their boundaries and their content, what one seeks to learn about and how one searches for this knowledge. They have been formalized in the course of intellectual history and bear the marks of the history of ideas within a civilization, being thus inseparable from a world view rooted in particular concepts. The history of ideas may revise and radically alter the content, interpretation and understanding of concepts, yet those concepts are specific, the patrimony of a civilization and its world view. The labels applied to disciplines of knowledge call to mind the process by which continuity and change of ideas rooted in concepts has occurred within the intellectual and academic tradition of a civilization.

Within western civilization the label anthropology conveys a potted biography sufficient to locate the activities and general concerns of the anthropologist. If the general public is often confused about the exact nature of anthropology, it is still true that their confused images are directly related to what has been done and said in pursuit of anthropology in the course of its intellectual history, that these ideas still inform the research of professional anthropologists, even if they understand them and relate to them in a markedly different way to the lay person. Within academic circles the label anthropology is sufficiently expressive of its boundaries and content to enable it to be refined and classified to encompass a host of different paradigms and orientations, as well as specializations that were or are currently operative. The label signifies, and what it signifies can be classified to enable informed discourse. So anthropology is the general field dominated in Britain and the United States by social anthropology, whereas in France anthropology is restricted to physical anthropology, while social anthropology is conducted under the title of sociology. While British and American anthropologists are concerned with society, for Americans the terminology cultural anthropology, with its strong links with their concern for ethnology, is more common. Signifier and signified, anthropology and its content, match because the signifier is understood as a study of mankind pursued through the investigation of other cultures by means of distinctive concepts of man and culture. On the basis of these two concepts the variety and diversity of all anthropological enquiry can be classified and located as a mutually intelligible discourse, utilizing common theories and terminology even when they are expressed as different paradigms. In other words, western anthropology is a field where eclecticism can run rife because the boundaries and content of anthropology are secure matters of convention. What is signified as anthropology is also available to other disciplines and is able to interact with other disciplines within the whole context of western ideas because they share a common intellectual history, and a common fund of conceptual thought.

The Islamic anthropology we have been concerned with does not signify in the same way. From a discussion of the conventional nature of knowledge we sought to demonstrate that the knowledge of the dominant discipline of anthropology is conventional only to the civilization of its origin, that is, western anthropology. By redefining anthropology as subordinate to a distinct conceptual and civilizational fabric, that of Islam, we began to examine the concepts that would determine the boundaries and content of a new discipline. This discipline would be the corollary of the entirety of western anthropology, not merely a variant. We have used the label Islamic anthropology as an investigative tool to establish the necessity of a distinct discourse of social enquiry based upon Islamic concepts and to examine the content and concerns it would encompass. The label has been a useful tool in arriving at the threshold of a new discipline; if that discipline is to flourish, we must seriously question whether the label appropriately signifies this future potential and the work that must be undertaken to realize that potential.

In seeking to shape an Islamic anthropology what has been uncovered are the fundamental building blocks common to any social science arising from the world view of Islam. To label this conceptual outline Islamic anthropology and leave the matter there would compound the many layers of confusion that presently bedevil the enterprise of the islamization of knowledge. The most important function of the naming of things is to signify the conceptual load that determines the boundaries and content of a discipline. To describe our subject as Islamic anthropology without further comment or refinement appears to locate the discipline most clearly by reference to western anthropology, whose predominant concerns and orientations it does not share. Within western anthropology it also raises confusion. There is a growing interest in the anthropology of Islam, often loosely designated Islamic anthropology, amongst western anthropologists, by which we mean those who utilize the conceptual premises of western anthropology as their starting point and methodology, whatever their national or ethnic origin. Constructive dialogue with western disciplines is not merely possible, it is an essential aspect of the intellectual growth of modern Muslim scholarship. Dialogue is not helped when the starting point of debate is obscured. The label Islamic anthropology does not make it sufficiently clear, given the conventions that already exist, that the source of discussion is to be found in the implications and consequences that arise from pursuing our enquiries from different conceptual starting points.

Furthermore, within the sphere of Muslim scholarship and the process of the islamization of knowledge the unqualified label 'Islamic anthropology' would seem to signal that interdisciplinary relations among islamized disciplines would merely follow the pattern set by western knowledge. In the current islamization of the social sciences the objective is to devise Islamic anthropology, sociology, psychology, economics, and so on with no hint that the classification and connections of these disciplines, once islamized, might acquire a different rationale and therefore relationship in the process from the one derived from western disciplines. As we have already tried to make clear, this must be the case. For example, Islamic concepts allow no meaningful distinction between Islamic anthropology and sociology, where such a distinction can be made and sustained in western scholarship. Conceptually, we have argued, Islam recognizes all communities as analogous. No relevance is attached to nor can there be any possible basis for recognizing stages of development in the form of communities as demarcating conceptually significant types of human organization. From an Islamic perspective the study of mankind in community is a unitary enquiry where the same relevant questions and topics of concern apply to all communities, whatever their type, organization or technological expertise. A classification of types of community within an Islamic enquiry is a recognition of important variations in the constraints that influence the patterns of human organization and action. Yet the objective of questioning the constraints particular to each class or type of community is the same: to develop an evaluative study of the way in which human organization and action enables, sustains and fulfils or disables, undermines or impedes the moral purpose of existence that is common to all mankind whatever kind of community they live in. Therefore, not only is information from all types of community relevant to this unitary enquiry but the terminology and methodology must be developed to generate information from all types of community as a single discourse if the significance of the diversity of human community is to be understood.

The problem of naming and classifying that faces Muslim scholars is part of constructing a whole spectrum of social sciences based upon Islamic conceptual premises. It is a comment on the contemporary state of Muslim scholarship that despite a decade of exhortation and discussion under the rubric of the islamization of knowledge, the literature is stalled at stating the need for Islamic social science and pointing to the problems of western disciplines, but lacks serious consideration of the Islamic concepts that would enable naming and classification to begin.

Even more perplexing is the fact that we have a flourishing discipline of Islamic economics, with all the attendant intellectual paraphernalia of university departments, lectureships, professorships, learned journals, conferences and seminars, entirely unsupported by any serious body of work on the nature of community and social process from the perspective of Islam. Economic behaviour is part of social behaviour, monetary choices and monetized relationships are directed and respond to a whole range of social influences beyond the comparative advantage sought by the rational, amoral, conceptual abstraction that is economic man. Economic man, within the conventions of western scholarship, is identifiable and classifiable for study precisely because he exists within a particular conception both of the nature of man and the nature of society; without that support structure economic man does not make sense. The scope of economics, whether in western knowledge or on the basis of Islamic economic injunctions, embraces far more than monetized activity and thereby obviously forms part of the basic conception of society and community. Thought, enquiry and planning within an Islamic economics, let alone an Islamic economy, cannot exist in a vacuum where the nature of community and the effect of economic activity within that community is an assumed afterthought.

Homo Islamicus does not exist solely because Muslims must answer to a set of economic injunctions in the Qur'an. Whether we properly understand the nature of Homo Islamicus and appropriately direct his economic affairs in the implementation of those injunctions can be considered only when we comprehend how the whole range of the 'economic' integrates and interacts with the entire conception of Islamic community. Islamic economics exists not because of economics as a sphere of knowledge but because Islam informs us that mankind cannot live by bread alone and the getting of our daily bread is part of the exercise of our whole being—biological, physical, social, intellectual, moral and spiritual—and as such we are accountable to the Creator for all activities within our natural, communal setting. If Islamic economics is to survive it cannot continue by perpetual activation of the Indian rope trick, it needs to be anchored in, and a contributory element of, an Islamic social science, where the whole range of 'economic' injunctions and exhortations in the Qur'an and Sunnah cause us to reflect on the nature of mankind and community, as well as the implementation and application of these regulations to actual human communities. This enquiry will take Islamic economics into new areas of questioning, quite distinct from those of western economics and intimately related to the enquiry of other Islamic social sciences. Where and how the boundary lines will be drawn, how the concerns of these different disciplines will be classified, will be established by convention in the endeavours of Muslim scholars. The convention will arise from the questions we ask and the theories we put forward, but their origin will be in the consequences of the conceptual premises of Islam that generate the questions and orientation of enquiry. Islamic social science cannot come of age until it gets beyond the convenience of using western disciplinary labels in the naming of things, and establishes a classificatory structure of ideas and disciplines upon the basis of Islamic conceptual enquiry.[1]

Naming and classification is all about establishing relationships and getting things in their right place and order, another vital reason why the unqualified title Islamic anthropology is a liability for the future of the discipline. In part this is merely a reflex of the familiarity of the dominant western usage of terms, while the concepts and terminology of an Islamic social science are, if not completely unfamiliar, then certainly a less frequented area of our mental outlook. Unchecked, this reflex renders islamization in its entirety a hollow exercise. Retaining the familiar terminology of western disciplines, even with a revised, islamized meaning, is a precarious procedure. Nor is it a practice likely to get easier as time goes on; subtlety of meaning is hard enough to achieve in the first place let alone having to express it in a complicated double code.

The best cautionary lesson on the problems of advancing an Islamic discipline on the basis of western terminology is provided by the work of Ali Shariati, a major figure whose work must be studied by anyone interested in an Islamic social science. What makes Shariati difficult is that one has to read his work very carefully to realize that he is using familiar social science terminology in a new way, not just giving basic definitions based on Qur'anic conceptual principles and then carrying on regardless with the accepted conventions of western social science, but carrying these definitions through in the manipulation of western terminology. It is a significance many Muslim writers, who refer to Shariati, seem to have missed. Shariati was an outstanding thinker whose career was sadly circumscribed by the times in which he had to live and work. He has left no major coherent social science study yet his lectures clearly demonstrate a creative imagination, one that was looking for conceptual starting points of enquiry from Qur'anic sources; his use of the concept of *al nas*, the people, is one all Muslim social scientists will have to start thinking about. A scholar with the stature of Shariati could, perhaps, use conventional western social science terminology and mean something different by the terms and make the procedure work but it is no guarantee this is the best way forward for Islamic social science. At present and for a long time to come Muslim scholars are likely to approach the field through a western dominated education, thus having a mind already groomed in conceptual meaning through paradigms that establish relationships and their associated questions. To use terms with an accepted western meaning to mean something else calls for a tortuous double-think that holds the dangerous prospect of having to fall back upon the established practice of western disciplines even when the logic of Islamic implications should be leading us to investigate new questions and new relationships.

Definition of terms is the fundamental procedure of a social science discipline. This is even more the case for western anthropology and sociology since they labour under the burden of using common language with technical implications. The words society, culture, class are both common parlance and terms with specific implications for the specialist. Further, each school, trend or paradigm within these disciplines has a refinement of definition that signifies major differences of orientation and implication in the manipulation of information. To add to this overcrowded field an Islamic conceptual definition of society, culture, and so on, using only these terms would compound the problem. It is possible to have discussion at cross purposes, where participants are unaware that they are talking about different realities because they are using the same words, but this negates the insight and stimulation that can occur in trying to understand the implications that follow from seeing reality differently.

But the real defect in holding to the familiar western terminology is the relationship implied and assumed that follows from expressing an Islamic discipline in the terminology of a western discipline. In effect it elevates the terminology to the level of universals with neutral definitional characteristics that any scholar can utilize in any manner he or she likes, without doing violence to sense and meaning. What scholars do in pursuing their study then becomes a matter of providing meaning by adding refinements to a universal neutral terminology. The meaning and the specific significance of the use of a term, its actual definition in the course of intellectual enquiry, is then of lower status than the term itself in its neutral state of minimal definition. The neutral terms that are accepted as universals and supposedly available for Islamic discourse are the conventional terminology of dominant western discourses of knowledge. It is understandable that Muslim scholars who approach these terms from a different civilizational history do not share the same response to the redolence of words as their western colleagues, but it is no excuse for being totally blind to their conceptual significance. There is nothing scientifically neutral about the terms 'man', 'culture' and 'society' or even 'science'; even as common English words they are tied to conceptual origins with meaningful definitional significance, as well as being tied to a whole western civilizational history of ideas wherein their conceptual meaning and implications have been discussed.

In effect what Muslim scholars are doing when they use western scientific terminology and the methodology that is invariably linked to these words, is to delink terminology and methodology from discourse. Since discourse is a convention of knowledge that is historically specific to a civilization, this delinking renders terminology totally meaningless. The procedure amounts to accepting the argument of the neutrality and value-freeness of 'scientific' enquiry. This would consequently be meaningless, however, for it would entail imposing western terminology and methodology upon Islamic enquiry. The gateway to contemporary Islamic knowledge is via a scientific understanding developed elsewhere. The procedure of islamized knowledge is to delink these terms and methods from the associations attached to them in western discourse, their secular and materialist interpretation, and instead overlay them with the values of Islam and incorporate into them the specific injunctions that constitute the operative aspects of Islam.

The only matter for an islamized discipline becomes procedure, resulting in an unenlightening discussion whose only discernible objective is the application of Islamic injunctions to modern Muslim society. Instead of a way of thought we are offered a way of discussing the possibilities of doing a certain limited set of things to Muslim society. Islamized knowledge is therefore made particular and specific to Muslims, a parochial concern, a way of looking inward at ourselves as Muslims in the modern world that claims to be a synthesis of knowledge but, in fact, is a rag-bag collection of mismatched assumptions. This is what we are offered as Islamic sociology by Ba-Yunus and Ahmad.[2]

In such an approach to islamization the relationships are the wrong way round. It is the Islamic concepts that should give rise to the definition of terms and the devising of methodology. We have tried to emphasize the distinctness of Islamic concepts by working from Arabic terms, such as *fitrah, ummah, din,* for this forces one to deploy one's development of the implications of the concept in discrete terminology. We have tried, as far as possible, to be consistent in this practice, not using the term society but rather community as the English rendition of *ummah,* for example, to signify that what follows from the concept of *ummah* is not the same as the assumptions entailed in the term society. Where we have examined a characteristic of the Islamic outlook for which we have, as yet, no obvious Arabic term then we have chosen a word with no associations within western social science, as in the use of the word consonance. The point of the exercise is not pedantry but a recognition that we are dealing with a conceptual fabric, that of Islam, that is a totality, a whole system of interconnected and interrelated terms that are mutually defining. Our enquiry begins with the concepts and relationships set out in the sources of Islam and is directed by their logic and orientations, not by some idealized 'scientific' necessity established by the conventions of western scholarship.

Western scientific terminology is neutral and value-free only when the value load of its concepts are taken for granted. Far from being above value commitment, operating in some rarefied atmosphere of pure logic and reason the western scholar is operating within a specifically value-defined arena of knowledge that depends entirely upon conceptual values. Islamization is not a procedure, it is a leap of imagination, the leap out of the assumed universal imperative of the western defined interpretation of knowledge as neutral and value-free and into an acknowledgement that an intellectual convention can be created and sustained in pursuit of knowledge only by commitment to concepts and their value load. This shift, this imaginative leap into a different mindset, we see as the sum total of the process of islamization. Once made, the leap of imagination must be signified by a change in the language of discourse, that is by the use of a specific and distinct terminology if that discourse is to be intelligible. Thereafter, instead of looking for islamization, one will be involved directly in pursuit of knowledge. A convention will then have been opened that must properly be described as Islamic enquiry.

Once our terminology is composed of Islamic concepts in their original language and the essence of an islamized discipline becomes clear, it is all about asking relevant questions. The relevant questions concern the meaning of accepted Qur'anic terms: what do they imply? What are their consequences in ordering our understanding of reality? How do the terms lead us to see the world around us? What do they make significant in the action, organization and practice of human existence? This might seem the most self-evident of commonplaces; in fact, it is in marked distinction to what is offered by much of the literature under the heading of islamization of knowledge.

Most of the small body of literature on islamizing the social sciences has a very particular stamp.[3] The overriding impression it creates is of seeking to reassure the Muslim by the restatement of certain Islamic verities that social science is a permissible undertaking. The trouble is that the Islamic verities are presented as static, stating formal necessities such as the way a Muslim must think or act, and they therefore pose problems for the existing practice of social science. Now a formal necessity exists because Islam is taken as a static repository of truth, a given as formulated in Muslim history and as applying to Muslims. An Islamic social science on this basis will only give the appearance of being dynamic; it will be dynamic because the social reality of Muslim society has been changed from the outside, creating the need for a certain flexibility in the application of Islamic techniques, the operation of Islamic injunctions in society. The only other dynamism such a discipline can demonstrate is the dynamic of complaint because the means of studying society as received through the conventions of western social science do not conform to certain essentials of the static Islamic eternal verities. With this kind of islamization the relationship of the Muslim scholar to Islam is in the wrong order, for the convention of Muslim history, from which modern Muslim scholars see themselves as ruptured, is subsumed within the basic conceptual definition of Islam. The hierarchy of relationships we considered earlier has been omitted.

The fixity from which a hierarchy of relationships derives is that the concepts of Islam are the eternal created verities which are actual and therefore discernible in the world around us, whether in the workings of the natural world or in the workings of mankind in community. Since the verities are universal, they are not confined to Muslim society, but apply to and are a way of knowing about all human community throughout the whole of human history. The truth is actual as created by God; Islam, as revealed in the Qur'an and exemplified in the Sunnah, is a guidance to understanding and learning about this actual truth, of which only God knows all. So the Muslim in any time or place, in any generation or human social condition relates to Islam as a belief in the actual truth that must be sought through the exertion of understanding and enquiry by conscience, logic, reason, intellectual rigour and intuition. Belief in a revealed actual truth is not the same thing as understanding it, which can come only by questioning and critical enquiry. This quest for understanding must always be an open system, not one closed by the rigid restatement of its basic propositions. God alone knows all, and even if the Muslim believes that mankind is perfectible according to the guidance of Islam in time and space he also believes that mankind is fallible and therefore can never indulge himself by assuming that he has attained perfect understanding. Perfect understanding awaits us outside time and space on the Last Day. Within the confines of the human condition we can only do our best to achieve understanding of the actual truth with the resources at our disposal and in the context of our own times and circumstances. This puts the Muslim scholar of today in exactly the same relationship to the concepts of Islam as the great minds of Muslim history—a fact the scholars of the past were more conscious of than most of the contemporary ones seem to be.

There are no Islamic propositions that can be stated as self-evident with fixed implications. Contemporary enquiry is the pursuit of the meaning of these very statements and propositions and therefore must begin with our asking questions about them, not making unquestioned assumptions on the basis of them. The use that is made of Islamic concepts, or the statement of Qur'anic *ayat* in the literature on islamizing the social sciences, is either taking them for granted as enabling legislation or relying upon the tradition of understanding of these concepts and statements in Muslim history. Taking meanings for granted is obviously no basis for a thriving intellectual discourse, but rather its negation. It is the relationship to classical Muslim discourse that needs to be carefully considered. The classical Muslim scholars were perfectly clear that the Qur'an and its meaning are not self-evident; the entire development of Islamic enquiry that is *fiqh*, the conceptual training ground of all the great Muslim thinkers, is a demonstration of this fact. They enquired critically and carefully into the circumstances of the revelation of the Qur'an and the nature of Makkan society at the time of the Prophet in order to inform their understanding of the meaning of concepts and injunctions. Just as they made clear the need to contextualize one's understanding of the circumstances of revelation to appreciate the distinction between the universal and the particular, or the way the particular made clear a general principle, so the enquiry of the classical scholars was itself contextual. Their understanding was derived by asking questions based on the problems they perceived. Before we can understand the thinking of the great Muslim scholars of the past we need to know more about the past history of Muslim society. The nature of their community and its problems is part of making comprehensible the understanding they derived from their Islamic enquiry.

Just as the questions asked by the classical Muslim scholars have relevance by reference to their historical context, so too must the significance of their answers be related to their historical context. Rather than having answered all questions for all time, as is the oft-heard boast made on their behalf by their successors, the traditional Muslim scholars or *ulema* of today, they asked and answered specifically defined questions of historic relevance that also have a general validity for other times and places, with different social circumstances. This general validity, as well as the specific historical relevance, are both matters that have to be investigated. In short, we desperately need a

Muslim quest into the history of Islamic ideas if the legacy of the great Muslim scholars is to have a role in furthering and forwarding Islamic studies today.

The classical Muslim scholars asked all the questions they found relevant, not all the questions it is possible for human beings to ask. They certainly could not have asked questions relevant to circumstances they never encountered or could not have imagined, such as those applicable today. Many classical scholars raised hypothetical topics for speculation, the famed angels on a pinhead kind of questions that al-Ghazzali condemned as irrelevant even in his own day. Some of these hypothetical questions may be considered to cover circumstances that have actually occurred in Muslim society since that time. But when a hypothetical situation actually occurs the host of circumstances and constraints involved may be quite different from those of the hypothetical speculation. How classical Muslim thinkers speculated is certainly informative, but it is not the sum total of what it is possible or necessary to think. That is to heap on the heads of an undeserving group of thinkers the same kind of presumption contemporary Muslims are fond of finding fault with in modern western scholarship, namely the elevation of the human intellect to the same level as the Divine.

The great issue that has to be resolved by contemporary Muslim scholars is the question of authority. In an earlier chapter we discussed the authority of the Islamic concepts and the sources of Islam and developed the notion of hierarchy whereby all Muslims stood in an interpretive relationship to the created Islamic concepts and the sources of Islam. Contemporary Muslim thought is not as concerned with these issues as it is with the meaning and content of the authority of the interpretive thought of classical Muslim scholars and thinkers. Most writers merely accept the scholars' authority without recourse to defining the meaning or content of that term; others grant them authority, again without defining the term itself, to emphasize the greater intellectual and spiritual exertions undertaken by the classical scholars than are evidenced by their latter day followers in pursuit of knowledge. In neither usage does the term authority significantly assist the accumulation of Islamic knowledge today. In the first instance it leads to mere repetition of familiar formulations of what is called Islamic thinking without these formulations eliciting any further insight into meaning, implications and consequences that would inform their applicability or relevance to the conditions of the modern world. The authority of classical Muslim scholars is used in statements that do not generate relevant questions by those writers who claim to be islamizing the social sciences. In the second use of authority, while we may agree that the great classical scholars were superior to modern scholars, they are not unchallengeable and should not be invested with significance that is not based on careful argument related to specific things they said or thought—this use of the term authority implies they are.

Authority is an acquired characteristic conferred and confirmed by a community. A convention of intellectual enquiry is indeed a process of conferring authority upon certain agreed ideas, modes of interpretation and so on, but the process must involve the actual scrutiny of ideas for the insight they offer, for the way they enable the manipulation of information that tells us more about the world around us and elucidates how we relate to the world or other people in such a way that it enables a better understanding of right action. The authority of the great scholars of the past lies not in the restatement of what they said but in the relevance of what they said for a better understanding of the reality in which we live.

Nothing illustrates better the misuse made of the work of classical Muslim scholars than the almost universal assertion made by those who would islamize the social sciences that anthropology and sociology were really founded by Ibn Battuta, al-Beruni and Ibn Khaldun. This argument of legitimation and reassurance from authority is made with no visible signs of any critical questioning into what these scholars wrote to substantiate the claim, or even to explain what it could possibly mean. It is quite sufficient, it would seem, that the great scholars wrote about other societies and Muslim community, and therefore they must have been engaged in sociology and anthropology. The terms sociology and anthropology are assumed to have a universal and obvious meaning and therefore, Islamic scholarship must have its own tradition of these disciplines. Where this tradition could possibly be located, since it is not mentioned in the work of the contemporary writers who announce its existence, remains a mystery. Presumably the Islamic tradition has been in suspended animation for a few centuries while the terms were formulated and gained currency elsewhere.

Those Muslim writers who labour under the delusion of seemingly thinking the mere names of great scholars are enough to secure the authority of an Islamic tradition in social science find their clearest example in the case of Ibn Khaldun who wrote in the fourteenth century CE. His work was discovered by Orientalists in the nineteenth century by which time western scholarship had already laid the foundations of its conventions of both sociology and anthropology. Because Ibn Khaldun wrote before the western foundation of these subjects, commentators in both western scholarship and Muslim writing have called him the 'Father of Sociology'. Only the most nominal kind of paternity by forced adoption after the fact is involved; there is nothing in the way of blood ties and *asibiyyah*. There is no evidence that any of Ibn Khaldun's ideas or approaches to the study of mankind played any part at all in the theoretical formation of either western anthropology or sociology; they gained currency amongst western scholars far too late for this to be the case and the origins of these disciplines within western ideas is too clearly known for there to be any doubt. If Ibn Khaldun founded a 'sociology' then it could not have been western sociology.

By glibly accepting Ibn Khaldun and the other great writers as founders of anthropology and sociology modern Muslim writers are showing they have no real regard for islamization as a conceptual process, and are reluctant to wrestle with ideas and meanings. The question is just what kind of anthropology or sociology were the classical scholars engaged in? What did they mean by the terminology they used? What were the conceptual orientations of their work? What kinds of assumptions did they make? What kinds of questions did they ask? What was the acknowledged objective of their enquiry? These are the questions that enable us to define and locate the kind of anthropology or sociology they were doing and on that basis decide whether it is best described by the words anthropology and sociology as they are understood in the western intellectual convention or require some new label. None of the writers whose purpose is islamizing the social sciences demonstrates any awareness of these questions. The only writer who has studied them is Aziz al-Azmeh, whose two books on Ibn Khaldun should serve as a reprimand to the would-be Islamic social scientists.

In his first study, *Ibn Khaldun in Modern Scholarship*, al-Azmeh looks at how the Orientalists responded to Ibn Khaldun, and how he entered into the discourse of modern western social science through their work. He makes it quite clear that the reputation of Ibn Khaldun in western social science is based upon the translation of his ideas according to the concepts and concerns of western convention, not upon understanding his thought within its own context. So ideas have been taken from Ibn Khaldun to fit in with the orientations of western social science, deploying arguments about the nature of society based on entirely secular and materialist propositions. And it is this use of Ibn Khaldun, a complete by-passing of his belief and thought process and Islamic concepts that is being hailed by our would-be Islamic social scientists. The point al-Azmeh misses is that even in the translation of his ideas to suit their purposes Ibn Khaldun has been of marginal interest to western social scientists, not a central thinker from whom theoretical insight must be drawn. Ibn Khaldun is made to move along with the western history of ideas, not contribute to its development. Probably the only leading western scholar who has used Ibn Khaldun's ideas in forming a theory is Ernst Gellner in his interpretation of Muslim society, thus making parochial an approach that Ibn Khaldun saw as universal.[4]

In his second book, *Ibn Khaldun: An Essay In Reinterpretation*, al-Azmeh presents a more contentious argument. Having satisfied himself that Ibn Khaldun was not questing after western social science nor laying its foundation, he then seems to fall into a common trap. Al-Azmeh accepts that sociology, indeed social science, can mean only the western convention, that there can be no other kind of sociology based on different conceptual principles. So his reinterpretation of Ibn

Khaldun within an Islamic context of his time cannot admit, even as a possibility, that Khaldun could point the way to a different kind of sociology. While there is a great deal in al-Azmeh's book that needs to be carefully considered, what he does by placing Ibn Khaldun in context is to destroy any possible significance of his ideas for future Muslim scholarship. Having used the history of ideas as a central technique, al-Azmeh seems determined to end it. His central argument is that Ibn Khaldun's objective was to establish a discourse of history that *ilm ul umran* was not a study of mankind in community in the sense of a social science but a serial narrative of human action, or, as al-Azmeh puts it, historical consecution.

This conclusion puts Ibn Khaldun beyond the thoughtless use made of his name by would-be Islamic social scientists. It settles little else. The world of significance al-Azmeh draws from his conclusion relies on the conventions of the disciplinary boundaries and attendant conceptual classification of knowledge devised in western scholarship. There, history and social science are distinct intellectual species. Western social science is ahistorical in its orientation, when it is not virulently anti-historical. Western social science could be described as the speculation on and search for those ahistorical regularities that explain contemporary conditions, thereby rendering history insignificant. We have pointed out that the relationship to history is a central problematique of modern western social anthropology, precisely because much of its terminology and concepts originated by abstracting differences occurring in history, and on the basis of these differences defining conceptual differences in the condition of mankind and society. The reaction against this evolutionary framework led to the rejection of history, or the reduction of history to a social category, Malinowski's manipulative social charter. The problem of history remains because the historical framework is embedded in the terms and concepts of the ahistorical western social sciences of today.

On the other hand the idea that history, even when it is dealing with the serial narration of action and events, is or must be blind to general speculation and the formulation of ideas about the nature of mankind and community as general principles, is a highly particular and partisan notion of history. It is perfectly clear from the contextualized interpretation of Ibn Khaldun's ideas that he did draw points of general principle from his examination of history and used general principles to order his examination of history. It is these ideas and orientations, that al-Azmeh argues were unconnected in Ibn Khaldun's mind, that can be examined by scholars involved in a critical enquiry of Islamic social science.

History is a major matter of classification facing the Islamic social sciences. From our discussion of basic concepts it is evident that we are convinced that history is an integral part of an Islamic social science understanding. The basic concept of mankind, *insan*, as defined by *fitrah*, *khilafah* and *din*, as well as the concept *ummah* describe the created capacities, status and condition in which mankind enters time and space, the realm of history. These concepts have explicatory power, the potential to unfold meaning and implications; they are an evaluative scale for the ordering, manipulation and classification of information and the accumulation of knowledge because they express actual truths about the nature and condition of mankind that are constant and underpin all the diversity of human action and events in history. Ali Shariati bases his entire anthropology upon the Islamic concept that mankind has free will, the ability to rise to be higher than the angels or to be lower than the brute beasts.[5] The evaluation and investigation of human action and events can make sense of mankind in their diversity and activity only when this possibility of variation, of following or deviating from a straight path, has the means, the investigative conceptual tools, to relate the mutable and changing to that which is constant and significant. Created actual truths are ahistorical because they are eternal and transcendent, but they can be appreciated only in history and by the way they render history meaningful. What is apparent in historical context and social circumstance has to be questioned for the similarities and differences it contains in relation to those conceptual principles that are always sensible to mankind, even if only in their violation. Quite simply, from the viewpoint of Islam, history is not an aimless, random succession of human actions and events but an ever-changing pattern whose sequence is continual and constantly related to actual verities embedded within them. Mankind can be properly understood only in relation to the transcendent eternal when comprehended within an historical setting. History is essentially part of the same enquiry for an Islamic social science.

In part it is al-Azmeh's insistence that Ibn Khaldun was concerned with history that confirms our view that the best label to describe the Islamic anthropology we have been shaping is *ilm ul umran*. This is not to say that contemporary Muslim scholarship should do only what Ibn Khaldun did but that the range and scope of what he did embraces the various elements that must necessarily be part of Islamic social science enquiry today. When we advance the label *ilm ul umran* it is as an appropriate description coined by Ibn Khaldun for a discourse of knowledge that both includes the matters he wrote about and goes far beyond the topics he considered, but without doing violence to the sense and meaning of the term he coined. The only way Muslim scholars can signify to themselves and others the nature of the task they are engaged in in islamizing the social sciences is in the development of our own terminology and methodology from a critical enquiry into the definition of basic concepts and conceptual propositions. From this task of definition a discrete system of classification and relationships arises that lead us to pose questions of actual human action in community. To call this enquiry *ilm ul umran*, an endeavour that can be described loosely in English as Islamic anthropology, carries a greater significance, a clearer indication of relevant questions and is a better basis for both discourse and dialogue than is the unqualified label Islamic anthropology. When the name of our discipline changes to *ilm ul umran* we signify that an entire system of Islamic thought is necessary to carry it forward. All our relationships of naming and classification can be got in the right order and right place to set an agenda of the relevant questions we need to address.

Accepting al-Azmeh's strictures that *ilm ul umran* has particular significance as used by Ibn Khaldun we feel that the rendition al-Azmeh gives of this significance is no block to the use we wish to make of the term. The intent of Ibn Khaldun's *Muqaddima* that introduces his *ilm ul umran*, al-Azmeh translates as 'a narrative of human aggregation which is the organized habitation (*umran*) of the world'. Not only does this seem to cover all the salient points we have discussed in relation to Islamic anthropology but to fit exactly to the logic of the conceptual building blocks we have outlined. Let us take the matter of 'a narrative', the point at which al-Azmeh sees Ibn Khaldun as locked into history rather than into anything approximating to social science. We have already made the point that there is no such thing as pure description or pure narrative, for they involve a selection, an ordering of pieces of information and this is done according to a theory-led interpretation of conceptual principles. A history or an ethnography begins with concepts and their definition and is deployed through the use of terminology and methodology arising from those concepts; both are always theoretically structured narrative. The function of *ilm ul umran* we are advancing then is based on the critical investigation into the significant points established by a narrative of the organized habitation of mankind. The conceptually structured narrative is subjected to questioning about the constraints that affect human action, how the nature, pattern and organization of human action presented in the narrative relates to and causes us to reflect upon and evaluate the nature and condition of mankind in community, how it explicates the concepts that are the origin and objective of enquiry. To have any utility or meaning a narrative must study and clearly establish the context of events, it must be both history and ethnography and identify significant historical and ethnographic elements.

As for 'human aggregation' being 'the organized habitation of the world' this is exactly the necessary consequence of the Islamic concepts we have considered as the basis of our enquiry. The created condition of mankind is to exist in human aggregation, that is, in relationship to other human beings. This necessary condition of existence is also created upon the basis of organized habitation, *umran*. The term *umran* is related to *ummah*, community, and the definitional significance of both terms is that all communities and therefore their individual members possess a *din*, with its attendant concepts of *shariah* and *minhaj*. The *din* is the body principles of organization, ways of thinking and doing that stem from a relationship to the Universal. The function of our enquiry is not a pure narration of these principles but critical questioning into how these principles are to be understood, the interpretations they have been given that enable us to develop an evaluative study that explicates meaning, implication and consequences.

Human beings cannot exist in isolation from each other, nor apart from an evaluative system of rules that define their identity and manner of living, a necessary conceptual proposition of the Islamic outlook. So the pursuit of *ilm ul umran* is universal in all significant applications of that term. Its conceptual premises are universal, applying to all mankind throughout all time and space because they express actual truths that enable information to be rendered meaningful. It is also universal in the sense that information must be gathered from all kinds of organized habitations that have existed in time and space if we are properly to understand and explicate these conceptual principles and their actual truth. The notion of diversity is subsumed within all these concepts, so our enquiry is properly concerned with studying the diversity of human community and explicating the significance of this diversity. Diversity is both the differences that stem from communities possessing different *din*, and the differences arising from diverse interpretations of the *din*. History is a necessary part of the focus; we are engaged in the diachronic, not merely the synchronic study of mankind in community because we are concerned to explicate and evaluate the significance of both continuity and change. Without integrating history as a fundamental perspective of our study we would be unable to distinguish what constitutes continuity or change, factors of central importance in an evaluative, explicatory study. Only a social science that is diachronic, that carefully investigates continuity and change, seeks to define these terms, their nature, causes and consequences and to this end entails historical study, can hope to gain any precision in seeking after the actual truths that remain constant and underpin all diversity in time and space. It must be able to discriminate and differentiate between apparent and actual change, the differences of fashion that signify nothing, from those that have significantly different consequences.

One point that should be made about the term *umran* is that it is most often used in contemporary Muslim writing in relation to human environment and the form of physical habitation, this application being a necessary part of its definition. It is also obvious from an Islamic perspective that the physical form of human environment cannot be dissociated from the whole system of which it is part and whose expression it is. The total system that explicates *umran* and gives it its organizational characteristics is biological, physical, social, moral, and spiritual, a system derived from *din*. The work being done on environmental studies and Islamic architecture therefore needs the support of, and falls within the confines of, Islamic social science. Here again the classification of disciplinary boundaries and relationships will be developed as our conventions are carried forward by sound contemporary scholarship.

Probably the greatest advantage gained by recognizing the Islamic anthropology we have been shaping as *ilm ul umran* is the redolence of the term *ilm* within the civilizational fabric of Islam. To locate our discourse as a branch of *ilm* firmly establishes the conceptual foundations as those of Islam, and therefore conditions the mindset of the Muslim scholar undertaking this branch of knowledge. Furthermore, one of the basic characteristics of the history of ideas in Muslim civilization on the subject of *ilm* has been the emphasis given to classification, virtually every classical thinker of note having advanced a classification of *ilm*, knowledge. Classification can go forward only by means of careful definition and by establishing the relationship of terms within a system. These associations of the term *ilm* are reminders and indicators of the task facing contemporary Muslim scholarship if it is not merely to parrot the formulations of its forebears on some indefinite and unquestioned authority, but to emulate them by furthering the accumulation of knowledge they were engaged upon.

The Islamic anthropology we wish to identify as *ilm ul umran* is a radical break from western anthropology and sociology. We maintain this is the only way to have a constructive and productive dialogue with these western disciplines. It is possible for an Islamic social science to be discerning about the usefulness and insight of questions, orientations and approaches employed in western social science only when it is clear that our interest in those western disciplines is based upon different conceptual premises. The idea that knowledge is one and therefore can be pursued only by the rules already laid down by one civilization in the course of its history is a narrow as well as imperialist notion.[6] The fact that the western conventions of knowledge have been developed in the context of a physical and intellectual domination of other approaches to knowledge, and therefore their domination must be unquestionably supported even if we do not accept they are right, a fallacious argument. This often heard debate about the oneness of knowledge confuses the human quest for knowledge with the knowledge that is the objective of the search. It conflates two senses of the word knowledge with each other. The knowledge we are concerned with is the human structures of understanding, the man-made conventions of enquiry. The knowledge we seek to identify through these human conventions is indeed one, but it is too large and irresponsible a claim to say that it is the actual possession of any one conventional approach to that end. What different approaches to the accumulation of knowledge do indicate is distinct perceptions of what is relevant and important about that one knowledge we all seek; these perceptions condition the means and necessary procedures to attain to that one knowledge.

We note with interest the work of British sociologist David Lyons who seeks a more humane sociology based on the premises of Christian belief.[7] Lyons' work is an attempt to resacralize, reintroduce central spiritual concepts into the practice of western sociology. He signals that it is possible to pursue sociology as a conventional approach to the accumulation of knowledge only when one's terms and means reflect and arise from what is considered relevant to the one knowledge one hopes to elucidate. Western anthropology and sociology have not established as 'scientific fact' that mankind is solely a biological and material being and that therefore all the spiritual perceptions of mankind are a human devised answer to a psychological characteristic. Western anthropology and sociology have asserted this proposition and have created a convention of questioning on this basis as a result of a particular history influenced by peculiarities of the western conceptual fabric and its civilizational expression. Because of the intellectual convention information is gathered in conformity with the relevant secular and materialist propositions about mankind and society and manipulated to fit the model. There is no place in that western model for a definition of mankind that integrates the biological, material and spiritual. The only way questions relevant to such a conceptual premise can be raised is within a different model. Only from radically different conceptual premises can challenging questions be posed to the western convention, the kind of questions that marshall a different body of information and call for a re-examination of long-accepted premises, and that is a definition of constructive dialogue. It is not the oneness of knowledge that is thrown into question by this radical departure, it is the adequacy of human constructed conventions to appreciate and discern the nature of that one knowledge. We maintain that only a genuine *ilm ul umran* can provide a stimulus for the re-examination of the assumptions of western conventions of knowledge.

There is no evidence in the literature directly concerned with islamizing the social sciences that other writers conceive of islamization in the way we have defined it. What they offer looks like an oddly-constructed halfway house where the overall design of the discipline, be that Islamic sociology or Islamic anthropology, is provided by the dominant western defined convention while certain special rooms have been added on to accommodate concerns of interest to Muslims. This is hardly surprising since their motivation in advancing the islamization of social science is not concerned with the conventions of knowledge as such but with a more generalized concern, one they share with the majority of social scientists from Muslim lands. They are concerned with the condition of contemporary Muslim society and with finding ways to improve it according to an agenda informed by the dictates of Islam. Their use of the disciplines and their stance in relation to them is geared to this end; they are looking for an applied social science. The central problem the Muslim and Arab social scientists have identified is a lack of fit between the descriptions of social reality in Muslim society in western social science and the perception of that social reality implicitly held by the Muslim and Arab social scientists.[8] This discrepancy between description and implicit response is then identified as a block to achieving constructive 'scientifically' informed practical means of improving the condition of Muslim society.

Whether we look at those who welcome the label Islamic or those who shun that label in favour of other ideological orientations, or those of no clear orientation, there does appear to be a common trend amongst the social scientists from Muslim or Arab society. The choice of terminology, Muslim or Arab, is a handy but not infallible indication of ideological orientations of those writing about Muslim or Arab society; it represents two dominant approaches but what it divides are spheres containing numerous shades of opinion and distinct groupings. The central experience they are all wrestling with is colonialism, the consequent marginalization and underdevelopment as well as misdevelopment, and the failure of independence to stem the consequences ushered in by colonialism. This is the nature of the social reality they grapple with. Colonialism is seen as a whole complex responsible both for the present condition of their societies and for the faulty description of their societies in western social science. This brings us back to the familiar territory of the denunciations of anthropology as a discipline formed by the reports of missionaries and colonial officials we considered in an earlier chapter. The censure of colonialism and its still potent legacy is, however, a discrete topic, one that does not raise the question of the nature of western social science. Ultimately for the Muslim and Arab social scientists of whatever hue, the problem comes down to the perfidy of the individual social scientists in western society who, in the context of colonialism and the mind set it created, lacked sensitivity to the social reality of Muslim and Arab society. It was colonialism as a complex that created the biased interpretation of Muslim/Arab society, being influenced by the tradition of Orientalism, a discipline distinct from social sciences. The individual western practitioners are distinct from the concepts and rules of social science.

Since the description of social reality is faulty because of the individual failings of the western social scientists the solution to this problem must lie in the hands of the indigenous social scientists. Whatever identity or ideological orientation they adopt or declare, or whether this is unspecified, the indigenous social scientists are important actors on the contemporary scene, but what is urgently required is a more rigorous consideration of their status and significance. Just what is it they bring to the practice of social science when they uniformly hold to the supremacy of social science as a received convention, when they all maintain the concepts and rules of social science as currently constituted have a universal validity and applicability? This bald statement is made by Laroui just as much as by Akbar Ahmad.[9] Since as a group the indigenous social scientists cover a great spectrum of ideology and orientation and yet all have the advantage that can be designated 'indigenous social scientist', the advantage cannot be a function of ideas; the answer can only be their person. Where the person of the western social scientist labours under handicaps in the manipulation and operation of the disciplines of social science the person of the indigenous social scientist does not.

The point to analyse is the nature of this relationship to social reality that confers superior insight and operative ability upon the indigenous social scientist. At one level this advantage is reduced to the level of nothing more than better access, a claim made by Soraya Altorki who is determined to have the best of both possible worlds.[10] For while maintaining the importance of 'scientific objectivity', the distance between observer and observed, she makes the indigenous social scientist one who has the right colour or language or ethnic background to merge with the setting, thus presumably being allowed into more situations than would a western social scientist. It is not clear from Altorki whether it is merely the case in her instance but implicitly it would seem to be a general proposition that training in scientific principles functions as a break from one's own social setting and thus makes a distinction between observer and observed. The brief of the indigenous social scientist is no different from that of the western social scientist, so the faulty description of social reality in western social science must be the result of a lack of rapport between observer and observed, causing vital information to be withheld or obscured.

One fails to see, if this is the case, why any credence should be given to a system of social science enquiry constructed and formed upon partial information or misinformation. If even Altorki's minimal claims are correct then there is no point in holding to the established and dominant conventions of social science; what the indigenous social scientist does must be superior and the claims to the universality of social science as received from the west collapse.

One could argue that Altorki is speaking of a very specific and long-standing phenomenon in anthropology. This is the famed conundrum 'how to study the women' that gave rise to that invaluable intellectual asset, the anthropological wife.[11] Altorki's own field work was amongst Saudi women where one can certainly see her point about accessibility of the field material.[12] But then anthropology more than any other discipline has thrown up many women as fieldworkers in their own right, rather than as adjuncts to their husbands. So even as she tries desperately to backtrack and minimize, Altorki is making a significant claim beyond her own gender for the indigenous anthropologist. She is making just the same claim as Akbar Ahmad in relation to his field work amongst the Pushtu.[13] In Ahmad's case such are the advantages of being an indigenous anthropologist that it allows him personally to violate central tenets of anthropological propriety by being an actor in the setting he describes. Not any actor either. He makes it clear he gathered his material while working as the Political Officer in the North West Frontier Territories of Pakistan, that is, as the encumbent of a system of administration of Pathan affairs that had not been altered since colonial times. Neither his position nor the structure of relationships that follow from his position, it would seem, are sufficient to outweigh the advantage of his being an indigenous anthropologist. Clearly it enables him to do what no non-indigenous professional anthropologist would dare even to think of, let alone attempt, in this day and age.

But neither Altorki nor Ahmad are talking about mere access to field material. What they are really speaking of is the accessibility of the field material to the indigenous social scientist. This is a distinction they would do well to ponder. For to have any relevance at all the indigenous social scientists must do more than being invisible in the social setting they study. The accessibility must be one of understanding and that understanding can arise only from shared meanings, a common fund of responses that can be recognized by the observer in the words and action of the observed. What the indigenous social scientists brings to their tasks, when compared with the non-indigenous, is a different history of socialization. As social scientists they should recognize that this socialization is composed of conceptual principles and values, or else it would not be socialization at all. These conceptual principles and values are distinct from the supposed value-freeness and neutrality of the rules of social science as well as the concepts and values that compose the socialization of the western or non-indigenous social scientist. It is this socialization that makes them conclude there is a lack of fit between the description of the social reality of Muslim or Arab society in western social science and what actually exists in that social reality but enables them to respond to the social reality of their own societies.

If we look at the ethnography, the basic information reports of indigenous anthropologists, or the social studies of the indigenous sociologists, then we find that not only do they read like the work of their non-indigenous counterparts, but they mirror the structures of description common in the complained of western social science. Somehow at the level of basic information gathering the indigenous social scientists have not gleaned anything significantly different by virtue of being indigenous; their better access has not been utilized to tell us things we did not know. By using the received conventions of social science and its paradigms they have eradicated the shared meanings they should have been bringing forth for analysis, the actual bricks and mortar of information to change the basis of description of their societies. All they are left with is advancing arguments for difference of interpretation in the application of particular theoretical propositions. Again Ahmad provides the obvious example. His quarrel with Barth is over the applicability of a particular theory to interpretation of the Pathan, the issue of charisma.[14] It is a particular argument that does nothing to suggest any mismatch between western social science description of Muslim society as a whole because it operates entirely within the boundaries of western social science itself. In his study *Religion and Politics in Muslim Society*, he applies exactly the same structural and conceptual referents to the study of religion, authority and power in Pathan society as any non-indigenous anthropologist would.

The locus of identification for the indigenous social scientist seems not to involve the doing of social science in a different way because they are indigenous but in criticizing western non-indigenous social scientists in general terms. In this critique a number of interesting features emerge. We find Nadia Abu Zahra, for example, correcting western anthropologists on the status of women in Muslim society.[15] The foundation of her argument is the ideal meaning of the Qur'anic sources, for to her this opens up more possible interpretive patterns of action that should be recognized as Islamic than merely those seen in contemporary Muslim society. Furthermore, this wider spectrum of possible interpretation recognized by Abu Zahra gives different nuances of meaning to the action observable in contemporary Muslim society, discernible to her as an indigenous anthropologist but ignored by the non-indigenous anthropologists. In making reference to an ideal meaning that is other than the abstracted description of what is observable in Muslim society she is explicitly and implicitly responding in a different way from that required by social science in its western convention, for the realm of meaning she utilizes to make her criticism simply does not exist according to the conceptual structure of that social science convention.

This is a very different line to the one taken by Akbar Ahmad, who actually claims to be engaged in islamizing anthropology. Ahmad advances the advantages of indigenous anthropology and the practical benefits it can bring as applied social science and in this respect nominates the undertaking of Islamic anthropology, while at the same time maintaining there is no realm of the Islamic ideal to mobilize the work or thought of the Islamic social scientist. Indeed, in his construction the person is all that distinguishes an Islamic anthropologist from a non-Islamic anthropologist. He can, for example, triumphantly proclaim that Islam has become the observer of other societies for the first time in centuries through the person of the eminent Turkish anthropologist Nur Yalman.[16] Yalman has given no evidence of any stance in relation to Islamic anthropology and his study of Sinhalese society, *Under the Bo Tree*, that so enthuses Ahmad, is an entirely conventional piece of excellent ethnography of western social anthropology. The statement made by Ahmad is redolent of the confusion that runs through his writings on the subject of Islamic anthropology, a subject he consequently manages to reduce to redressing the prejudicial slurs heaped upon Muslims for not eating pork.

A critique that does seem to address the central problem is Talal Asad's *The Idea of an Anthropology of Islam*.[17] While Asad works within the conventions of western anthropology, he nevertheless relates the interpretation of Islam found therein to its origin in the concepts of an entirely conventional piece of western civilization. Asad's argument is that to understand how western anthropologists have interpreted Islam one must examine the concepts of power and authority in western civilization and the institutional structures that derived from them. The western anthropologists have taken these conceptual definitions and their institutional consequences and then interpreted Islam as their obverse. It is a thoroughly convincing exposition of how western anthropologists have come to see Islam as they do; an explanation that has nothing to do with individual perfidy or prejudice, but everything to do with the centrality of Judeo-Christian thought and tradition and its civilizational history to the construction of the convention of anthropology. Asad makes no claim to be advancing or seeking an Islamic anthropology in our terms that is as a discipline distinct from western anthropology. What he is engaged in is critique of the western anthropological convention, but one that focuses upon conceptual premises and their influence upon the formation of the convention. Asad declares his intention to pursue this course of critique by further study of the interpretation of concepts in the civilizational history of western society.

Asad's critical analysis raises a host of questions indigenous social scientists should be investigating. In passing he also mentions a major topic we ought to be considering. He notes that the objective of understanding for which knowledge is accumulated is defined differently by western civilization than by the tradition of scholarship of Muslim civilization. While the objective for western knowledge has been to elucidate the nature of society, the point of focus for Islamic scholarship was the moral person. Indigenous social scientists would do well to question whether their socialization has not left them with a different perception of the objective of knowledge that conditions their stance to the received western conventions of social science by endowing them with expectations it is no part of western social science to fulfil. Does this different socialization, that echoes different concepts and values and their orientations, not have some explanatory relevance to their location of the problem of social science description in the person of the western social scientist rather than in the system of thought? Whether indigenous social scientists choose to address these questions in this form or not they must begin a far more searching analysis of the nature of social science as received convention. It is only in questioning meanings that they can get nearer to understanding how to construct a social science that will answer their objective of appropriate applied knowledge. The best way to propel this discussion to a higher level would be to establish a flourishing discourse of *ilm ul umran*, whose intellectual agenda would serve to clarify many of the issues in indigenous critique and learning that are currently submerged rather than debated.

In the course of shaping and identifying *ilm ul umran* as a radically different kind of Islamic anthropology we have touched upon many matters that comprise its intellectual agenda for the future. The most fundamental picks up the point mentioned by Talal Asad, the centrality of the moral person. This argument is also made by Naquib al-Attas in his exposition of *din*, where he maintains that while western civilization has been interested in what makes the good citizen, Islam's interest is in the good man, the moral person. Significantly he points out that the moral person is not an isolate but a microcosm of the Islamic vision of the moral universe. It is with this distinction that *ilm ul umran* must begin. While focusing on the moral person, the collective and communal has been subsumed as an appendage of the individual. For this reason there is little direct tradition of discourse upon the nature of community, little awareness of a distinct concept of community or social thought at the communal level. Today we urgently need to explore the relationship between the individual as moral person and the concept of community as moral domain to expand our perception of social thought.

Nothing better demonstrates the obscuring of the relationship between the individual and community in traditional Islamic thought than the voluminous literature on the Islamic state. Without an active tradition of social thought or consideration of the communal dimension, the discourse has become an arid and endlessly perplexing matter of discussing political form and institutions. The Islamic state becomes an abstract, a thing to be made or done at some future date and contemplating it fails to reveal more about how community works now in its absence, just as it fails to give insight into how an Islamic state would be different in practice if it were established. The political speculation on the Islamic state is not the same thing as a convention of communal, social thought. But no political science can be informative or relevant without the support of an active and enquiring discourse of social science.

The business of *ilm ul umran* must be to explore the consequences that follow from the identity of both the person and the community as moral entities. The moral person is not charged with nor conceived as having solely individual responsibilities. The concept of the moral duties of the individual embraces communal and collective responsibilities, therefore, the individual is tied firmly to the communal setting. Not only is the isolate individual inconceivable, but incapable of being a fully moral person. There is an identity of interest in understanding the moral person and the community as a moral domain. The question we need to be exploring through reflection upon the basic sources and in devising questions to gather information from social studies is whether a moral person can exist without a morally responsible communal setting. This enquiry does not involve abstract speculation but the asking of practical questions that seek to identify the constraints that influence and affect the relationship between the individual and the community. It means devising a whole series of questions aimed at identifying the points of articulation and interaction between the individual with his collective responsibilities and the community with its duties to the individual to see how action that occurs in our communities, or in any community, affects the quality of life of the individual and the community as a whole. Where we are gathering information, what we are investigating is the real world, the world of newly-industrializing nations, of dependent economies, of famine-stricken agricultural nations, as well as nations struggling towards the post-industrial era. It is in the context of how people live today that we pose a new set of questions to gain insight into how community works, how it impinges upon the individual and how it enables or disables the moral purpose that should be a unified frame of reference for both community and individual. If what we are questioning is whether the moral individual can exist without a moral community then the information we gather should lead us to thinking about ways in which both community and individual can be brought together to improve the practical moral action of both.

Exploring the relations between the individual and community from the perspective of *ilm ul umran* changes the conventions and requires not just new terminology and methodology but a change from the evaluative loading of questions as currently posed in the received convention of social science. The major area we are thinking of is urban studies. At present the urban setting has a significant value load derived from western convention that influences both social science studies and urban planning. The city and urban life are implicitly viewed as a higher form of communal existence. Now for *ilm ul umran*, we would suggest, the significance of how a community is organized, whether rural or urban, is not its form but the moral action that occurs and is affected by that form. Both have their characteristics, being subject to constraints arising from the physical environment, the technological capacity, the system of communal organization and socialization. It is the way in which community is adapted to these constraints, the way a whole system of living operates within these settings, that is the stuff of evaluation. The framework of enquiry sees both the rural and the urban as a moral domain; they are brought together as sharing consonant features for investigation and evaluation rather than divided. The kind of social science questioning that results from this perspective will entail a very different kind of urban studies, because what it is relevant and significant to ask of the social action and communal formation in cities will be changed. The city cannot be assumed to be a superior communal setting; it must be questioned about living conditions, the housing patterns, the access to the means of livelihood and the provision for the fulfilment of communal moral responsibilities. Our conceptual perspective on the nature of community is loaded with values, our questions must be designed to understand the meaning and implications of these values in the actual patterns of on-going human action in actual communal settings.[18]

An Islamic social science must by its very nature have applied implications and give rise to more informed discussion of policy and planning for actual communities. The significant point we would make about the applied nature of *ilm ul umran* is that it must create a broader context for understanding the meaning and implication of specific Islamic injunctions. It is only when we develop a more informed analysis of the nature of community that we can begin to appreciate the flexibility, the permissible possibilities of Islamic injunctions in relation to the actual state and condition of Muslim society. Then, instead of viewing the ideal of Islamic legislation as an agenda that requires sweeping away the contemporary condition of Muslim society to make way for a new communal order, we can consider how that legislation enables reform, can guide us to a practical programme of action where change occurs that is institutionally and organizationally appropriate to the present predicament and enables the individual members of the community and the community as a whole to enact right action to carry themselves into the future. It is the difference between seeing Islamic injunctions as an imposition upon a communal setting, no matter what its condition or resources, and seeing the Islamic injunctions as as outgrowth of action that can occur within the given constraints of a particular communal setting.

A further topic for *ilm ul umran* is to devise studies that examine the nature of tradition and convention in community. A conception of tradition is formed in the socialization of the individual in a communal setting; the institutions of community also maintain a tradition. Yet these traditions can and do change, often by the introduction of new patterns of behaviour justified as having been handed down from time immemorial or instituted in such a way as to appear so. We need to study how tradition is transmitted between generations, how individuals in a community understand the rules and limits of tradition as opposed to the possibilities of novel action. In what kind of situations are the limitations and restraints of tradition seen as crucial, are there particular kinds of situations where tradition is considered to be flexible and mutable, what constraints and circumstances give rise to different responses to tradition? In examining tradition we are concerned with the transmission of values, whether they are impeded or encouraged. In effect what we are seeking to explore is the nature of social action as interpretation. We cannot see tradition as a fixed form, but as a pattern of action that is defined by values in a communal setting. These values are to be enacted in diverse circumstances by a diversity of actors. How people understand themselves as relating to tradition in individual and communal behaviour is the basic building block of developing insight into how traditions live, how eternal necessary propositions are or whether they can be endlessly reintegrated in their applicability to communal existence.

Social studies that examine the nature of tradition are the beginning of the study of change, a study that no genuine *ilm ul umran* can avoid. As a study rooted in conceptual premises and their entailed values that are eternal verities, the area of investigation for *ilm ul umran* is mankind in time and space, the relationship of mankind in community to eternally valid propositions through observed diversity, whether that is the diverse nature of the forms of different communities or the diversity of particular communities through their history. The doing of *ilm ul umran*, the making of a convention of knowledge, is concerned with devising questions to be applied to contemporary reality and the record of human history. Our questions are indeed ordered and structured by the logic of our premises but the purpose of questioning and the necessity of a critical outlook is to test whether we can demonstrate the validity of our premises as a way of making sense of the world in which we live and the human action that takes place there. This questioning and critical enquiry must establish whether we as intelligent beings can understand what is significant and important about the concepts and values we maintain are eternally valid. There can be nothing parochial about this study; it must range over all the communities that exist today or have existed in the past. The validity we claim for our premises of enquiry is their universality, not their particularity to Muslims. Indeed the greatest impetus *ilm ul umran* can give to contemporary Muslim thought and discussion is by lifting it out of its parochialism. Most Muslim critique makes very little effort to understand the nature of western society. There can be no debate and no dialogue on the basis of excoriation and denunciation devoid of any common human sympathy and understanding. Viewing all mankind in all its diversity as consonant does not mean there is not genuine difference between communities and serious points of disagreement. It does mean setting these differences in a context of understanding where the common challenge facing all people, no matter what kind of community they live in or views or beliefs they hold, can be clarified to promote mutual understanding about what is right action for people anywhere in the increasingly interdependent world in which we live.

The great challenge for *ilm ul umran* as Islamic social science is to develop a convention of social studies that demonstrates the nature and relevance of the quest for knowledge as a function of a world view, a human construct conditioned by our communal origin. It is only by the quality of the studies we produce in pursuit of *ilm ul umran* that we can conclusively demonstrate that this is not relativizing ourselves into a narrow, exclusive identity separate from the rest of mankind. The way we undertake and develop our convention of *ilm ul umran* must be the positive demonstration that we do not see any system as 'other' but all systems of thought and action as consonant endeavours of a common humanity where our particular enquiry opens the way for dialogue and debate.

Shaping Islamic anthropology from the sources of Islam has been the task of today, a function of the disrupted state of Islamic thought; constructing *ilm ul umran* is the task of the future. We must either engage in and employ Islamic thought as our way out of present difficulties or resign ourselves to seeing Islam wither into an arcane body of dissociated rituals, remote from the pressing concerns of modernity. As a body of ritual and spiritual experience Islam is a means of giving emotional support to the perplexed individual in a frightening and senseless world. Recognizing Islam as a way of thought is a means of infusing its guidance into the resolution of our problems and nurturing the potential of individuals and communities by suggesting the possibilities for making sense of their life in this world.

Notes

1. For an excellent discussion of classification from the Islamic perspective see Parvez Manzoor, 'Limits to Information', p.44.

2. Ba-Yunus and Ahmad, *Islamic Sociology*.

3. Here we have chosen to exclude the rapidly growing literature on Islamic economics since it is a discrete topic. So the main texts on islamizing the social sciences are indeed very few. The work of Ismail al-Faruqi and the contributions to the book he edited, *Social and Natural Sciences*, constitute the bulk of the literature. Akbar Ahmad has written two papers on Islamic anthropology while a number of the contributors to al-Faruqi's book have contributed articles to the *American Journal of Islamic Social Science*. We also have a number of works on social sciences from the Iranian Ayatullah Murtaza Mutahhari. The central importance Faruqi attached to the social sciences seems to have elicited very little response from Muslim thinkers.

4. Gellner, *Muslim Society*.

5. See 'Anthropology: The Creation of Man and the Contradiction of God and Iblis', or 'Spirit and Clay' in Shariati, *On the Sociology of Islam*. In his use of the terms sociology and anthropology Shariati obviously is holding to the French convention gleaned from his education in that country.

6. This is the rather defeatist notion advanced by Ninian Smart in his review of Sardar's *Islamic Futures*, See 'Islam and the Future', Futures, Vol. 8 (6), December 1986. Smart regards with interest the ideas presented by islamization but somehow this is not sufficient to challenge the dead hand of conformity to knowledge as conceived and dispensed by western society.

7. Lyon, *Sociology and the Human Image*.

8. For a general introduction to themes in Arab social science that includes contributions by many of the leading Arab social scientists see Ibrahim and Hopkins, eds. *Arab Society*.

9. See Laroui, Crisis of the Arab Intellectual and Akbar Ahmad, 'Defining Islamic Anthropology', RAIN (65) December 1984.

10. Soraya Altorki, 'The Anthropologist in the Field: A Case of Indigenous Anthropology', in *Arab Society*, ibid. pp 76–84.

11. One is thinking of course of Laura Bohannon's Return to Laughter, Mary Smith's *Baba of Karo* and Elizabeth Fernea's Guests of the Sheikh as some of the well-known published examples of the phenomena.

12. Altorki, *Women in Saudi Arabia*.

13. See Ahmad, *Religion and Politics in Muslim Society*, pp.107–48.

14. See Ahmad, *Millennium and Charisma among Pathans*.

15. See Abu Zahra 'On the Modesty of Women in Arab Muslim Villages', pp. 1079– 92.

16. Ahmad, *Toward Islamic Anthropology*.

17. Talal Asad, 'The Idea of An Anthropology of Islam', Occasional Papers Series, Centre for Contemporary Arab Studies, Georgetown University, Washington D.C., 1986.

18. These ideas have been discussed in more detail in my paper, 'Beyond Catastrophe, The Muslim Urban Condition', published in Ziauddin Sardar, ed. *An Early Crescent*, Mansell, London.

Bibliography

Abd al-Ati, Hammudah. *The Family Structure in Islam*, American Trust Publication, Indianapolis, 1977.

Abdalati, M. Islam in Focus, North American Trust, Indianapolis, 1975.

Abdel-Malek, Anouar. *Civilisations and Social Theory*, Vol. 1 of *Social Dialetics,* Macmillan, London, 1981.

Abu Zahra, Nadia. On the Modesty of Women in Arab Villages, A Reply, *American Anthropologist,* 72 (5) Oct, 1970.

Ahmad, Aziz, ed. Religion and Society in Pakistan, *Contributions to Asian Studies*, Vol. 2, Brill, Leiden, 1971.

Ahmad, Khurshid, ed. *Islam, Its Meaning and Message*, Islamic Foundation, Leicester, 1976.

_____ed. *Studies in Islamic Economics*, Islamic Foundation, Leicester, 1980.

_____and Zafar Ishaq Ansari, eds. *Islamic Perspectives, Studies in Honour of Mawlana Mawdudi*, Islamic Foundation, Leicester, 1979.

Ahmad, Akbar S. *Millennium and Charisma among Pathans*, A Critical Essay in *Social Anthropology*, Routledge, London, 1976.

_____*Pieces of Green, The Sociology of Change in Pakistan*, Royal Book Company, Karachi, 1977.

_____*Pukhtun Economy and Society, Traditional Structure and Economic Development in a Tribal Society*, Routledge, London, 1980.

_____*Religion and Politics in Muslim Society, Order and Conflict in Pakistan*, CUP, Cambridge, 1983.

_____Defining Islamic Anthropology, *Royal Anthropological Institute News*, 65, December 1984.

_____*Pakistan Society*, OUP, Karachi, 1986.

_____*Toward Islamic Anthropology*, New Era Publications, Ann Arbor, 1986.

Ali, S. Ameer. *The Spirit of Islam*, OUP, Oxford, 1965.

Ali, Shaukat. *Intellectual Foundations of Muslim Civilisation*, Publishers United, Lahore, 1977.

Altorki, Soraya. *Women in Saudi Arabia*, Columbia, New York, 1986.

Anees, Munawar Ahmad, Islamic Values and Western Science: A Case of Reproductive Biology, in Z. Sardar, ed., *The Touch of Midas*, MUP, Manchester, 1984.

_____Laying the Foundation of Islamic Science, *Inquiry*, 2 (11) 1985.

_____Science and Gender, *Inquiry* 2 (8) 1985.

_____Illuminating Ilm, *Inquiry*, 3 (5) May 1986.

Arens, W. *The Man Eating Myth, Anthropology and Anthropophagy*, OUP, Oxford, 1979.

Aron, Raymond. *Main Currents in Sociological Thought*, Penguin, Harmondsworth, 1968, 2 vols.

Asad, Muhammad. *The Message of the Quran*, Dar al-Andalus, Gibraltar, 1980.

_____*The Principles of State and Government of Islam*, Dar al-Andalus, Gibraltar, 1980.

Asad, Talal, ed. *Anthropology and the Colonial Encounter*, Ithaca Press, London, 1973.

_____and Roger Owen, eds. *Sociology of Developing Societies', The Middle East,* Macmillan, London, 1983.

Asaria, M.I. Constructing the Edifice of Homo Islamicus, *Inquiry*, 2 (4) April 1985.

al-Attas, Syed M. Naquib. *Islam, Secularism and the Philosophy of the Future* Mansell, London, 1985.

Augé Marc. *The Anthropological Circle, Symbol, Function, History*, Cambridge Studies in Social Anthropology, 37, CUP, Cambridge, 1982.

Ayoob, Mohammad, ed. *The Politics of Islamic Reassertion*, Croom Helm, London, 1981.

Azami, M.M. *Studies in Hadith Methodology and Literature,* American Trust Publications, Indianapolis, 1977.

_____*Studies in Early Hadith Literature,* American Trust Publications, Indianapolis, 1978.

al-Azmeh, Aziz. *Ibn Khaldun in Modern Scholarship, A Study in Orientalism,* Third World Centre, London, 1981.

_____*Ibn Khaldun, An Essay in Reinterpretation,* Cass, London, 1982.

Azzam, Abd-al-Rahman, *The Eternal Message of Muhammad,* Quartet, London, 1979.

Azzam, S., ed. *Islam and Contemporary Society,* Longman, London, 1982.

Badawi, M.A.Z. *The Reformers of Egypt,* Croom Helm, London, 1978.

Baer, Gabriel, *Fellah and Townsman in the Middle East,* Cass, London, 1982.

Balandier, Georges, *Political Anthropology,* Penguin, Harmondsworth, 1972.

Banton, Michael, ed. *The Relevance of Models for Social Anthropology,* A.S.A. Monographs 1, Tavistock, London, 1965.

_____*The Social Anthropology of Complex Societies,* A.S.A. Monographs 4, Tavistock, London, 1966.

Barnes, Barry. *T.S. Kuhn and Social Science,* Macmillan, London, 1982.

_____and David Bloor. Relativism, Rationalism and the Sociology of Knowledge, in Martin Hollis and Stephen Lukes, *Rationality and Relativism, Blackwell,* Oxford, 1982.

Barth, Fredrik. *Political Leadership Among Swat Pathans,* LSE Monographs on Social Anthropology 19, Athlone, London, 1965.

_____*Selected Essays of Fredrik Barth,* Routledge, London, 1981, 2 vols.

Ibn Battuta. *The Travels of Ibn Battuta,* translated by Rev. Sammual Lee, Darf Publishers, London, 1984.

Ba-Yunus, Ilyas. Sociology and Muslim Social Realities, in LR. al-Farugi and A.O. Naseef, eds., *Social and Natural Sciences: The Islamic Perspective,* Hodder, London, 1981.

_____and Farid Ahmad. *Islamic Sociology: An Introduction, Hodder,* London, 1985. Beattie, J. *Other Cultures,* Free Press, New York, 1964.

Beck, Lois and Nikki Keddie, eds. *Women in the Muslim World;* Harvard, Cambridge, 1978.

Belshaw, Cyril. *Traditional Exchange and Modern Markets,* Prentice Hall, Englewood Cliffs, 1965.

Benedict, Ruth. *Patterns of Culture, Routledge,* London, 1935.

Berger, Peter L. *Invitation to Sociology, A Humanistic Perspective,* Penguin, Harmondsworth, 1966.

_____*Facing Up To Modernity,* Penguin, Harmondsworth, 1979.

_____and Hansfried Kellne *Sociology Reinterpreted,* Penguin, Harmondsworth, 1982.

_____and Thomas Luckmann. *The Social Construction of Reality, A Treatise in the Sociology of Knowledge,* Penguin, Harmondsworth, 1967.

Bloch, Maurice. *Marxism and Anthropology,* Clarendon Press, Oxford, 1983.

Bloor, David. *Knowledge and Social Imagery,* Routledge, London, 1976.

Boas, Franz. *Race, Language and Culture,* Macmillan, 1948.

Bovill, E.W. *The Golden Trade of the Moors,* OUP, Oxford, 1970.

Braudel, Fernand. *The Mediterranean and the Mediterranean World in the Age of Phillip II,* Fontana, London, 1972, 2 vols.

_____*On History,* Weidenfeld, London, 1980.

_____*Civilization and Capitalism, 15th–18th Century,* Fontana, London, 1985, 3 vols.

Brown, Dee. *Bury My Heart at Wounded Knee,* Barrie and Jenkins, London, 1971.

Bujra, A.S. *The Politics of Stratification, A Study of Political Change in a South Arabian Town,* Clarendon, Oxford, 1971.

Carr, E.H. *What is History?,* Penguin, Harmondsworth, 1964.

Chapra, M.U. *Towards a Just Monetary System,* Islamic Foundation, Leicester, 1985.

Chaudhuri, K.N. *Trade and Civilization in the Indian Ocean,* CUP, Cambridge, 1985.

Clarke, Peter B. *West Africa and Islam,* Edward Arnold, London, 1982.

Cohen, Percy. *Modern Social Theory,* Heinemann, London, 1968.

Coles, Paul. *The Ottoman Impact on Europe,* Thames and Hudson, London, 1968.

Collingwood, R.G. *The Idea of History,* OUP, Oxford, 1946.

Coulson, N.J. *A History of Islamic Law,* EUP, Edinburgh, 1964.

Daniel, Norman. *Islam and the West, The Making of an Image*, EUP, Edinburgh, 1960.

_____*Islam, Europe and Empire*, EUP, Edinburgh, 1966.

_____*The Arabs and Mediaeval Europe*, Longman, London, 1975.

_____*The Cultural Barrier*, EUP, Edinburgh, 1975.

Davies, Merryl Wyn. The Legacy of Mawdudi and Shariati, *Inquiry*, 2 (10) October 1985.

Diamond, Stanley. *In Search of the Primitive, A Critique of Civilization*, Transaction Books, New Brunswick, 1981.

Dobbin, Christine. *Islamic Revivalism in a Changing Peasant Economy*, Scandanavian Institute of Asian Studies Monograph Series no. 47, Curzon Press, London, 1983.

Doi, Abdur Rahman I. *Shari'ah: The Islamic Law*, Ta Ha, London, 1984.

Donohue, John J. and John L. Esposito, eds. *Islam in Transition*, Oxford UP, New York, 1982.

Douglas, Mary, Cultural Bias, Occasional Paper no. 35, Royal Anthropological Institute, London, 1978.

Dumont, L. *From Mandeville to Marx, The Genesis and Triumph of Economic Ideology*, UCP, Chicago, 1977.

Durkheim, E. *Elementary Forms of Religious Life*, Allen and Unwin, London, 1915.

_____*The Rules of Sociological Method*, Free Press, New York, 1950.

Eickelman, Dale F. *Moroccan Islam, Tradition and Society in a Pilgrimage Center*, UTP, Austin, 1976.

_____*The Middle East, An Anthropological Approach*, Prentice Hall, Englewood Cliffs, 1981.

_____*Knowledge and Power in Morocco*, PUP, Princeton, 1986.

Enayat, H. *Modern Islamic Political Thought*, Macmillan, London, 1982.

Epstein, A.L. *The Craft of Social Anthropology*, Tavistock, London, 1967.

Evans-Pritchard, E.E. *Witchcraft, Oracles and Magic among the Azande*, Clarendon Press, Oxford, 1937.

_____*The Nuer, Clarendon Press*, Oxford, 1940.

_____*The Sanusi of Cyrenaica*, Clarendon Press, Oxford, 1949.

_____*Social Anthropology*, Cohen and West, London, 1951.

_____*Essays in Social Anthropology*, Faber, London, 1962.

_____and M. Fortes. *African Political Systems,* OUP, London, 1940.

Faghirzadeh, Saleh. *Sociology of Sociology, In Search of Ibn Khalduns Sociology Then and Now,* Soroush Press, Tehran, 1982.

Fakhry, Majid, *A History of Islamic Philosophy, Longman*, London, 1983.

al-Faruqi, Ismail. Islamizing the Social Sciences, in I.

al-Faruqi and A.O. Naseef, eds., *Social and Natural Sciences:* The Islamic Perspective, Hodder, London, 1981.

_____*Islamization of Knowledge: General Principles and Workplan,* International Institute of Islamic Thought, Washington, D.C., 1982.

_____*Tawhid: Its Implications for Thought and Life,* International Institute of Islamic Thought, Pittsburgh, 1982.

Fernea, Robert and James A. Malarkey. *Anthropology of the Middle East and North Africa, Annual Review of Anthropology*, 4, 1975.

Firth, Raymond. *Elements of Social Organization,* Greenwood, Westport, 1981.

_____ed. *Themes in Economic Anthropology*, A.S.A. Monograph 6, Tavistock, London, 1967.

Islamic Revivalism in a Changing Peasant Economy,

_____ed. *Man and Culture, An Evaluation of the Work of Malinowski,* Routledge, London, 1968.

Foucault, Michel, *Madness and Civilization*, Tavistock, London, 1967.

_____*The Order of Things*, Tavistock, London, 1970.

_____*The Archaeology of Knowledge,* Tavistock, London, 1972.

Freeman, Derek. *Margaret Mead and Samoa,* Penguin, Harmondsworth, 1984.

Fyzee, Asaf A.A. *Outlines of Muhammadan Law,* Oxford UP, Delhi, 1964.

Gardiner, Patrick, *The Nature of Historical Explanation,* OUP, Oxford, 1961.

Gauhar, A., ed. *The Challenge of Islam,* Islamic Council of Europe, London, 1978.

Geetz, Clifford. *The Religion of Java,* UCP, Chicago, 1960.

_____*Agricultural Involution,* UCalP, Berkeley, 1963.

_____*Peddlars and Princes,* UCP, Chicago, 1963.

_____*Islam Observed,* UCP, Chicago, 1968.

_____*The Interpretation of Cultures,* Basic Books, New York, 1973.

Gellner, Ernest. *Muslim Society,* CUP, Cambridge, 1981.

_____Concepts and Society, in Bryan R. Wilson ed., *Rationality,* Blackwell, Oxford, 1970.

_____Relativism and Universals, in Martin Hollis and Stephen Lukes, eds., *Rationality and Relativism,* Blackwell, Oxford, 1982.

Gerholm, Thomas. *Market, Mosque and Mafraj,* Stockholm Studies in Social Anthropology 5, UniSt, Stockholm, 1977.

al-Ghazali. *The Book of Knowledge,* trans. by Nabih Amin Faris, Ashraf, Lahore, 1962.

_____*Ihya Ulum-id-Din,* trans. by Fazul-ul-Karim, Sind Sagar Academy, Lahore, n.d., 4 vols.

Gibbs, James L. *Peoples of Africa,* Holt, New York, 1965.

Gilsenan, Michael. *Recognizing Islam,* Croom Helm, London, n.d.

Gluckman, *Max. Politics, Law and Ritual in Tribal Society,* Blackwell, Oxford, 1967.

_____*Custom and Conflict in Africa,* Blackwell, Oxford, 1956.

Goody, Jack. *The Domestication of the Savage Mind,* CUP, Cambridge, 1977.

_____*The Developmental Cycle of Family Groups,* CUP, Cambridge, 1958.

Gullick, John. *The Middle East, An Anthropological Perspective,* Goodyear, Pacific Palisades, 1976.

Haddad, Yvonne Yazbeck. *Contemporary Islam and the Challenge of History,* SUNYP, Albany, 1982.

Haider, Gulzar, Habitat and Values in Islam: A Conceptual Formulation of the Islamic City, in Z. Sardar, cd., *The Touch of Midas,* MUP, Manchester, 1984.

_____Heritage and Harmony, *Inquiry,* 2 (2) 1985.

_____The City Never Lies, *Inquiry,* 2 (6) 1985.

_____Man and Nature, *Inquiry,* 2 (8) 1985.

_____Utopianism and Islamic Ideals, *Inquiry,* 2 (9) 1985.

_____The City of Learning, *Inquiry,* 2 (7) 1987.

Hakim, K.A. *The Ideology of Islam,* Institute of Islamic Culture, Lahore, 1965.

Hamidullah, M. *Introduction to Islam,* Centre Cultural Islamique, Paris, 1959.

_____ *The Muslim Conduct of State,* Ashraf, Lahore, 1969.

Haque, Ziaul. *Landlord and Peasant in Early Islam,* Islamic Research Institute, Islamabad, 1977.

Harris, Marvin. *The Rise of Anthropological Theory*, Routledge, London, 1969.

Haykal, Hussain. *Life of Muhammad,* trans. by Ismail Faruqi, American Trust, Indianapolis, 1976.

Hill, Christopher, *The English Revolution 1640*, Lawrence and Wishart, London, 1940.

_____ *The World Turned Upside Down*, Penguin, Harmondsworth, 1975.

_____ *The Century of Revolution*, Abacus, London, 1978.

Hindes, Barry and Paul Q. Hirst. *Pre-Capitalist Modes of Production,* Routledge, London, 1975.

Hobsbawm, EJ. *The Age of Revolution,* Abacus, London, 1977.

Hodgen, Margaret T. *The Doctrine of Survivals*, Allenson, London, 1936.

_____ *Early Anthropology in the Sixteenth and Sevenieenth Centuries*, UPP, Philadelphia, 1964.

Hodgson, Marshall G.S. *The Venture of Islam,* UCP, Chicago, 1974, 3 vols.

Hollis, Martin and Steven Lukes, eds. *Rationality and Relativism, Blackwell*, Oxford, 1982.

Hooykaas, R. *Religion and the Rise of Modern Science*, Scottish Academic Press, Edinburgh, 1973.

Hourani, George F. *Averroes, On the Harmony of Religion and Philosophy,* Gibb Memorial Trust, London. 1976.

Huizinga, J. *The Waning of the Middle Ages,* Penguin, Harmondsworth, 1955.

Husaini, S. Waqar Ahmed. *Islamic Environmental Systems Engineering*, Macmillan, London, 1980.

Hussain, Asaf, Robert Olsen and Jamil Qureshi, eds. *Orientalism, Islam and Islamists,* Amana Books, Vermont, 1984.

Hymes. D. *Reinventing Anthropology,* Random House, New York, 1973.

Iqbal, Allama Muhammad. *Reconstruction of Religious Thought in Islam, Ashraf,* Lahore, 1971.

Ibrahim, Saad Eddin and Nicholas S. Hopkins, eds. *Arab Society*, AUCP, Cairo, 1985.

Jalibi, Jameel. *Pakistan: The Identity of Culture,* Royal Book Company, Karachi, 1984.

Jamali, Muhammad Fadhil, *Letters on Islam*, OUP, Oxford, 1965. Jarvie, I.C. *The Revolution in Anthropology,* Routledge, London, 1964.

_____*Rationality and Relativism, In Search of a Philosophy and History of Anthropology,* Routledge, London, 1984.

Johnson, Paul. *A History of Christianity,* Penguin, Harmondsworth, 1978.

Kaplan, D. and Robert A, Manners. Culture Theory, Prentice Hall, Englewood Cliffs, 1972.

Keddie, Nikki R. *An Islamic Response to Imperialism*, UCalP, Berkeley, 1968.

_____ed. *Scholars, Saints and Sufis,* UCalP, Berkeley, 1972.

Ibn Khaldun. *The Mugaddimah: An Introduction to History,* translated by F. Rosenthal, Routledge, London, 1967.

Koto, Sayed. *Social Justice in Islam,* Octagon Books, New York, 1970.

_____*Islam, The Religion of the Future*, IIFSO, Kuwait, 1971.

_____*Milestones*, IIFSO, Kuwait, 1978.

_____*The Characteristics of the Islamic Concept,* Hindustan Publications, Delhi, 1984.

Kroeber, A.L. *Anthropology*, Harrap, London, 1948.

Kuper, Adam. *Anthropology and Anthropologists*, Routledge, London, 1983. rev. ed.

Lacoste, Yves*, Ibn Khaldun*, Verso, London, 1984.

La Fontaine, Jean. *What is Social Anthropology?* Edward Arnold, London, 1985.

Lapidus, Ira M. *Muslim Cities in the Later Middle Ages,* CUP, Cambridge, 1984.

Laroui Abdullah. *The Crisis of the Arab Intellectual*, UCalP, Berkeley, 1976.

Last, Murray. *The Sokoto Caliphate,* Longman, London, 1967.

Leach, Edmund. *Rethinking Anthropology,* LSE Monographs on Social Anthropology 22, Athlone, London, 1966.

_____*Social Anthropology,* Fontana, London, 1982.

Leaf, Murray J. Man, Mind and Science, *A History of Anthropology*, Columbia, New- York, 1979.

Lerner D. *The Passing of Traditional Society*, Free Press, New York, 1958.

Lévi-Strauss, C. Structural Anthropology, Basic Books, New York, 1968.

Lewis, I.M. cd. History and Social Anthropology, A.S.S. Monograph 7, Tavistock, London, 1968.

Lienhardt. G. *Social Anthropology*, OUP, Oxford, 1964.

Lings, Martin. *Muhammad, Allen and Unwin,* London, 1983.

Lowie, Robert H. *The History of Ethnological Theory,* Farrar and Reinehart, New York, 1937.

Lyon, David. *Sociology and the Human Image,* Inter-Varsity Press, Leicester, 1983.

Maalouf, Amin. *The Crusades Through Arab Eyes,* Al Saqi, London, 1984.

Mahmudunnasir, Syed. *Islam, Its Concepts and History,* Kitab Bhavan, New Delhi, 1981.

Mair, Lucy. *Anthropology and Social Change,* LSE Monographs on Social Anthropology 38, Athlone, London, 1969.

_____*Anthropology and Development,* Macmillan, London, 1984.

Makdisi, George. *The Rise of the Colleges: Institutions of Learning in Islam and the* West, EUP, Edinburgh, 1981.

Malinowski, B. *Argonauts of the Western Pacific*, Routledge, London, 1950.

_____*A Scientific Theory of Culture*, UNCP, Chapel Hill, 1944.

Mandrou, Robert. *From Humanism to Science,* Penguin, Harmondsworth, 1978.

Manzoor, Parvez. Environment and Values: The Islamic Perspective, in Z. Sardar, ed.,

The Touch of Midas, MUP, Manchester, 1984.

_____Islam and the Challenge of Ecology, *Inquiry*, 2 (2) 1985.

_____Reeducating the Muslim Intellectual, *Inquiry*, 2 (7) 1985.

_____Thinking about a Future Civilization of Islam, *Inquiry* 2 (12) 1985.

_____Studying Islam Academically, *Inquiry*, 3 (4) 1986.

_____The Quest for Sharia, Past and Future, *Inquiry*, 4 (1) 1987.

_____Liberating the Institutional Mind, *Inquiry*, 4 (4) 1987.

_____Limits to Information, *Inquiry*, 4 (5) 1987.

Markus, George. *Marxism and Anthropology,* Van Gorcum, Assen, 1978.

Marwick, Arthur. *The Nature of History,* Macmillan, London, 1970.

Mauroof, Saibo Mohamed. Elements for an Islamic Anthropology, in al-Faruqi and

A.O. Naseef, eds., *Social and Natural Sciences: The Islamic Perspective,* Hodder, London, 1981.

Mawdudi, A.A. *Islamic Law and Constitution,* trans. by Khurshid Ahmad, Islamic Publications, Lahore, 1960,

_____*Fundamentals of Islam,* Islamic Publications, Lahore, 1975.

McDonough, Sheila. Muslim Ethics and Modernity, Wilfred Laurier UP, Ontario, 1984.

Merton, R.K. Science, Technology and Society in Seventeenth Century England, *Osiris,* 4, 1938,

Midgley, Mary, *Evolution as a Religion,* Methuen, London, 1985.

Mishkat al-Masabih, trans. by James Robson, Ashraf, Lahore, 1975, 2 vols.

Murdock, G. *Social Structure,* Macmillan, New York, 1949.

Mutahhari, Murtaza. *Fundamentals of Islamic Thought, Man, God and the Universe,* trans. by R. Campbell, Mizan, Berkeley, 1985.

_____*Society and History,* trans. by Mahliqa Qarai, Islamic Propagation Organization, Tehran, 1985.

_____*Social and Historical Change,* trans. by R. Campbell, Mizan Press, Berkeley, 1986.

Musallam, B.F. *Sex and Society in Islam,* CUP, Cambridge, 1983.

Nadel, S.F. A Black Byzantium, OUP, Oxford, 1942.

_____*The Foundations of Social Anthropology,* Free Press, New York, 1951.

Naqvi, S. Nawab Haider. *Ethics and Economics, An Islamic Synthesis,* The Islamic Foundation, Leicester, 1981.

Nasr, S.H. *Ideals and Realities of Islam,* Allen and Unwin, London, 1966.

_____*Islamic Life and Thought,* Allen and Unwin, London, 1981.

Nisbet, Robert A. *Emile Durkheim,* Prentice Hall, Englewood Cliffs, 1965.

Orme, Bryony. *Anthropology for Archaeologists,* Duckworth, London, 1981.

Overing, Joanna, ed. *Reason and Morality,* ASA Monograph 24, Tavistock, London, 1985.

Parry, J.H. *Trade and Dominion,* Cardinal, London, 1974.

Parsons, Talcott *Societies*, Prentice Hall, Englewood Cliffs, 1966.

Pelto, P. and G.H. Pelto. *Anthropological Research: The Structure of Inquiry*, Harper and Row, New York, 1970.

Penniman, T.K. *A Hundred Years of Anthropology*, Duckworth, London, 1965, rev. edn.

Peters, Emrys. Aspects of Rank and Status among Muslims in a Lebanese Village, in Julian Pitt-Rivers, ed., *Mediterranean Countryman, Greenwood*, Westport, 1977.

Pickthall, M.M. *Cultural Side of Islam,* Ashraf, Lahore, 1927.

_____*The Meaning of the Glorious Quran, New American Library*, New York, 1953.

Piscatori, James P. *Islam in the Political Process,* CUP, Cambridge, 1983.

Pitt-Rivers, J. ed. Mediterranean Countryman, Greenwood, Westport, 1977.

Popper, K. *The Poverty of Historicism,* Routledge, London, 1957.

Radcliffe-Brown, A.R. *Structure and Function in Primitive Society,* Cohen and West, London, 1952.

_____and Daryll Forde, eds. *African Systems of Kinship and Marriage,* OUP, London, 1967.

_____*A Natural Science of Society,* Free Press, Glencoe, 1957.

Rahman, Fazlur. *Islam and Modernity*, UCP, Chicago, 1982.

_____*Islamic Methodology in History,* Central Instinute of Islamic Research Karachi, 1965.

_____Quranic Exegesis, *Inquiry*, 3 (5) 1986.

Raison, Timothy, ed. *The Founding Fathers of Social Science*, Penguin, Harmondsworth, 1969.

Ramadan, Said. *Islamic Law: Its Scope and Equity*, Macmillan, London, 1970.

Redfield, R. *The Little Community/Peasant Society and Culture*, UCP, Chicago, 1973,

_____The Folk Society, in *American Journal of Sociology*. 52.

Riley, G. *Values, Objectivity and the Social Sciences,* Addison-Wesley, Eading, Mass., 1974.

Rosenthal, F. *Knowledge Triumphant,* Brill, Leiden, 1970.

al-Sadr, Baqir. *Islam and Schools of Economics*, Islamic Seminary Publications, Accra, 1982.

Saad, Elias N. *Social History of Timbuktu*, CUP, Cambridge, 1983.

Sahlins, Marshall, *Tribesmen*, Prentice Hall, Englewood Cliffs, 1968.

_____*Culture and Practical Reason,* UCP, Chicago, 1976.

_____*The Use and Abuse of Biology,* Tavistock Press, London, 1976.

Said, Edward W. *Orientalism*, Routledge, London, 1978.

Said, H.M. and A.Z. Khan. *Al-Biruni, His Times, Life and Works*, Hamdard Academy, Karachi, 1981.

Sardar, Ziauddin. *Science, Technology and Development in the Muslim World,* Croom Helm, London, 1977.

_____ed. *The Touch of Midas*, MUP, Manchester, 1984.

_____Is There an Islamic Resurgence? *Inquiry*, 1 (1) 1984.

_____*Arguments for Islamic Science*, Centre for Science Studies, Aligarh, 1985.

_____*Between Two Masters: Quran and Science? Inquiry,* 2 (8) 1985.

_____The Other Jihad, *Inquiry*, 2 (10) 1985.

_____*Islamic Futures, The Shape of Ideas to Come,* Mansell, London, 1985.

_____*The Future of Muslim Civilization,* Mansell, London, 1987, new ed.

_____*Information and the Muslim World,* Mansell, London, 1988.

_____Reformulating the Sharia, *Inquiry*, 4 (1) 1987.

_____and Zaki Badawi, *Hajj Studies,* vol. 1, Croom Helm, London, 1978.

Schacht, Joseph and C.E. Bosworth. *The Legacy of Islam,* OUP, Oxford, 1974, 2nd ed.

Schmidt, Nathaniel. *Ibn Khaldun, Historian, Sociologist and Philosopher,* Universal Books, Lahore, 1978.

Shariati, Ali. *On the Sociology of Islam,* trans. by Hamid Algar, Mizan Press, Berkeley, 1979.

_____*Marxism and Other Western Fallacies, An Islamic Critique,* trans. by R. Campbell, Mizan Press, Berkeley, 1980.

Sheikh, M. Saeed. *Islamic Philosophy*, Octagon Press, London, 1982.

Siddiqui, Kalim. *Towards A New Destiny*, Open Press, Slough, 1971.

Siddiqui, Nejatullah. *Muslim Economic Thinking,* Islamic Foundation, Leicester, 1981.

Islamic Economics: Annotated Sources in English and Urdu, Islamic Foundation, Leicester, 1983.

Smith, M.G. Government in Zazzau, OUP, Oxford, 1960.

_____*Corporations and Society*, Duckworth, London, 1974.

Southern, R.W. *Western Views of Islam in the Middle Ages*, Harvard, Cambridge, 1962.

Sperber, Dan. *On Anthropological Knowledge,* CUP, Cambridge, 1985.

Stocking. Jr., George W. Race, *Culture and Evolution, Essays in the History of Anthropology,* UCP, Chicago, 1982.

_____ed. *History of Anthropology,* Vol. 1, UWP, Madison, 1983.

Sweet, Louise E. *Peoples and Cultures of the Middle East,* Natural History Press, New York, 1970, 2 vols.

Taleghani, Ayatullah S.M. *Society and Economics in Islam,* trans. by R. Campbell, Mizan Press, Berkeley, 1982.

Ibn Taymiya. *The Public Duties in Islam,* trans. by Muhtar Holland, Islamic Foundation, Leicester, 1982.

Tax, Sol. ed. *Horizons in Anthropology*, Aldine, Chicago, 1964.

Terray, Emmanuel. Marxism and Primitive' Societies, Monthly Review Press, New York, 1972.

Thomas, Keith. *Religion and the Decline of Magic,* Penguin, Harmondsworth, 1973.

_____*Man and the Natural World, Penguin,* Harmondsworth, 1984.

Tibawi, A.L. *Arabic and Islamic Themes*, Luzac, London, 1976.

Trimmingham,J.S. *Islam in West Africa,* London, 1959.

_____*The Influence of Islam upon Africa*, London, 1968.

Turner, Brian. *Weber and Islam, Routledge,* London, 1974.

Watt, W.M. *Islamic Political Thought,* EUP, Edinburgh, 1968.

Weber, Max. *The Sociology of Religion,* trans. by Ephraim Fischoff, Beacon Press, Boston, 1963.

_____*The Protestant Ethic and the Spirit of Capitalism,* trans. by Talcott Parsons, Allen and Unwin, London, 1976.

_____*The Theory of Social and Economic Organisation,* trans. by A.M. Henderson and Talcott Parsons, Free Press, New York, 1964.

_____*Weber Selections in Translation*, trans. by Eric Matthews, CUP, Cambridge, 1978.

Wilson, Bryan, R., ed. *Rationality, Blackwell,* Oxford, 1970.

Wilson, Edward O. *Sociobiology: The New Synthesis,* Harvard, Cambridge, 1975.

Wilson, G. and M. Wilson. *The Analysis of Social Change*, CUP, Cambridge, 1968.

Wolf, Eric R. Social Organization of Mecca, *Southwestern Journal of Anthropology*, 7 (Winter 1951).

_____*Peasants*, Prentice Hall, Englewood Cliffs, 1966.

_____*Europe and the People without History*, UCalP, Berkeley, 1982.

Worsley, Peter. *The Third World,* Weidenfeld, London, 1964.

_____The End of Anthropology? Paper for the 6th World Congress of Sociology, 1966.

el-Zein, Abdul Hamid. *The Sacred Meadows*, Northwestern, Evanston, 1974.

_____Beyond Ideology and Theology: The Search for the Anthropology of Islam, Annual Review of Anthropology, 6 (1977).

Index

The index contains entries for persons and subjects; books discussed in the text have been indexed, but not the bibliographical references; books are entered in the index under the author. Terms from the Arabic language, and titles of published books, are given in italics. Filing in the index is word-by-word; a hyphen is regarded as a space; in Arabic names the prefix 'al-' is ignored in filing.

abudiyyah 143–4
Africa, portrayal of 5
Ahmad, Akbar
    Millennium and Charisma
    Among Pathans 195–6
    Religion and Politics in
    Muslim Society 194–6
Ahmad, Kurshid 90
Altorki, Soraya 193–4
America, discovery of 35
American Indians
    portrayal by cinema films 4
    portrayal by early Western
    writers 41–45

Amerigo Vespucci, on American
    Indians 42
animal behaviour 2–3 (*see also*
    socio-biology)
anthropologists, role of 192–3
anthropology
    history and methodology
    33–5
    Islamic definition of 169–171
    Western definition of 167–8
anthropology, economic 13–14
anthropology, physical 2
anthropology, social 3–4
Arens, W.
    The Man Eating Myth 46

art, in Islamic society 75
Asad, Talal
  Anthropology and the Colonial Encounter 36
  The Idea of an Anthropology of Islam 197–8
al-Ati, Hammudah Abd
  The Family Structure in Islam 129
al-Attas, Naquib 198
Auge, Marc
  The Anthropological Circle 45
al-Azmeh, Aziz
  Ibn Khaldun: an Essay in Reinterpretation 183–7
  Ibn Khaldun in Modern Scholarship 183–7

Barley, Nigel
  The Innocent Anthropologist 8
Berger, Peter L.
  Facing up to Modernity 56–7
  The Homeless Mind 88–89
biology, *see* evolution;
socio-biology
Braudel, Fernand 23
Brazilian Indians, described by Montaigne 42

Calvinism 26
cannibalism 46–7
Christianity 21–22, 38–40
cinema 4
cities 200–201
civilization, definition of 24–5

classical scholarship, Islamic 179–181
colonialism
  and anthropology 35–39, 192
  effect on Muslim countries 83–86
communities, *see ummah*
cultural anthropology 2–3
cultural determinism 55 (*see also* socio-biology)
'culture', anthropological concept of 50–55
culture, popular (Western) 4–5

development, *see* economic development; Westernization
Diamond, Stanley
  In Search of the Primitive 8
din (religion) 109 ff, 151–3

economic anthropology 13–14
economic development 87–89
  before colonialism 82–3
economics, Islamic 89–90, 171–2
education (*see also* literacy)
  in Islamic society 79–80
  of Muslim jurists 73
  Western influences 83–6
ethnography 34–35, 50
  Islamic approach to 159–161
evolution (*see also* socio-biology) 43–5
  Qur'anic description of 95

al-Faruqi, Ismail
    Islamization of Knowledge 91
Films 4
fiqh (jurisprudence) 70–73
Firth, Raymond
    *Elements of Social
    Organisation* 54
fitrah (human nature) 102–6
Foucault, Michel 15, 17–18
free will, Qur'anic concept of
    106–8
Freeman, Derek
    Margaret Mead and Samoa 3

Gellner, Ernst
    Muslim Society 183
Goody, J.
    *The Domestication of the
    Savage Mind* 47–9

hadith 68–70
Harriott, Thomas 45
history, and anthropology 184–5
Hodgen, Margaret
    *Early Anthropology in the
    Sixteenth and Seventeenth
    Centuries* 29–30
Hooykaas, R.
    *Religion and the Rise of
    Modern Science* 26–8

Ibn Khaldun 181–7
Ibn Taymiya *Public Duties in
    Islam* 80
ilm (knowledge) 159

ilm ul umran 184–8
Imperialism, *see* colonialism
Indians, American 4–6, 38–41
individual, and the community
    199–200
industry, *see* economic
    development
institutionalization, in Islamic
    society 142

Jarvie, Ian
    Rationality and Relativism
    7–8
jurisprudence, *see* law

khilafa 102–6, 143–4
Kirk, James T. 6
Koran, *see* Qur'an
Kuhn, T.S. 15–17, 41
Kuper, Adam
    *Anthropology and anthropolo-
    gists* 36

law, Islamic 70–1, 80–81, 155–8
    Western influences 86–7
law schools 72
Leach, Sir Edmund
    Social Anthropology 6
Leaf, Murray J.
    Man, Mind and Science 15
literacy 48 (*see also* education)
Lyons, David
    *Sociology and the Human
    Image* 190

Magic 49
Malinowski, B. 55–6
Mawdudi, Maulana 90–1
Mead, Margaret 3
Midgley, Mary
  Evolution as a Religion 24–5,
  64
minhaj 158–9
modernization 85
monogenism 43, 52
Montaigne, Michel de
  On the Cannibals 42–3
More, Thomas
  Utopia 38
Morris, Desmond
  The Naked Ape 2

Naqvi, S. Nawab Haider.
  Ethics and Economics 90
non-Muslims, Islamic attitude to
  126–7

Pathans 194–5
Peyrere, Isaac de, and polygenism 43
physical anthropology 2
polygenism 43, 52
popular culture, Western 4–6
Protestantism, and Western science 26–30

Qur'an 6, 65–8, 89 f

race, *see* evolution; socio-biology

Rahman, Fazlur
  *Islamic Methodology in
  History* 141–2
rationalist/relativist debate 56
Reformation, the 22–27
religion, Islamic concept of 110
  f, 151–2
Renaissance, the 27
rural life 200–1

Sahlins, Marshall
  Culture and Practical Reason
  51
Sardar Z.
  Islamic Futures 89–91, 148
Scholarship, classical 179–81
  School of law 72
Science and scientific philosophy
  15 ff, 21
sharia, see law, Islamic
Shariati, Ali 173
Shia Musims 73
social anthropology, definition
  of 2–3
societies, *see* communities
socio-biology 51–54(*see also*
  evolution)
sociology 19–20, 182–3, 190
'Star Trek' 5–6
Stocking, George W.
  Race, Calture and Evolution
  52
Sunnah 65

taqlid 77–80
'Tarzan' films 5
tawhid (unity) 91, 136–7
terminology 173–7
trade, *see* economic development
tradition 202–3
Tylor, E.B.
    Primitive Culture 53–4

ulema, role in Islamic society 74, 78
ummah 126–7, 151–2
urban studies 200–1

Vespucci, Amerigo 42
Weber, Max 26–8

Westernization 88–91
westerns (films) 5
White, Lynn 39
witchcraft 49
Wolf, Eric
    Europe and the People
    Without History 37
writing, see literacy

Yalman, Nur *Under the Bo Tree* 197

Zahra, Nadia Abu 196
el-Zein, Abdul Hamid
    Beyond Ideology and Theology 14

www.ingramcontent.com/pod-product-compliance
Lightning Source LLC
Chambersburg PA
CBHW031504270326
41930CB00006B/248